Teaching and Learning with Virtual Teams

Sharmila Pixy Ferris
William Paterson University, USA

Susan H. Godar
William Paterson University, USA

Information Science Publishing
Hershey • London • Melbourne • Singapore

Acquisitions Editor:	Michelle Potter
Development Editor:	Kristin Roth
Senior Managing Editor:	Amanda Appicello
Managing Editor:	Jennifer Neidig
Copy Editor:	Bernard J. Kieklak, Jr.
Typesetter:	Diane Huskinson
Cover Design:	Lisa Tosheff
Printed at:	Yurchak Printing Inc.

Published in the United States of America by
Information Science Publishing (an imprint of Idea Group Inc.)
701 E. Chocolate Avenue
Hershey PA 17033
Tel: 717-533-8845
Fax: 717-533-8661
E-mail: cust@idea-group.com
Web site: http://www.idea-group.com

and in the United Kingdom by
Information Science Publishing (an imprint of Idea Group Inc.)
3 Henrietta Street
Covent Garden
London WC2E 8LU
Tel: 44 20 7240 0856
Fax: 44 20 7379 0609
Web site: http://www.eurospan.online.com

Library of Congress Cataloging-in-Publication Data

Teaching and learning with virtual teams / S. Pixy Ferris and Susan Godar, editors.
p. cm.
Summary: "This book investigates issues around teams in the virtual and hybrid classroom, offering a view of current research and practice on the subject of virtual and collaborative teams in teaching and learning"--Provided by publisher.
Includes bibliographical references and index.
ISBN 1-59140-708-7 (hardcover) -- ISBN 1-59140-709-5 (softcover) -- ISBN 1-59140-710-9 (ebook)
1. Group work in education. 2. Team learning approach in education. 3. Teaching teams. 4. Distance education--Computer-assisted instruction. I. Ferris, Sharmila Pixy. II. Godar, Susan Hayes, 1948-
LB1032.F39 2005
371.39'5'0285--dc22

2005020631

British Cataloguing in Publication Data
A Cataloguing in Publication record for this book is available from the British Library.

All work contributed to this book is new, previously-unpublished material. The views expressed in this book are those of the authors, but not necessarily of the publisher.

Teaching and Learning with Virtual Teams

Table of Contents

Section III: Teams in Action: International Collaboration

Section IV: Teams and Technology

Preface

With the growth of e-learning and distance education, there is an increasingly pressing need for research and writing on the pedagogy of e-learning today. Teams are, or should be, an integral component of e-learning. This book develops this concept by investigating many issues around teams in the virtual and hybrid classroom, bringing together in a single accessible source a variety of current research and practice on the subject of virtual and collaborative teams in teaching and learning.

Teams and E-Learning in the 21st Century

Electronic education is rapidly becoming a fixture in higher education. Today it is clear that the use of computer and digital technologies in teaching and learning is here to stay—not just through the increase of distance learning or virtual courses, but through the use of cyber-education as an adjunct to the traditional classroom. This is clear in the increased access to technology in higher education, and the continuing growth of online courses globally. Teaching is irrevocably changed, with access to computers and Internet technologies now all but universal for faculty members in the United States (Higher Education on the Web, 2002). Learning is similarly impacted, with over 1.9 million students in the U. S. studying online in the fall of 2003 and a projected growth in online enrolment of 20% a year—a growth rate exceeding the overall expected growth for the entire higher education student population (Sloan Consortium, 2004). Institutions of higher education clearly accept the importance of virtual education. The "instructional integration of information technology" was reported by CIOs in the U. S. as the "single most important IT issue" confronting their institutions over the next two-to-three years (National Survey of Information Technology in US Higher Education, 2004). This raises some important considerations for educators. Ultimately, the issue is whether we as educators are prepared to incorporate and use technology effectively in our teaching.

While extensive literature on the use of virtual teams in business and industry does exist, the literature on educational use of teams is scarce. Some of the lessons for virtual teams from industry are useful in educational settings, but there are important differences. Virtual teams in a business are set up to primarily accomplish a goal, while education involves an additional dimension: that of helping students learn how to operate in teams. This book gives multiple examples of how students can effectively learn to work in teams in universities around the globe.

As we have previously noted, there is a relative lack of research on the pedagogy of e-learning. However, we believe that existing "traditional" pedagogy can be used to improve teaching and increase student online learning. One important and enduring pedagogy available for improvement of e-learning and teaching is collaborative learning. Various names have been given to this form of teaching, and there are some distinctions among these: cooperative learning, collaborative learning, collective learning, learning communities, peer teaching, peer learning, reciprocal learning, team learning, study circles, study groups, and work groups. This book focuses on collaborative learning with virtual teams.

Collaborative learning through the grouping of students for the purpose of achieving an academic goal has been widely researched and advocated throughout the professional literature. Here the term "collaborative learning" refers to an instruction method in which students at various performance levels work together in small groups or teams toward a common goal. The students are responsible for one another's learning as well as their own. Thus, the success of one student helps other students to be successful.

Collaborative learning is particularly effective in teaching and learning with virtual teams. As Davis (1993) points out in her classic text, *Tools for Teaching*, active learning occurring in small groups is the best method of learning. She cites extensive research that has found student learning and retention in small group or team learning to be stronger than through other instructional and learning techniques.

It may be noted that we have, thus far, been using the terms "teams" and "groups" somewhat interchangeably, as is the accepted convention in much of the pedagogical literature on collaborative learning. Specifically, we define teams or groups by their generally accepted definition (and following our earlier book—see Godar & Ferris, 2004). By this definition, teams or groups have specific characteristics, including: size, groups should be small enough for mutual awareness; interdependence, or a mutually interdependent purpose/goal; and interaction, or active communication and feedback among group members. Additionally, cohesion, or a sense of belonging, and cooperation among the members, help define group identity.

In this book, the common definition of teams and groups is, of course, modified to incorporate the element of virtuality, or working either partially or wholly in the medium of cyberspace. Virtual teams avail themselves of an array of computer, digital and telecommunication technologies. They can be utilized in virtual classes as well as an added pedagogical element in "traditional" classes. In teaching and learning environments, virtual teams can take several forms that include, but are not limited to, the following:

- Activity groups/teams or temporary groups, formed to accomplish specific activities, and/or to meet affiliation needs.
- Problem-solving groups/teams, formed to address some condition or problems.
- Personal growth groups/teams, which help members engage in personal learning and growth through the development personal insights, overcoming of problems, and growth through feedback and support.
- Learning groups/teams, which are formed as a medium for learning and participants' growth. Such teams may complete their work in a single class (such as a laboratory experiment) or over a length of time (for example, by carrying out a project, conducting research).

The chapters in this book provide excellent examples of all these types of virtual groups/teams.

The Contribution of This Book

This book continues the cross-disciplinary and collaborative conversations begun in our previous book about the potentials of virtual teams. We bring together academics from a variety of disciplines, including business, communication, education, psychology and information technology. They represent perspectives on teaching and learning from a broad range of academic institutions—from private to public comprehensive, teaching to research, and from state and national to international. Excitingly, our authors also represent the power of both student and author collaborations. Not only do chapters provide examples of international collaborations between student virtual teams, but a number of our authors have written chapters "virtually," collaborating in their writing with colleagues across the United States and the world. International academic perspectives represented here range from France, Belgium and Poland to South Africa and Singapore.

In innovative and visionary ways of discussing issues of teaching and learning in virtual education in general, and virtual teams in particular, the authors in this book provide a transformative view of academia. They epitomize the revolutionary Carnegie Model of scholarship (Boyer, 1990; Ferris, Minielli, Phillips, & Mallard, 2003) in their treatments of teaching and learning. Their various chapters demonstrate a rethinking of basic notions of teaching and illustrate the concept of teacher as scholar and teacher as learner. As knowledgeable scholars who integrate teaching into, rather than separate it from, research, the authors in this book not only provide excellent examples of the Carnegie Model of scholarship, but exemplify the potentials of collaborative, inter-disciplinary research.

The Organization of This Book

This book has 12 chapters, divided into four sections. Here we briefly describe each section and its accompanying chapters.

Section I: From E-Learning to Learning in Virtual Teams

Not only has it become vital that we deal with issues of e-learning and its accompanying pedagogy in education today (as we have discussed quite extensively above), but it is equally essential that we expand the pedagogy on the use of virtual teams in the classroom. Research has repeatedly and consistently found small group or team learning creates engaged and successful students, but pedagogical research on the issue is scarce. The authors in the four chapters in this section demonstrate the importance of moving from e-learning to learning in virtual teams.

In Chapter I, Diane Boehm of Saginaw Valley State University in Michigan and Lilianna Aniola-Jedrzejek of the Poznan University of Technology in Poland build on Chickering and Gramson's popular article, "Seven principles of good practice in undergraduate education," extending and "distilling" these principles to virtual student collaborations. Using their experiences with projects involving several different teams of Polish and American students, Boehm and Aniola-Jedrzejek offer both detailed examples and concrete advice for instructors interested in successful virtual and international collaborative student projects.

In Chapter II, Pieter du Toit of the University of Pretoria in South Africa and Peter van Petegem of the University of Antwerp in Belgium present a psychological model for e-learning in virtual teams through a consideration of Learning Style Flexibility. Building on Herrman's Whole Brain theory, they consider the potential of learning style flexibility to enhance virtual team learning. Du Toit and van Petegem not only present a framework for developing learner's full potentials through such methods as action learning, but provide concrete strategies for facilitators' use in actively facilitating e-learning through the development of team roles and social skills.

In Chapter III, Robert Zheng of Temple University in Philadelphia brings an interdisciplinary perspective to his consideration of WebQuests in e-learning. He discusses four constructs critical to WebQuests: constructivist problem-solving, social interaction, motivation, and scaffolding in e-learning. Zheng tests these constructs using both quantitative and qualitative methods. His findings identify concepts underlying virtual learning, and he draws on his research to suggest strategies for improving the effectiveness of virtual team design.

The final chapter in this section takes a theoretical approach to virtual team effectiveness. Pnina Shachaf and Noriko Hara of Indiana University in Bloomington, Indiana, provide an ecological theoretical framework of virtual learning environments that accounts for the factors of team boundaries management, technology use, and external environment and properties. Drawing upon both theoretical and empirical research, their study provides teachers with tools for managing virtual team effectiveness.

Section II: Strategies for Effective Teaching and Learning in Virtual Teams

Educators interested in improving teaching and learning using virtual teams are faced with significant issues that go beyond work in virtual teams to the broader issues of learning. Instructors must deal with issues ranging from ensuring students' mastery of conceptual, analytical, and theoretical knowledge to developing students' ability and comfort with the use of technologies. They face the problem of engaging students in higher order learning, and of maximizing the potential benefits of interaction and collaboration between virtual team members. The chapters in this section address these issues, focusing on strategies for teaching and learning in virtual teams.

In Chapter V, Rashmi Assudani of Xavier University in Cincinnati, discusses e-learning in management education. Using an ethnographic study of a Web-based graduate course, she explores the circumstances that encourage learning in virtual teams. The practical implications of Assudani's study for teachers and learners include the importance of developing familiarity, building community as a means of creating successful outcomes, and developing social and technological competencies among learners.

Virtual study groups are the subject of Chapter VI, by Gregory B. Northcroft of the University of Illinois, Terri L. Griffith of Santa Clara University in California, and Mark A. Fuller of Washington State University, who discuss the potentials and benefits of virtual study groups. Drawing on their own experiences with virtual study groups composed of "working adults" at a large university, Northcroft, Griffith, and Fuller provide some strategies for effective design, training, and management of virtual study groups.

In Chapter VII, Kara L. Orvis of the U. S. Army Research Institute and Andrea Lassiter of Minnesota State University in Mankato consider the role of the instructor in identifying and directing learner-learner relationships in computer supported collaborative learning environments. Orvis and Lassiter identify potential problems (motivational, cognitive, and affective) for learners, and make clear and concrete recommendations for instructors to increase their effectiveness in facilitating learner-learner processes.

For teaching and learning in virtual teams to be academically legitimate, instructors must incorporate replicable and accurate assessment tools. In Chapter VIII, Patricia J. O'Connor of Queens College, City University of New York, and Susan H. Godar of William Paterson University, New Jersey address the assessment of virtual teams for the purpose of maximizing student learning. Moving from an explication of the concepts and strategies of outcomes assessment, they present specific examples of assessment tools and a "blueprint" for faculty to use in assessing virtual teams.

Section III: Teams in Action: International Collaboration

To educators, one of the most exciting potential uses of the Internet can be to enable students from different countries to exchange information and come to know one another and each another's cultures. In this section, authors address global issues in international collaborations. They present effective models of students who work in international virtual teams to learn both strategies and tactics for presenting themselves, and to become successful cross-cultural communicators.

In Chapter IX, Anne-Laure Fayard of INSEAD in France discusses her experiences of working with virtual student teams on two continents: Europe and Asia. Building on her own experience working with student virtual teams composed of members from France and Singapore engaged in collaborative consulting projects, Fayard discusses issues around course design and implementation. Using examples from her classes, she offers strategies for effective teaching and learning using international virtual teams.

In Chapter X, a second example of effective international student virtual team work is offered by Kathryn Hashimoto of the University of New Orleans in Louisiana and Jean-marc Lehu of Panthéon Sorbonne Université in Paris. They discuss their experiences with a well developed and several-year-old Student International Collaboration Project (SICP). The SICP is a problem-solving project where students work with each other and with faculty mentors to provide lessons in virtual teams' problem solving, communication skills, team management, and cross-cultural communication. Hashimoto and Lehu draw upon their own experiences with, and experiences of, past projects within SICP to offer a guide for teachers in initiating and effectively managing similar projects. Readers interested in issues of international collaboration among student virtual teams should also re-visit Chapter I, where Boehm and Aniola-Jedrzejek discuss their work with several different virtual teams composed of Polish and American students.

Section IV: Teams and Technology

By their very nature, virtual teams are reliant on technological tools. In the 21st century a wide range of technologies exist to facilitate the functioning of virtual teams. Not only can virtual teams in higher education routinely access course management software at their institutions of learning, but they can also utilize commercial freeware, commercial software and hardware, and are constantly exposed to the potential of emerging new technologies. The two chapters in this section provide different perspectives on the role and place of technological tools in virtual teams.

In Chapter XI, Karen Rohrbauck Stout of Western Washington University in Bellingham applies an analysis of tools as cultural artifacts to the understanding of learning in virtual teams. She uses Wartofsky's framework of primary, secondary, and tertiary tools to provide a typology of tools used in distance learning, and analyzes technological tools in terms of virtual team cognition and interaction. Stout's work offers a framework for considering the value of different technological tools for teaching and learning.

In Chapter XII, Stephen Rains and Craig R. Scott of the University of Texas at Austin develop the theme of technology in virtual teams, moving from the theoretical to the applied in a comprehensive examination of the range of technological tools available to, and used by, virtual teams. Drawing on examples from their own courses, they consider the importance of technology-based training and address practical implications and lessons for student team members.

Sharmila Pixy Ferris
Susan H. Godar
June 2005

References

Boyer, E. L. (1990). *Scholarship reconsidered: Priorities of the professoriate.* San Francisco: Jossey-Bass.

Davis, B. G. (1993). *Tools for teaching.* San Francisco: Jossey-Bass.

Ferris, S. P., Minielli, M., Phillips, K., & Mallard, J. (2003). *Beyond survival in the academy: A practical guide for beginning academics.* Cresskill, NJ: Hampton Press.

Godar, S. H., & Ferris, S. P. (2004). *Virtual and collaborative teams: Process, technologies and practice.* Hershey, PA: Idea Group Publishing.

Higher Education on the Web. (2002, February). Research Center Update, 7(1). Retrieved from http://www.campuscomputing.net/summaries/2004/index.html

National Survey of Information Technology in US Higher Education. (2004). Retrieved from http://www.campuscomputing.net/summaries/2004/index.html

Sloan Consortium. (2004). Entering the mainstream: The quality and extent of online education in the United States, 2003 and 2004. Retrieved from http://www.sloan-c.org/resources/survey.asp

Acknowledgments

First and foremost, we thank our authors and reviewers. We thank our authors for their outstanding contributions. They were a real pleasure to work with! We are equally grateful to those who helped with the collaboration and blind review process, without whom we would not have achieved a book of this caliber. Among the reviewers were many of the authors of chapters, who expertly served as referees for articles written by other authors. But our special thanks for reviewing go to our colleagues who gave unstintingly of their knowledge and time to provide constructive and comprehensive feedback. They include:

David Arentsen, LIM College and Baruch College

Karen Mallia, University of South Carolina

Maureen C. Minielli, Indiana University-Purdue University at Indianapolis

Len Presby, William Paterson University

Milda Yildiz, William Paterson University

We would also like to thank our editor Kristin Roth for her efficiency and generosity in working with us, and the publishing team at Idea Group Inc. for their competence and expertise. Finally, we are grateful for the understanding and support of our partners who helped us survive this process, and to our canine and feline menageries for grounding us in reality by being their own unforgettable selves.

Section I

From E-Learning to Learning in Virtual Teams

Chapter I

Seven Principles of Good Practice for Virtual International Collaboration

Diane Boehm
Saginaw Valley State University, USA

Lilianna Aniola-Jedrzejek
Poznan University of Technology, Poland

Abstract

This chapter presents seven principles of good practice for conducting virtual international collaborations with students. The authors have conducted such collaborations with several different groups of American and Polish university students using different models. The collaborations were the basis for distilling these seven principles: develop cross-cultural awareness and mutual understanding of the culture of each group; create a multifaceted virtual environment; coordinate calendars; require intermediate level of English language proficiency; create relevant, engaging collaborative assignments with rubrics and shared understandings for evaluation of student work; establish methods for successful group interactions, including information-sharing and relationship-building; evaluate project outcomes. These seven principles of good practice can assist instructors to develop successful virtual intercultural collaborations that prepare students for the workplace of the 21st century.

Introduction

"Think globally—act locally." This slogan, popular among environmentalists, has equal validity for today's institutions of higher education, where preparing students for the future must embrace both the global and the local. As we teach and mentor young people preparing to enter the workforce, we act locally to prepare them for a global community very different from previous generations. It is clear that the workplace of the 21st century will increasingly demand employees who bring a global perspective as well as a multiplicity of abilities to their work, including an understanding of world cultures, an ability to work collaboratively, and the capacity to integrate technology into many facets of their work.

If students are to develop these capabilities, they must have real-world learning experiences, including opportunities to develop understanding of the barriers that can complicate intercultural interactions:

> *At the present time there is a greater need for effective international and cross-cultural communication, collaboration, and cooperation, not only for the effective practice of management but also for the betterment of the human condition. Ample evidence shows that cultures of the world are becoming more and more interconnected and that the business world is becoming increasingly global. As economic borders come down, cultural barriers will most likely go up and present new challenges and opportunities in business. When cultures come into contact, they may converge on some aspects, but their idiosyncrasies will likely amplify.* (House, Hanges, Javidan, Dorfman, & Gupta, 2004, p. 1)

The desire to give students real-world experience in surmounting cultural barriers as they developed collaboration and technology skills became the impetus for virtual international collaboration between university students in our two countries, the U.S. and Poland. Saginaw Valley State University (SVSU) in Michigan is a regional state university with about 9,450 students. Poznan University of Technology (PUT) in Poznan, Poland, is the fourth largest technological university in Poland, with about 20,000 day and weekend students. PUT is likewise regional, as the majority of its students come from the west-central Wielkopolska region. It also has students from small towns in northern Poland, and a small number from eastern Poland. Over the span of the past several years, we have conducted English language cross-cultural collaborative learning projects with students from both universities in multiple online contexts and, by trial and error, have learned a great deal about what makes such collaboration successful or not.

Recognizing that globalization has permanently changed national perspectives as well as international relationships, the idea of collaboration between students of both our universities has focused on two goals. Our first goal has been to build mutual understanding and openness to other cultures. This understanding of other cultures, already familiar to most Polish students who have traveled to neighboring countries, has become a priority for Poland, as it entered the European Union on May 1, 2004. Such understanding is equally important but less common for American students, whose sphere of interest may stop at U.S. borders, with limited awareness of the dramatic changes globalization has already begun to bring about within and beyond those borders.

How can students build cultural understanding and openness in this new international environment? What has changed? What has stayed the same? Journalist and historian Tom Friedman, in *The Lexus and the Olive Tree: Understanding Globalization* (2000), provides some context. Friedman has charted the beginning of this era of globalization as the 1989 fall of the Berlin Wall, which permanently shifted not only political boundaries but also human possibilities. Friedman contrasts the image of the ultramodern Lexus luxury automobile, representing ever-evolving global technologies, with the gnarled roots of the ancient olive tree, a symbol of the age-old needs for community and personal freedoms characteristic of human learners. Friedman cautions thoughtful world citizens to weigh priorities in this new global environment:

Globalization emerges from below, from street level, from people's very souls and from their very deepest aspirations. Yes, globalization is the product of the democratizations of finance, technology and information, but what is driving all three of these is the basic human desire for a better life—a life with more freedom to choose how to prosper, what to eat, what to wear, where to live, where to travel, how to work, what to read, what to write and what to learn. (p. 333)

Even the most futuristic emerging technologies, Friedman reminds us, evolve from innate human needs. Thus attention must be paid to the human side of globalization, to helping students build the mutual understanding and openness to other cultures that has been our first goal.

Our second goal has been to make the required courses we teach (composition in the U.S., and English as a Second Language in Poland) more challenging and engaging for students. Because English has become the *lingua franca* of international trade and communication, Americans have not had to stretch their language capacities, and composition students do not always see the immediate value of the hard work required for success in such courses. In contrast, students in the rest of the world often see the learning of English as a door to the future, and English language instruction is becoming a requirement around the globe. But helping non-native speakers learn English (which encompasses multiple dialects/world Englishes, as well as five times the vocabulary of many other languages) can pose a significant challenge for teachers of the language in other countries.

Thus international collaboration among students from our two countries has offered intriguing possibilities to expand student learning and understanding in both our contexts. For this goal, PUT and SVSU were well-suited for collaboration for several reasons: mid-Michigan has a significant number of people of Polish descent; both universities have many first-generation college students; furthermore, the instructors had already gotten to know each other personally prior to the first project and shared similar outlooks. Intercultural classroom collaborations, we have discovered, present many challenges, but they can become a transforming learning experience for students.

What we have learned from several years of collaboration is rooted in well-researched principles of teaching and learning. The idea of "seven principles for good practice" had its origins in the publication of Arthur W. Chickering and Zelda Gamson's "Seven Principles for Good Practice in Undergraduate Education" in the March 1987 *AAHE (American Association of Higher Education) Bulletin*. Based on extensive research of what constitutes good teaching and learning in undergraduate education, Chickering and Gamson identify seven qualities of good teaching:

1. Encourages contact between students and faculty
2. Develops reciprocity and cooperation among students
3. Encourages active learning
4. Gives prompt feedback
5. Emphasizes time on task
6. Communicates high expectations
7. Respects diverse talents and ways of learning.

Subsequently, as new technologies became integrated into higher education in multiple ways, these seven principles were expanded in "Implementing the Seven Principles: Technology as Lever" by Chickering and Stephen C. Ehrmann. "Implementing" provided strategies and examples of the ways in which technology could offer teachers new methods for achieving the seven principles of good practice. Since then, globalization—which both coincided with, and was precipitated by, the new technologies—has spurred dramatic changes in both technology and its multinational applications.

We have long valued and put into practice these seven principles. However, because they were based upon a traditional educational context, they could not answer our questions about best practices to develop successful international student collaborations. Thus teachers who seek to practice Chickering and Gamson's original seven principles, implement technology as a lever, and integrate a global perspective into their teaching and learning require a new set of principles on which to base best practices in this challenging new environment.

International collaboration is by its very nature an exercise in problem-solving. We have not — and may never — resolve all the issues such collaborations raise. The challenges of achieving Principle 7 of good teaching, for example, which calls for respecting "diverse talents and ways of knowing," increase exponentially when cross-cultural and second language factors enter the equation.

Take for instance the very basic vocabulary we use to describe this work. In the U.S., collaboration is viewed very positively as an essential component of successful teamwork, a familiar "way of knowing" in American universities. In European universities, however, the practice of working in teams is far less common. And in a country like Poland, which spent decades as part of the Soviet bloc, the very word "collaborator" is a reminder of a bitter chapter in history, a remembrance of those who betrayed their homeland. Thus, to respect our own diverse histories and individual ways of knowing, we use the term *collaboration* when presenting our work to an American audience, but for a Polish or European audience we discuss *cooperation*.

Similarly, developing the principle of "reciprocity and cooperation among students" from different countries must also take into consideration such complex factors as the differing educational systems and cultural values, the access to technology, as well as the language capabilities of the students. Students from any culture tend to assume that their international counterparts will approach collaborative work from a perspective like their own. They may be amazed to find out that the educational structures in another country often dictate very different student approaches and educational goals. For many American students, few of whom will have traveled to other countries or developed fluency in another language, this revelation also introduces them to previously unfamiliar global realities even as it piques their intellectual curiosity.

Adapting the "seven principles for good practice" model, we have developed a parallel set of seven principles for virtual international collaboration that can increase the likelihood that such collaborations will achieve their goals and work relatively smoothly. These principles of good practice for international collaboration provide a framework to guide faculty who wish to develop similar virtual collaborations in their own contexts. We will illustrate these principles with examples from our U.S./Poland collaborations, but we offer the principles as a foundation for any student collaboration that crosses international boundaries.

The essential base for cross-cultural virtual collaborations is, of course, the technological infrastructure. Recent educational technologies dramatically expand a teacher's options. Course management systems, for instance, have brought new ease to the work of virtual student groups. We have conducted our collaborative projects with students at SVSU and PUT using the Blackboard course management system (PUT students are enrolled into the SVSU course). From these experiences, we have distilled the seven principles we find essential for effective international student collaboration.

Principle 1. Develop cross-cultural awareness and mutual understanding of the culture of each group prior to collaboration.

Cross-cultural awareness and understanding set the stage for both instructors and students to engage in collaborative work. Consider especially the following four factors:

1. *Education Systems and Practices*

What educational system and practices are students in each country accustomed to? Is most teaching deductive or inductive in nature? Are courses traditionally taught in lecture format or are active learning strategies widely used? Problems we have encountered here, for example, are connected with the Polish/European approach of deductive rather than inductive learning; deductive approaches such as lectures provide limited student practice in group problem-solving. And because Polish students are accustomed to working on the basis of knowledge they acquire either during lectures or from literature they are given, most would rather rely on prepared materials than search independently.

Documentation of source materials has likewise been a persistent issue. Citation and avoidance of plagiarism are not emphasized in other countries as they are in American higher education. This can cause problems when students from both countries exchange research information for a project. An e-mail exchange between instructors demonstrates the dilemmas this can cause:

The [missing] source citations were a big problem for the SVSU students; they were reluctant to use information [from PUT students] which didn't have source citations, because they knew that would be considered plagiarism. (D. Boehm, e-mail communication, November 26, 2002)

The response:

We discussed the problems of the citations, and my students put them at the end of the article. I think the major misunderstanding was that my students thought that if they send the materials your students will work with them, because of their English. (L. Jedrzejek, e-mail communication, December 7, 2002)

2. *Cultural Context*

How can students develop understanding of cultural contexts when preparing for international collaboration? As Cushner and Brislin point out, "People experience strong emotional reactions when their cultural values are violated or when their cultures' expected behaviors are ignored" (p. 8). Edward Hall's analysis of context in culture is helpful here. Context is based on the degree to which members of a group share common values and background. High context cultures are generally homogeneous and rely heavily on implicit communication (Thomas, 2004). Poland's culture has high context characteristics. National holidays such as All Saints Day or Assumption, for instance, have shared religious as well as cultural significance, and successful interaction is built upon shared values as a foundation for mutual trust. Because relationship-building is important for Poles, the lack of nonverbal communication in electronic interaction is keenly felt.

Low-context cultures require more explicit communication, since the environment is heterogeneous and common values and background cannot be assumed; for example, the USA (Thomas, 2004). American students, coming from a low-context environment, consequently tend to be more direct, more task-oriented, and less patient with the time needed to build relationships and achieve consensus. Instructors must reflect: How can students from high-context cultures work most effectively with students from low-context cultures? (This reflection applies also to instructors. This very task-oriented American instructor has had to learn from her high-context Polish colleague to think far more strategically about how to help students establish personal connection as a necessary element for successful task completion.)

3. *Individualism*

A related cultural characteristic is individualism. Are students' cultures more individualistic or collective/group-oriented? Geert Hofstede (2003) of The Netherlands has scored countries on the basis of five Cultural Dimensions, including individualism. Not surprisingly, the USA ranks the highest of any country in individualism. Its score of 91 "indicates a society with a more individualistic attitude and relatively loose bonds with others. The populace is more self-reliant." Poland, with an individualism score of 56, values interpersonal relationships more highly due to its "more collectivist nature with close ties between individuals."

Related questions about student perspectives on collaborative work also merit consideration here. Is group work valued or considered unimportant? What group learning experiences have students previously had? How much structure is necessary for collaboration to be successful? Though working in groups is familiar to most American students, that does not mean they have learned how to function effectively to achieve group goals. Polish students may have had very limited experience with group processes. With each student project, we have become more aware of the importance of incorporating strategies that take these cultural characteristics into account.

4. *Educational Level of Students*

As could be anticipated, collaborations which involved PUT students with greater English language proficiency have gone more smoothly than those involving students still learning basics of the language. Likewise, collaborations with upper level SVSU students have been more satisfying and achieved better outcomes than those that involved freshman students, which is also not surprising, since freshmen are still learning how to navigate in their own university environment. The majority of our examples in this paper have been drawn from two collaborations involving PUT intermediate level English students and upper level SVSU students. However, PUT students with lower English language proficiency and SVSU freshmen have generally been positive about the collaborations, and often comment on the experience in their end-of-course evaluations.

Principle 2. Create a multifaceted virtual environment.

Creating the virtual environment for successful e-learning has three interrelated elements (see Figure 1):

- **Learners:** Recognizing the factual and conceptual knowledge students bring to the project, the level of experience with electronic learning tools, and the importance of cultural and individual differences (see Principle 1).
- **Pedagogy/Content:** Understanding how to align the process of content learning to the needs of students (see Principles 5, 6, and 7); this includes establishing goals and project outcomes (e.g., enhanced ability to understand issues, analyze problems, and apply skills) and determining the most effective instructional methods to achieve those outcomes.
- **Technology:** Employing the most user-friendly solutions for technology-enhanced learning, creating interactive social dimensions to enhance team effectiveness, and sequencing learning tasks so learners without technical expertise do not feel overwhelmed.

Figure 1. Inter-related elements of successful virtual learning environments

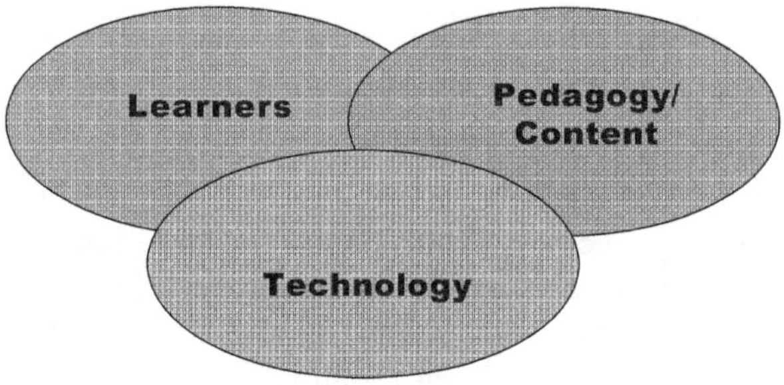

Since the instructional technology aspect is vital to the success of any virtual international project, it should be included in project goals and evaluated in project outcomes. Evaluating the learning outcomes of each collaborative project we have conducted has provided insight into how to establish a successful virtual environment.

One of our objectives has been to increase competence in the use of technology in collaborative settings. Our outcomes assessment has identified two issues. One is purely technological: when creating the virtual environment, computer and Internet access must also be taken into account. Whereas ready access can be assumed for most American students, that may not yet be the case in other countries, such as Poland. The second issue is psychological: regardless of the technology, the success of its use depends on the personal characteristics of the project participants, their reliability in collaborative environments, and their adherence to the assignment schedule. Even the most sophisticated technology will be useless if students are not committed to the project.

With each group of students, we also wanted to nurture discovery of both the pros and the cons of virtual collaboration. A further goal for the PUT students, most of whom were studying at the Faculty of Computing Sciences and Engineering Management, was to introduce them to the Blackboard platform. This would help them discover how effective and potent technology can be for finding resources and producing documents — technical knowledge that is directly relevant to their programs of study. This outcome has consistently been achieved, as Polish students have demonstrated a tremendous leap in their practical use of this technology by the end of each project. Students in both countries have also recognized its limitations and have often expressed a wish that they could meet face-to-face.

As educators, we had a further aim of making the virtual collaboration engaging for students who more and more are accustomed to living in a virtual world, thereby enhancing the value of the courses we teach. American students were often first intrigued by the novelty of the project, but later became far more savvy about the interrelationship between the human and the technological aspects of collaboration. The Polish students generally went through three phases that are perhaps typical of partners from different cultures working on a new project. At first, many were anxious and even frustrated for various reasons: language competence, Internet access, and the time needed to complete the assignment. The second phase was curiosity, as the project was introduced and students were organized into working teams. The final phase was either a sense of fulfillment, when the team worked together well and produced interesting results, or a sense of anxiety, when expectations of the group were not met. The latter has generally required instructor intervention and problem-solving.

When students come from significantly different cultures, multifaceted virtual interaction of learners becomes especially important. As Cramton's research (1999) points out, in a virtual environment, attention to team-building takes on special significance, given the lack of face-to-face conversation, body language, facial expression, or physical interaction to smooth out communication hurdles. With a Web interface such as a course management system, the student Web pages, course Web sites, virtual chats, asynchronous discussion boards, file exchanges, and e-mail all contribute to creating a virtual classroom atmosphere that fosters team-building, group problem-solving, discussion, and review and revision of documents, as well as student/faculty interaction.

Principle 3. Coordinate calendars (allow maximum time).

Timelines have consistently been the single most formidable challenge in our international cooperation. It is wise to anticipate a number of differences that might cause problems here:

- **Time Factors:** Students in different countries work on different academic schedules (see Table 1). Thus U. S. students are at midterm when Polish students are just starting their semester.

Table 1. University academic calendars

	First semester	Second semester
United States	Late August to mid-December	Early January to late April/early May
Poland/Europe	Early October to late January	Early March to late June

Furthermore, the time difference (six hours between Poland and the U. S.) limits the number of synchronous conferences that can be easily scheduled. European universities also observe more and longer holiday breaks than do American universities, which can further complicate timetables.

Thus time factors can become a critical issue when significant time is invested in relationship-building prior to carrying out the actual assignment. The maximum time window available for us to complete all phases of a project is usually four to five weeks. For SVSU students, the project deadline is likely to correspond with other end-of-semester deadlines as well.

- **Time Management:** Polish students, working on a project in English — a foreign language for them — need more time to complete the project. Furthermore, their limited experience with documentation practices and citation formats necessitates additional instructional time. To extend the time, however, means American students would likely be simultaneously involved in other class projects. Consequently, international collaboration also demands significant instructor time for dialogue, group monitoring, troubleshooting, follow-up, and assessment.

Principle 4. Require intermediate level of English language proficiency.

The quality and productivity of the students' interaction is directly related to the language fluency of the English language learners. When we have conducted collaborations with Polish students who were still developing basic English language proficiency, the collaboration became much more difficult for all. Polish students had to spend so much time struggling to understand and properly word messages that they were unable to adequately prepare the assignment itself. Limited vocabulary and weak command of grammatical structures can also cause cross-cultural misunderstanding in any language interaction. Such misunderstandings are amplified if language learners have not reached a necessary level of language acquisition.

The Polish students were also still becoming familiar with the CLIL (Content and Language Integrated Learning) approach to language learning, a relatively new concept in many countries, where a more traditional skill-and-drill method of instruction had been used in the past. The pedagogy used in CLIL integrates the acquisition of the subject knowledge as a means of language learning. CLIL is very effective in ensuring foreign language competence along with professional growth, as it creates a balance between linguistic, vocational, cultural and personal development. Thus it is a very important and efficient strategy to ensure that the teaching/learning of foreign languages is taking place in a real environment. However, this unfamiliar approach may unnerve students at the outset. Of course the range of proficiency and motivation to learn English will have a wide range in any class, so while some groups may forge ahead, others may need significant attention and coaching.

A further consideration is the British English dialect (vocabulary and spelling) widely used in European universities. (American English may be familiar to some because of American television, movies, and other popular media.) Thus American students may jump to the conclusion that their counterparts are not checking for errors when they see spellings such as *honour, favourite, organise*, and the like. And of course many American students are neither accustomed to calculating in metric units of measure, nor to telling time on a 24-hour clock; most are not familiar with different currencies and political processes.

And because many American students do not develop proficiency in another language, they fail to appreciate the challenge a collaborative writing assignment brings to non-native speakers of English. If they lack any second language learning experience, American students may not recognize that their counterparts will take everything they say very literally and sometimes construct meaning by compiling dictionary definitions of unfamiliar terms. American students may not realize how important simple, straightforward, and specific language is when seeking to avoid miscommunication. They may also be careless with grammar and punctuation, and use many idiomatic or slang expressions that their counterparts will not be able to find in a dictionary. If, for example, a Discussion Board posting includes expressions such as "on the fast track," "having a meltdown," "on a power trip," "pushing the envelope," and the like, English language learners face a quandary. Should they take time to ask for an explanation or just go on without really understanding the term?

Fortunately, some American textbooks are now beginning to address cross-cultural communication. Kolin's text *Successful Writing at Work*, now in its 7th edition and used in the SVSU Writing in the Professions class, emphasizes the need "to respect the cultural and communication needs and traditions of a global audience" (p. xxi). The textbook incorporates new information on thinking globally and multi-culturally throughout the chapters. It reminds American students, for example, that sports metaphors such as "out in left field" or "struck out" or "long shot" will have no frame of reference for students in most countries of the world. The text also aims to develop cultural sensitivity, warning writers to avoid pejorative ethnocentric terms such as "third-world country," "foreigner," or "Oriental." But students who have not previously been sensitized to multicultural issues may not be aware that their language could unknowingly offend their counterparts. And non-native speakers of English will likely need to invest much time to be successful team members.

Principle 5. Create relevant, engaging collaborative assignments and tasks with rubrics and shared understandings for evaluation of student work.

Assignments must take into account all of the other principles identified here. Over the past several years, we have developed, through instructor dialogue, several collaborative assignments based on the student population in each class for that semester. Our assignments have evolved as our experiences, coupled with student feedback, have led us in new directions.

One of the challenges we face is that we do not teach the same student populations each semester. At SVSU, the two student populations have been incoming freshman composition students in fall semesters, and upper level students with a mix of majors in a professional writing class in winter semesters. In both cases, this is a required course for the students, rather than an elective. At PUT, English courses are compulsory, but the mix of students has likewise varied. And because PUT is a technological university, students may not give language courses the same priority that liberal arts students might.

To date, we have used four different collaborative assignments:

1. **A Collaborative Research Project**
   - U. S. Participants: 19 students in an upper level Writing in the Professions course.
   - PUT Participants: 14 Polish students at intermediate level of English language competence, enrolled in compulsory English, a five-semester course for students studying at the Faculty of Computing Sciences and Engineering Management.
2. **Intercultural Interviews and Peer Review**
   - U. S. Participants: 20 first semester freshman honors composition students.
   - PUT Participants: 15 students at intermediate level of English language competence, enrolled in compulsory English, a five-semester course for students studying at the Faculty of Computing Sciences and Engineering Management.
3. **Contrast/comparison of the job market for targeted jobs in both countries**
   - U. S. Participants: 19 first semester freshmen in a regular composition course.
   - PUT Participants: 15 students at intermediate level of English language competence, approaching their final semester at the faculty of Technical Physics and Engineering Management.
4. **Intercultural Interactions Using Critical Incidents, based on the Cushner and Brislin model of Critical Incidents described below**
   - U. S. Participants: 18 students in an upper level Writing in the Professions course.
   - PUT Participants: 14 students at low intermediate level of English language competence, enrolled in compulsory English, a five-semester course for students studying at the Faculty of Computing Sciences and Engineering Management.

As we developed these assignments, we sought projects that went beyond gathering and reporting of information to those that demanded higher level thinking skills, such as application, analysis, and/or synthesis. Of the four assignments we have used, the Critical Incidents model used with upper-level students has generated the most interesting collaborative projects, perhaps because it is innovative and different from the typical formal research paper and because the application, analysis and synthesis that it requires make the perspectives from different cultures an integral part of the assignment task. This assignment, however, could be overwhelming for incoming American freshman students, since it is based on the expectation that students have developed a certain amount of skill with research, analysis, and critical thinking.

The Critical Incidents assignment is likely to be unfamiliar to most instructors, so we will illustrate it in detail. Since project-based learning and case studies are considered an "active learning" best practice, we based this assignment on the intercultural Critical Incidents model from Cushner and Brislin's *Intercultural Interactions: A Practical Guide* (1996). This model (analogous to a mini case-study) can be used to create a collaborative assignment that engages students and provides multiple types of learning experiences. The assignment is manageable for students who are non-native speakers of English, yet is based upon significant research, student exchanges, and relevant information from students in both countries. The Critical Incidents Assignment was designed to achieve the following student learning outcomes:

1. Develop an international perspective on relevant current issues
2. Enhance research and writing skills in a collaborative context
3. Build collaboration skills in multinational groups
4. Increase competence in the use of technology in collaborative settings
5. For PUT students, enhance second language skills through CLIL (Content and Language Integrated Learning) approach

The Critical Incidents assignment has four components:

1. An original Critical Incident followed by three to five possible response scenarios (using the Cushner and Brislin model), based on the topic chosen by the group
2. Rationales for the response scenarios, supported by research (also using the Cushner and Brislin model)
3. Supporting text (three to six pages), based on research and exchange of ideas, that explains and supports the rationales; these must include appropriate citations

4. A collaboratively created PowerPoint group presentation, to be presented in both countries.

Each phase of the project requires collaborative effort by all participants.

- **Phase 1:** To set the stage for interpersonal relationships, using the multifaceted virtual environment described in Principle 2, students begin the collaborative project by posting a personal Web site (with photo) telling about themselves. Students generally choose favorite photos that not only show their appearance but also characterize their values and interests, career goals, personal history and background, to provide a starting point for future online conversations. (An unanticipated experience demonstrates how easily cultural differences shape perceptions even here. When a nontraditional SVSU student posted a photo of herself with her two daughters, the PUT student assumed he was working with the older daughter, rather than the mother! Since nontraditional students are rare in European universities, the PUT student was making a natural cultural assumption that the SVSU student then had to address.) In our most recent collaboration, SVSU students also posted brief streaming video clips (three to four minutes) in which they introduced themselves to their Polish cohorts.
- **Phase 2:** Students then select general topics of interest, which are used to assign students to virtual working groups of 4-5 students, comprised of students from both countries with similar interests and complementary skill levels.
- **Phase 3:** This is followed by a group virtual chat, which has two purposes: acquainting student group members with each other and exploring potential ideas for the assignment. The chat includes discussion of a published Cushner and Brislin Critical Incident posted to the Course Documents. (We choose Incidents that would be relevant to students of both countries and remain within Fair Use Guidelines.)
- **Phase 4:** After discussion of the selected Cushner and Brislin Critical Incident, student groups begin the research and asynchronous discussion to develop their own Incident. Each Critical Incident must integrate a cross-cultural conflict, with sufficient detail to be clear and plausible. To create their original Critical Incident, each student group agrees on a relevant theme or topic (e.g., advertising; discrimination; business ethics; the impact of media; genetically modified foods) for its research and

project. Students then exchange ideas to develop a specific focus and generate a situation based on their research, personal experience, interviews with others, observation, and analysis.

The Critical Incident includes 3-5 possible scenarios to resolve the conflict. Each must likewise be plausible. Each scenario is then evaluated, with an explanation of the reasons why that scenario is more or less successful as a strategy for dealing with the conflict than the other scenarios.

- **Phase 5:** Upon completion, the final project with supporting text is submitted to the instructors, and the Critical Incident is presented to the classes in both countries for discussion via the collaborative Power Point presentation. Regardless of the culture, presentation skills are necessary in today's world. For the students it is an important element of the project, since it allows the whole group to find out what the other teams were working on. They are motivated to finish on time, since they know the groups will be comparing results. The presentation has been the highlight of the project for the Polish students, as they have a real sense of accomplishment giving presentations in English for invited guests and other students. As student groups discuss their Critical Incidents with each other, they become far more aware of the many ways in which cultural blinders can result in misunderstandings and missed cues, achieving Goals 1 and 2 of the assignment. As students have worked through the phases of the assignment, their collaboration and technology skills, Goals 3 and 4, have likewise been honed. Goal 5 is specific to the PUT students, and has also been accomplished, though with a wide range of success. Throughout the project, the instructors in both countries monitor student progress with both groups of students via e-mails, postings to discussion boards, and face-to-face conversations with local students. Student projects are evaluated using the project rubrics presented under Principle 7.

An example of one student group's Critical Incident project illustrates the effectiveness of this active learning model to stimulate student learning and engagement.

Advertising Strategies and Ethics

- **Critical Incident**[1]**:** Helmut and Stefan are employed in the advertising department of the Heineken Beer Company. Their base of operations is in Germany, and the company sent them to promote its product in Poland. They envisioned huge billboards on the streets and a series of entertaining commercials on Polish television to sell their product.

The first few weeks of their work went well. They prepared the advertisements and visuals that would be important for production of their commercial. Helmut and Stefan liked working with the Polish people, and the preparation went without any serious problems. However, they ran into trouble in their fifth week of work. When Helmut went to the public television station to get all the necessary documents reviewed, he discovered that Polish law bans all types of alcohol-related advertising. Helmut and Stefan didn't know how to tell their boss they could not promote Heineken products on TV as planned due to Polish advertising laws.

- **Response Scenarios:** Which best explains Helmut and Stefan's oversight?
  1. They did not respect Poland's commitment to substance abuse prevention.
  2. Their employers neglected to give them a workable assignment.
  3. They gave up too easily and should have challenged the Polish law since the rest of the European Union has no ban on advertising alcoholic beverages.
  4. Since the rest of Europe is very liberal about alcoholic beverage advertising, they saw no reason to consult the laws.
- **Rationales for Response Scenarios (Supported by Research):**
  1. The movement to curb substance abuse in Poland is relatively new; thus it may be unfair to assume Helmut and Stefan did not respect Polish commitment to substance abuse prevention. Poland has a nationally-documented substance abuse problem that is not widely known outside of the country. To stem problems associated with alcohol abuse, the legislative body in Poland, the *Sejm*, banned advertising containing alcoholic beverages in 2000.
  2. This is the best answer. A case can be made that it was an oversight on the part of Helmut and Stefan's bosses that led to their failure in Poland. Clearly, if a company like Heineken is going to pursue business in foreign countries, it should be knowledgeable about the culture and regulations that would affect their business, especially in a neighboring country.
  3. If Helmut and Stefan were really ambitious, they could challenge the Polish law banning alcoholic beverage advertisements as a form of

trade restraint. While they would have very little luck directly challenging the law in a Polish context, they may have a compelling case as Poland joins the European Union, since the Polish regulations are more stringent than in other countries in the European Union. The European Union is considering a uniform BAC (Blood Alcohol Content) level for drunk driving laws at .05%. In Poland, the legal limit is .02% (astounding compared to .08% in Michigan!). Poland seems very resistant to changing these limits. Also, alcohol prices are much higher in Poland than in all other European Union countries, a fact that may cause conflict between the European Union and Poland concerning alcohol policy and exports. However, it would not be a wise idea for Helmut and Stefan to fight this battle themselves. They should respect the laws instead of challenging them.

4. Because Helmut and Stefan are Germans, they did not consider Polish law. Since alcohol is accepted in most European cultures, it is likely Helmut and Stefan did not consider the possibility of Polish regulations banning alcoholic beverage advertising.

Principle 6. Establish methods for successful group interactions, including information-sharing and relationship-building.

The challenge of creating a structure for successful group collaboration is magnified because students must manage both cultural differences as well as the limitations of virtual interaction. The ideal would be for students to form their own groups based on their interest in a topic. However, groups of 4-5 (of both nationalities) need to be put together somewhat strategically, considering the different level of computer and Internet access and skills in both groups of students, as well as the broad range of English proficiency among non-native speakers of English.

Composition of groups is only one aspect that requires consideration. It is impossible to foresee all the possibilities that could impede group success. Cramton's studies (1999) have identified several types of information problems with which dispersed teams struggle. For example, team members often fail to share important information about their own context and constraints. Several such incidents in our collaborations demonstrate the importance of cultural sensitivity in information exchange. In our first collaboration, one of the

SVSU students sent the instructor a memo about a problem with the group; the PUT students, he said, were

> *...offended by our discussion of communism and democracy. What they didn't realize was that we were curious about the topic. It's not every day that one gets to ask someone with first-hand knowledge their thoughts on the subject. Once it became apparent that this was a sensitive subject, we discontinued the discussion.* (J. Leach, personal communication, November 11, 2002)

When this information was forwarded to the PUT instructor, she discussed it with her students and provided information that the SVSU instructor could then relay to her students:

> *I also noticed that...the U.S. students are interested in the subject of communism, and that's something Polish students don't want to write too much about and don't want to include into the project.* (L. Jedrzejek, November 5, 2002)

A subsequent instructor e-mail exchange suggested a reason for other miscommunications:

> *I'm glad you told them to communicate their wishes! I think many of the students from both our campuses failed to do that at the beginning, which made the collaboration much harder. They were trying too hard to be nice, and didn't express their wishes clearly.* (D. Boehm, e-mail communication, November 26, 2002)

Furthermore, Cramton (1999) suggests electronic communication may make it more difficult to produce the level and type of feedback necessary for achieving mutual goals. And relationship tensions, which are characteristic of any group interactions, may be more difficult with students who are still learning to function in teams, and whose problem-solving strategies may stem from different cultures. Such tensions can be magnified by language limitations and cultural differences in thought processes and project management. Typically, the

Table 2. Causes of difficulties in intercultural collaborative project

	Yes	No	Uncertain
1. Distribution of tasks	12	3	1
2. Expectations	11	4	1
3. Time component	10	5	1
4. Cultural differences	10	5	1
5. Understanding Language	4	10	2

American students, working comfortably in a familiar context and language, will want to exercise a "take-charge" attitude that moves the group forward, but often at the cost of substantive contributions by all participants.

In spite of—and perhaps because of—such issues, students themselves develop significant insight into the problems of virtual multicultural collaboration as they complete the projects. Upper-class SVSU students in our first collaboration during Fall 2002 are representative. They ranked their perceptions in response to the question of what caused the greatest difficulties (see Table 2 above).

Since distribution of tasks, expectations and time components are issues that frequently arise in any group project, it is not surprising that these would be ranked at the top of the issues by American students in our collaborations. Polish students, however, more often ranked time components and language as a frequent cause of difficulties.

Most students from both countries were quite sanguine about the challenges. Their anonymous evaluations identified numerous advantages to multinational collaboration: "Fun, interesting, new, insightful"; "Greater awareness of other cultures"; "Getting to know about another culture." They were equally aware of disadvantages: "Working with someone so far away"; "The differences between the Polish students and ourselves"; "Language barriers; uneven distribution of work." Our final conclusion was that the challenges provided a realistic learning experience: "Had there been no frustrations, the students would have learned far less about the challenges of this type of work" (Boehm, e-mail communication, December 7, 2002).

It is wise to anticipate such problems with efficient communication and division of tasks among the partners in the group and to establish guidelines for the process. Monitoring group progress is essential to success, and skillful intervention may become necessary when groups appear to be struggling to remain on schedule and accomplish assigned work.

Principle 7. Evaluate project outcomes.

Our evaluation has had two components:

- **Project Evaluation:** First, it is necessary to evaluate student work. With the Critical Incident assignment, each group's project was evaluated using the rubrics provided below in Table 3 and Table 4 (a rubric clearly "communicates high expectations" for student achievement, also a best practice).

Table 3. Collaborative project evaluation

Strong	OK	Weak	This collaborative project:
			Produced an engaging, relevant, original multicultural Critical Incident (Cushner & Brislin model)
			Presents an international perspective on a relevant current issue
			Presents credible and clearly stated Critical Incident response choices
			Provides researched rationales for the Critical Incident response choices
			Includes sufficient authoritative research to give rationales credibility and authority
			Properly cites references to all source materials used
			Presents an effective PowerPoint presentation of the Critical Incident
			Provides a valuable learning experience for both group members and presentation audience
			Demonstrates substantial, balanced contributions by all group members
			PUT: Enhances second language skills through CLIL approach

Table 4. Oral presentation evaluation

Strong	OK	Weak	For this class presentation:
			Presenters projected professional image
			Content was appropriate for audience
			Content included all information necessary for audience understanding of topic
			Presentation conformed to time limits
			Presentation included appropriate audio/visual component
			Presenters used effective presentation style
			Presenters' voice and rate of speaking were effective
			Presenters' eye contact, body language, and gestures enhanced presentation

- **Project Assessment:** The second type of evaluation assessed the outcomes of the entire collaborative project after completion. Students completed an anonymous questionnaire, also conducted on Blackboard, which assessed the development of cross-cultural awareness, the challenges and rewards of international student collaboration, and the strengths and limitations of collaboration via electronic media. (See Appendix A for questionnaire.) We then synthesized these responses using Bush, Maid, and Roen's six-part assessment matrix (Bush, Maid, & Roen, 2003, p. 312) to assess overall outcomes, with a goal to guide and improve future collaborations. Most of the changes we have made from project to project have been precipitated by student feedback. The questionnaire also creates an opportunity for the type of reflection and metacognitive analysis students and instructors rarely have time for during the press of project work. The summary matrix in Table 5 assessed the Critical Incidents assignment.

In addition to this synthesis of the students' responses, we have also reviewed our personal communications and reflections. Each collaboration has taught us some things we could apply in subsequent interactions. Each likewise motivated us to continue to refine our processes because we could see evidence of the benefits:

Table 5. A matrix for assessing e-learning pedagogy and curriculum[2]

Clear Goals (Questionnaire, #1-3, plus instructors' reflections)	Both Polish and American students reported that the collaboration achieved the stated outcomes: • Students increased understanding of each other's cultures • Students developed their ability to work collaboratively • Students identified both advantages and limitations of collaborating via electronic media • In addition, the Polish students significantly increased their communication skills. The level of achievement of outcomes varied widely from student to student in both cultures.
Adequate Preparation (Questionnaire, #4-7)	Student responses identified a need to pay more careful attention to project procedures: • Create a friendlier virtual environment to counteract the lack of direct communication (e.g., along with pictures of individual students, use student Web sites for students to share more about their backgrounds and goals as preparation for introductory chats and subsequent collaboration) • Provide more background on the other country, its educational practices, cultural characteristics, and the students participating in the project; give native English speakers more instruction in language issues which affect intercultural communication • Group students based on similar goals and professional interests as much as possible, with an equal number of students from each country • Take computer access into account when planning • Establish a longer timeline, to allow for relationship-building and more opportunities to exchange ideas and materials (especially if some Polish materials must first be translated, a time-consuming process).

Table 5. (continued)

Appropriate Methods (Questionnaire, #8-10)	Based on student feedback, we identified some changes in our methods which could enhance future projects: • Guide students' processes more directly by providing explicit guidelines and requirements for the project, including approaches to collaborative writing, guidelines for documentation of source materials, grading rubrics, and a detailed timetable that accounts for differences such as course calendars and time needed for preparation of presentations, especially by non-native speakers of English • Develop methods to resolve tensions, including strategies for working effectively as teams and formulating group procedures and responsibilities • Give non-native speakers of English the maximum possible time for preparation of the project, as they require adequate time to study exchanged materials and tackle new vocabulary, so that their work is fully thought-out and written with use of the newly acquired language • Monitor group interactions closely, intervening as necessary.
Significant Results (Questionnaire #11-14)	• Both students and instructors recognized to a much greater degree both the power and the limitations of course management system/Internet-based technology as a tool for international collaboration • Students in both countries learned in detail about important and relevant problems of both countries, developing a broader perspective and understanding of international trends and events.
Effective Communication (Questionnaire #15-16 plus instructors' observations)	• Polish students made a great leap in their communicating skill in English. All students agreed that learning language in a real context (CLIL approach) had positive impact on their overall language understanding. Most students stated that their vocabulary broadened significantly, as did their communicative skills. They noticed the difference, as they were able to exchange information and communicate much more fluently by the end of the project. The Polish students appreciated the fact that they could practice the language and get feedback from their American peers. As one student observed, "I've improved my [American] English in each aspect. Practise makes perfect. A real context of learning any language is very useful."

Table 5. (continued)

Effective Communication (Questionnaire #15-16 plus instructors' observations)	• American students observed the complexities of writing and working both online and with non-native speakers of English. They also viewed their native language through fresh eyes, realizing how easily common idioms, slang, or careless use of language can lead to misunderstanding. Many also started to pay attention to news about the European Union, and Poland specifically.
Reflective Critique	Each collaboration poses a unique set of problems. Can we establish some general guidelines to guide the process?

I'm really enjoying this project, because it gives us so much additional knowledge about the students' minds. (L. Jedrzejek, e-mail communication, November 5, 2002)

I'm really pleased with the [PUT] students....What I actually liked the most was the atmosphere; they were presenting materials in pairs, helping each other. My other colleagues present noticed, that it was so nice for a change [to see] students who enjoy doing something and are involved....And [the PUT students] all mentioned the names of their partners and when the American part was included into the presentation they always said: "and this is the part prepared by our American part of the team." (L. Jedrzejek, e-mail communication, November 20, 2002)

As we analyzed the wealth of qualitative data from student responses in our several collaborations, including the Critical Incidents model described above, we began to see patterns which ultimately have led to the seven principles we present here. Our experiences, both positive and negative, and the feedback we have received from each group of SVSU and PUT student participants, indicate that the complexities of cross-cultural communication and virtual cooperation require attention to critical specific factors if such collaboration is to achieve its goals. Thus we have developed these interrelated seven principles and suggested ways to implement each principle.

Conclusion

As with any challenging project, satisfaction and achievement in international collaboration are tempered by times of frustration and tension. However, we believe virtual international collaboration has the potential to grow exponentially and is far more likely to be successful when these seven principles of good practice for virtual international collaboration guide the process.

The rewards of such collaboration are great: students develop valuable cross-cultural understandings, create engaging project materials, and learn from each other in multiple ways, all of which lay a foundation for their future participation in the global workplace. For English language learners, the overall result is an astonishing qualitative increase in their language proficiency as well as in their oral presentation skills.

We invite readers to envision innovative ways to teach, connect, and transform their own students in the global community. We count ourselves fortunate to have the tools available to make such virtual intercultural collaboration possible. At the conclusion of one collaboration, Jedrzejek wrote:

> *I was very surprised (in a positive way) that my students feel so strongly about this project. The atmosphere is so warm, I can see the smiles on their faces when they talk about their experience....I really feel a deep satisfaction when I think of all the positive "side effects" the project has had on my students. Now they know the meaning of real cooperation and this way they are much better equipped for their future success at work....I hope your students have also experienced similar problems and joy.* (L. Jedrzejek, e-mail communication, November 27, 2002)

The eloquent words of one student completing the final anonymous project evaluation express the greatest advantage of such collaboration: "World Peace. I know, that sounds huge, but the more connected we are with people from somewhere else on the planet, the more likely we are to see them as friends."

References

Bush, L., Maid, B., & Roen, D. (2003). A matrix for reconsidering, reassessing, and shaping e-learning pedagogy and curriculum. In C. M. Wehlburg (Ed.), *To improve the academy, Vol. 21*. Bolton, MA: Anker.

Chickering, A. W., & Ehrmann, S. C. (2004). *Implementing the seven principles: Technology as lever*. The TLT Group: Teaching, Learning & Technology. Retrieved October 21, 2004, from http://www.tltgroup.org/program/seven.html

Chickering, A. W., & Gamson, Z. F. (2004). *Seven principles for good practice in undergraduate education*. Retrieved September 30, 2004, from http://www.aahebulletin.com/public/archive/sevenprinciples1987.asp?pf=1

Cramton, C. (1999). Crossing the international teaching divide: Evaluation of an Internet-based teaching project. *Journal of Teaching in International Business, 10*(3&4). Retrieved January 18, 2005, from http://www.som2.gmu.edu/cramton/PublishedPapers.htm

Cushner, K., & Brislin, R. W. (1996). *Intercultural interactions: A practical guide* (2nd ed.). Thousand Oaks, CA: Sage.

Friedman, T. L. (2000). *The Lexus and the olive tree: Understanding globalization*. New York: Farrar, Straus, Giroux.

Hofstede, G. (2003). *ITIM creating cultural competence*. Retrieved February 7, 2005, from http://www.geert-hofstede.com

House, R. J., Hanges, P. J., Javidan, M., Dorfman, P. W., & Gupta, V. (2004). *Culture, leadership, and organizations: The GLOBE study of 62 societies*. Thousand Oaks, CA: Sage.

Kolin, P. C. (2004). *Successful writing at work* (7th ed.). New York: Houghton Mifflin.

Thomas, J. (2004). *Guide to managerial persuasion and influence.* Upper Saddle River, NJ: Pearson/Prentice Hall.

Endnotes

1 Critical Incident composed by SVSU students Wayne Hofmann and Sarah Fortner, and PUT students Krzysztof Plotka, Piotr Pilarski, and Wojtek Zietek (Fall 2002).

2 The Reflective Critique presented in Table 5 became the genesis for this chapter.

Appendix A

Student Questionnaire

1. What were your expectations regarding cooperation with students from PUT/SVSU before the collaboration began?
2. Were your expectations the same or different after the collaboration concluded? Please comment.
3. In what way, if any, did the collaboration increase your cross-cultural awareness?
4. Please comment on the usefulness of each of the following for the online collaboration:
    - E-mail
    - Discussion Board
    - Virtual Chat
5. Did you encounter any problems with the technical aspects of the collaboration? Please comment.
6. Of what value to the collaboration, if any, were the personal Web pages?
7. How does virtual collaboration compare with face-to-face collaboration? Please comment.

8. What advantages do you see to online collaboration?
9. What disadvantages do you see to online collaboration?
10. What changes, if any, would enhance the type of online collaboration conducted in this class?
11. What were your personal priorities when you started working on the [Critical Incident] assignment?
12. Which of the course outcomes did you achieve while working on the [Critical Incident] assignment?
13. What was the most difficult part of the project? What was the most rewarding part of the project?
14. Were there any problems with the timing of the project? Please comment.

For PUT students:

15. Did this project have an impact on your English language skills? In what way?
16. How did the project affect your vocabulary, the comprehension of reading materials, writing skills and communication skills?

Chapter II

Learning Style Flexibility for Effective Virtual Teams

Pieter H du Toit
University of Pretoria, South Africa

Peter van Petegem
University of Antwerp, Belgium

Abstract

Changes currently taking place globally in education, training and all areas of human potential development where learning forms the crux, have implications for e-learning. Interactive participation in virtual teams has become an evident means of promoting the principles of deep and constructive learning, and the life-skill of working in teams. Team members working in virtual teams are interdependent of each other and learning to become independent learners as an end result. Value is added to learning in virtual teams when the principles of learning style flexibility

(LSF) are integrated with the principles of effective collaborative e-learning. The idea of learning style flexibility proposed in this chapter underpins the notion of developing learners' full potential and facilitating the process of becoming flexible in problem solving. The Ned Herrmann whole brain theory is used as the basis of the theoretical framework and adapted for learning style flexibility in virtual teams. In this chapter we discuss awareness of one's own learning style preferences, flexibility in terms of learning with the aim of developing one's full potential, formation of diverse e-learning groups according to learning style preferences for optimizing virtual group performance, and using collaborative action learning to promote constructive learning.

Introduction

What all visionary facilitators of e-learning should realize is that every learner has unique, unlimited potential. This fact challenges facilitators of e-learning to embark on a quest to explore the possibilities of discovering and developing learners' full potential. Moreover, facilitators should guide learners in maximizing their own potential. Collaborative action learning (O'Hara, Bourner, & Webber, 2004) could be used as a tool to achieve this.

Having a vision of innovating one's e-learning practice also necessitates being aware of the differences between the traditional and the more progressive approaches to teaching and learning as discussed in Brandes and Ginnis (1996). From their work it is clear that the most important question to be asked is not only *what* an e-learning opportunity or an assessment opportunity should consist of, but also *how* it should be informed by processes that would promote deep and holistic learning.

This chapter applies the theory on learning style flexibility (LSF) with the underpinning principles applied to the designing of opportunities for constructing meaning in the e-learning environment. In order to construct meaning, productive learning should be promoted. Characteristics of productive learning are exploring, discovering and experimenting. To discover and maximize e-learners' potential both the facilitator and learner need to become versatile and flexible partners. Members of virtual learning teams should become versatile and flexible peers.

Learning style flexibility forms the theoretical core of this chapter. Andrew, Pheiffer, Green, and Holley's (2002) idea of applying the principles of learning styles beyond the matching hypothesis and the idea of developing the full potential of learners are supported. This is provided for when learners are challenged to work beyond their comfort zones — executing tasks that do not match their preferences. In the e-learning environment it might be the very challenge of working in teams or participating in online discussions. The e-learner with a preference for working individually might not appreciate the interpersonal learning that comes along with virtual teamwork.

A holistic view of e-learning practices is key to innovation and it should be acknowledged that it is multifaceted. For the purpose of this chapter the focus is on some of the essential roles of the facilitator of e-learning — namely developer of learning programs, facilitator of learning, and assessor (South Africa, 1999), and their interrelatedness — as they are applicable to the context of e-learning.

Background

This chapter focuses on the concepts of multiple intelligences (MI). It includes: all latent human capacity that could be utilized for learning and problem-solving in an integrative way; learning style (an individual's preferred way of processing information and solving problems within a given context); learning style flexibility (the ability to adapt one's learning style according to the demands of the learning task at hand); and action learning (a process of continual constructing of meaning derived from and continuously monitored and modified by experience).

In this chapter we build on some key research, discussed below. First, Gardner's (1993) multiple intelligences (MI) theory provides convincing material that would urge any facilitator of e-learning to become more innovative in practice. Kolb's (1984) book, *Experiential Learning,* provides an overview of his entire learning style theory that is adapted to the context of virtual teamwork as collaborative action learning. In a more practical way the work of Ellis (1997) is a user-friendly application of the principles of Kolb's theory. The latter provides excellent complementary reading. For a thorough understanding of Ned Herrmann's (1995) theory on whole brain learning, *the creative brain* gives an excellent overview. It allows a reading beyond any restricting context of learning to explore the possibilities of applying the principles of whole brain learning as a life-skill, which can be practiced through collaborative virtual teamwork.

Additionally, Wagner's (1994) work on interaction and independence in distance learning should be read in conjunction with the literature on MI and learning styles. The common approaches to interaction are challenged by the notion of balanced learning as it is represented in Herrmann's (1995) whole brain learning model. De Verneil and Berge (2000) state that it is important in most online instruction contexts for the designer to situate the learning in a social context. It is argued in this chapter that such a social context should include learning style flexibility as adapted from Herrmann's (1995) work to add value to the learning context and to ensure positive social dynamics in an online classroom, as proposed by Woods and Baker (2004). Research confirms the need for learners to connect with one another (Atack & Rankin, 2002; Swan, 2001). This connectedness could be enhanced if the principles of learning style flexibility are applied.

Burge (1994) argues that different types of peer behavior are essential in an e-learning environment such as participation, response, provision of affective feedback and short, focused messaging. Again, value is added to this perspective if read in collaboration with the proposed model on learning style flexibility. For example: Participation implies that learners show interest in sharing their learning experiences in a balanced or whole brain way, and that their responses to questions from peers and feedback in general should be done in the same balanced way. Thus balanced e-learning is represented in the Herrmann (1995) model that is consequently discussed.

Herrmann's Whole Brain Theory Applied

An array of research on learning style theories exists, by various scholars such as Kolb (1984), Sternberg (1997), and Vermunt (1995). All these theories should be interpreted to the background of the theory on multiple intelligences, as proposed by Gardner (1993). He claims that we do not have a single, fixed intelligence that can be determined with a standardized IQ test—every person has a different combination of these intelligences. This has to be kept in mind when facilitating e-learning. One of the implications for facilitators of e-learning is that they have to design e-learning events in a wide variety of ways (Armstrong, 1994) offering learners the opportunity to learn in different ways. This is also true for virtual teamwork.

According to Sternberg and Zhang (2001) learning styles do not represent abilities, but rather a set of preferences. Renzulli and Dai (2001) view style constructs as an interface of cognitive ability and personality. Learning style is seen as characteristic of how a learner would prefer to learn. Facilitators of learning tend to facilitate learning according to their personal preferred style or predisposition.

In the literature the terms "learning style," "learning approach," and "learning strategy" are often used as synonyms. For the purpose of this chapter it suffices to refer to Schmeck's (cited in Miller, Imrie, & Cox, 1998, p. 45) distinguishing between "strategy" and "style":

> *A learning style is a predisposition on the part of some students to adopt a particular learning strategy regardless of the specific demands of the task. Thus a style is simply a strategy that is used with some cross-situational consistency. In turn, I define a* learning strategy *as a pattern of information-processing activities...*

Learning style flexibility would mean adapting one's style of learning in accordance with the nature and perceived demands of the task (Entwistle, McCune, & Walker, 2001) at hand. Using a flexible style of facilitating learning would mean being able to adapt one's style according to the nature and demands of the subject matter. Biggs (2001) is of the opinion that styles are flexible and can be learned and views learning styles as both a matter of nature and nurture.

In this chapter, the theory on LSF we propose is selected for its credibility in terms of the validation of the instrument used for determining learning style preferences and user-friendliness. The instrument used, the Herrmann Brain Dominance Instrument (HBDI), has been validated (Bunderson, 2004). It is viewed as user-friendly since it is widely applied in different fields from management, business, medical sciences, engineering to teaching, worldwide.

We approach the concept "learning style" from a full potential perspective, based on Gardner's theory, which promotes the idea that man's cognitive ability is multidimensional—it cannot be reduced to a single number on paper.

Analogous to Gardner's (1993) idea that we all have a combination of intelligences, one should keep in mind that man's learning style preference is multidimensional. It is of the utmost importance that we recognize and nurture all the varied learning styles and all the combinations of learning styles. Learners are all so different largely because they all have different combinations of learning styles. Recognizing this, and applying related principles will at least offer e-learners a better chance of dealing appropriately with the different types of problem that they have to solve. An important characteristic of the LSF theory is that every learner should be accommodated as a whole. Each learner's uniqueness should be respected and developed. Moreover, each learner's full, latent potential should be maximized.

We suggest Herrmann's (1995) theory on whole brain learning as a point of departure for effective virtual teamwork. Implementing the principles of learning style flexibility enhances collaborative virtual teamwork. This implies that learning style flexibility is used in helping virtual team members becoming independent, flexible learners through being interdependent on virtual teams. Effective learning forms the core of any task to be executed, problem to be solved, outcome to be achieved/demonstrated, or end product to be delivered. A virtual team's flexibility in terms of planning, monitoring, completing tasks, and assessing the process and outcome culminates in the coherence of learning styles.

The following adapted figure (Figure 1) represents our model. The original model is adapted to fit the notion of promoting a culture of collaborative learning in any virtual team activity.

Different scholars such as Knowles (1990), Buzan (1991), and Ornstein (1997) agree that effective learning takes place if the whole brain is involved in learning. Therefore effective e-learning is promoted when an appeal is made to all faculties of the brain. Interpreted in terms of Herrmann's metaphoric model of the brain, this presupposes that all four quadrants of the brain, represented by the brain dominance of each virtual team member, should be included in any virtual team effort. Lumsdaine and Lumsdaine (1995) identify the following four modes of learning, which could be applied to the context of e-learning in the following way:

- External learning is related to virtual learning from authority through fact-based e-texts. It is predominantly A quadrant learning.

Figure 1.

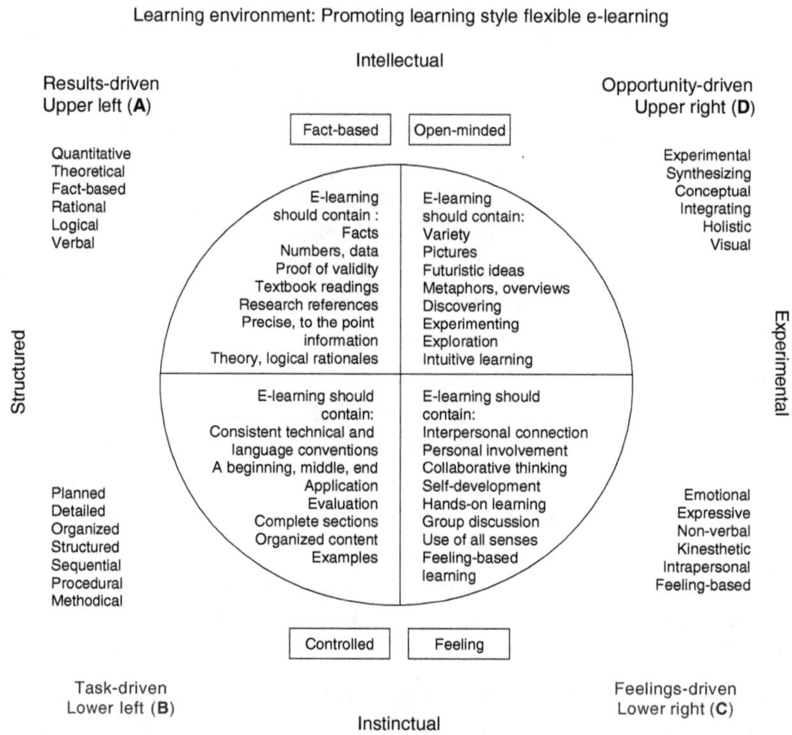

- Procedural learning is characterized by a methodical step-by-step way of mastery, practice and repetition to improve skills and competence, and following virtual guidelines. It is predominantly B quadrant learning.
- Online discussions, "hands-on" activities and sensory-based experiments and simulations bring about interactive virtual learning, where a virtual team member can execute a task with an opportunity for verbal feedback and encouragement. Interactive e-learning is predominantly C quadrant learning.
- Internal learning can be described as an insight, visualization and the synthesis of data or through the understanding of concepts holistically or intuitively. Online brainstorming and creativity exercises could serve this purpose. This is predominantly D quadrant learning.

These four learning modes emphasize that a learner is a whole-brained person and therefore a virtual team may represent all four quadrants of the Herrmann whole brain model. Cognitive functions are accommodated when e-learning activities/tasks are constructed to comply with a learner's preferred mode of learning. Cognitive functions are utilized and challenged when e-learning activities are constructed in such a way that the cognitive functions associated with all four quadrants of the Herrmann model are used.

Virtual team activities should cater for all the modes of Herrmann's model, ensuring that virtual team members' preferred thinking styles are accommodated and less preferred thinking modes are utilized. It necessitates facilitators of virtual teamwork to becoming aware of their own thinking preferences and the implications thereof for their e-learning practices.

Research done by scholars such as MacLean, who proposed the triune brain theory, and Sperry's left-brain right-brain theory (cited in Herrmann, 1995) gave impetus to the development of Herrmann's metaphoric whole-brain model. This research eventually brought about the specialized functions that are associated with the left and right hemisphere. The left, structured mode is categorized by processing dealing with logical, rational, critical, quantitative issues and activities. The procedural, planned, sequential and organized elements of e-learning activities are found in the structured left mode. The learning activities of the left mode are depicted in the cultural and social environment of e-learning by achievements and fact-based knowledge. Processes dealing with visual, conceptual, emotional and interpersonal activities, categorize the experiential right mode. In the cultural and social environment of virtual teamwork the learning activities of the right mode can be described as participative and future-oriented. The inclusion of all these modes in e-learning comprises a full range of activities.

Herrmann (1996) and Gazzaniga (1998) confirm that physical connections secure integrated brain activity, that each hemisphere is specialized in a different way, controls vastly different aspects of thought and action, and thus has its own limitations and advantages. The left and right hemispheres are divided into different processes that represent different ways of learning, dividing the human brain into four quadrants. Each quadrant has very distinct groupings of learning functions. Preference for the A quadrant means that a learner favors activities that involve logical, analytical and fact-based information — referred to as the intellectual self. A preference for the B quadrant implies a linear approach to activities. Learners with a B quadrant preference favor organized, sequential, planned and detailed information — referred to as the safekeeping self. They are conservative in their actions and like to keep things as they are. A preference for the C quadrant indicates favoring information that is interpersonal, feeling-based and involves emotion — referred to as the emotional self. A preference for the D quadrant is mainly characterized by a holistic and conceptual approach in thinking — referred to as the experimental self.

Analogous to Felder's (1996) remarks, if facilitators of e-learning facilitate the learning process exclusively in a manner that favors their learners' less preferred learning style modes, the learners' discomfort level may be great enough to interfere with their learning. On the other hand, if facilitators of e-learning facilitate the learning process exclusively in their learners' preferred modes, the learners may not develop in such a way that they need to reach their potential for being successful in life. To be successful in life we need to become more flexible in terms of our learning and problem-solving styles.

When facilitators of e-learning want to afford learners the opportunity to monitor their own learning, a metacognitive theory of learning (Pesut, 1990) should be developed. Metacognition forms an important part of self-regulated learning as it enables learners to plan and organize their learning, engage in self- and peer instruction, and monitor their progress through continuous self-assessment. In conceptualizing self-regulated learning, learning styles are an indispensable, integral part. Being metacognitively aware of one's learning implies an awareness and knowledge of one's learning style preferences, which forms part of metacognitive knowledge. Learners would have to keep their learning styles in mind when planning for learning; they have to monitor their style, and may have to adapt.

Learning style flexibility would mean that a learner is able to adapt the style of learning in accordance with the nature and perceived demands of the task at hand (Entwistle, McCune, & Walker, 2001). Likewise, if a flexible style of facilitating e-learning were used, facilitators would be able to adapt their style according to the nature and demands of the subject matter and related outcomes. Biggs (2001) is of the opinion that styles are flexible and can be learned. Learning style flexibility, therefore, should not only form part of the learning outcomes, but should also be embedded in the learning strategy that is used. In this way learners learn how to adapt their learning styles.

Collaborative Action Learning in Virtual Teams

Alignment between the way in which facilitators of e-learning facilitate learning and how their learners learn is important. What we view as more important, though, is the constructive realignment in the case of a misalignment, which would include challenging e-learners to work beyond their comfort zones (De Boer, Steyn, & du Toit, 2001).

E-learners need to master different kinds of skills necessary to add value to how they learn. Learning how to think creatively and critically, and gaining insight into the subject matter or a future profession at an intellectual, structural, emotional and creative level (Herrmann, 1995) would mean gaining value-adding attributes. This would for example imply skills needed to work/learn with others. E-learners need "time and space for reflection, and the opportunity to learn with and from others who are also trying to manage their own problems" (O'Hara, Bourner, & Webber, 2004, p. 31). Being subjected to such e-learning events will be conducive to mastering thinking strategies, methods and skills needed for competence in problem solving in teams (interdependently), and as an individual (independently).

Taking responsibility for their own development and developing a sense of lifelong learning (Olivier, 1998) form part of becoming such an independent learner and professional. Facilitators of e-learning have the responsibility to design activities for developing the necessary competencies related to independent learning. E-learners should master and demonstrate the managing of their growth regarding self-regulating competencies and professional development by means of the basic strategies of action learning, namely planning, implementing, monitoring and assessing.

Facilitators of e-learning need to facilitate interdependent and action learning with the aim of developing independent learners and therefore need to provide their learners relevant experiences. This should be integrated with the assessment strategy being used such as electronic portfolio development (Cambridge, 2001) that expects independent learning, evidence of peer assessment and action learning. A useful developmental process supporting the idea of developing independent learners is collaborative virtual teamwork. It can be destructive when the distance between the independent learning the facilitator of e-learning expects from learners, and the competence of the learners in learning independently, is too big. Facilitators of e-learning should constructively align the curriculum, their approaches to facilitating e-learning and their assessment practice with the principles of learning style flexibility, action learning, collaborative teamwork and developing independent learners.

While the facilitator of e-learning and learners are seen as equal partners, the action learning process of the learners could be complemented by action research of the e-learning practice, done by the facilitator. This serves as a synchronous model of learning—both the learners and facilitator are learning in tandem. While the learners are learning by using the strategies of action learning, facilitators use the same strategies to learn more about their e-learning practices. Here the model of Zuber-Skerritt (2000) is integrated with the ideas of constructivist learning and self-reflection (York-Barr, Sommers, Ghere, & Montie, 2001).

We regard critical reflection (York-Barr, Sommers, Ghere, & Montie, 2001) as an important thread throughout the action learning process. The learner could do reflection individually or in collaboration with others. There are different directions reflection takes. York-Barr, Sommers, Ghere, and Montie (2001) refer to reflecting in the present (reflection-in-action), reflecting back (reflection-on-action), reflecting forward (reflection-for-action) and reflecting within (intrapersonal reflection).

Our conceptualization of collaborative action learning in the context of e-learning is aligned with the aim of developing reflective learners. Learning-centeredness (Olivier, 1998) necessitates learners becoming metacognitively (Biggs, 1985) aware of how they learn and how they manage their learning. Kolb (1984) suggests that learners should go through the process of experiential learning. In the context of e-learning the model can be used to promote collaborative action learning in virtual teams. The principles of cooperative learning (Johnson & Johnson, 1992) could be used. Cooperative learning helps learners in becoming independent learners by first being collaboratively interdependent.

Managing one's learning includes determining one's role in the individual or collaborative learning process, and includes determining what is important to learn, how it must be learned, what is expected of you, and what must be done to achieve set outcomes under certain circumstances. In the process of collaborative virtual teamwork learners learn from each other how to learn and construct meaning in an LSF way.

Models for LSF Learning

Some example of models for constructing meaning in an LSF way include Biggs' (1999) 3-P model, York-Barr, Sommers, Ghere, and Montie's (2001) five states of mind model, and the action learning model.

The 3-P "presage-process-product phase" model of Biggs (1999), used by different authors, such as Valcke (2000) could be adapted into one that would include Learning Style Flexible Action Learning (LSFAL) in the e-learning process. This is distinguished as the process phase. The learner needs to be subjected to a challenge, such as compiling an electronic portfolio. The development of the electronic portfolio is based on the principles of action learning. As product learners are expected to submit an electronic portfolio, as proposed by Costantino and Lorenzo (1998). The first phase, or entry level, consists of factors within the learner, such as abilities and learning style; and e-learning context factors such as the nature of the field of specialization, the facilitator, styles of facilitating learning, and learning climate. At entry level the learners become part of the learning process with different learning styles and different thinking skills. Facilitators should intentionally try to align their facilitating of e-learning and assessment with the principles of action learning, and creating a climate conducive to authentic action learning and developing an electronic portfolio. Action learning and developing a portfolio on one's growth are emancipatory and are useful for intrapersonal development (du Toit, 2002).

In the conceptual framework of collaborative action learning, learning styles are an indispensable, integral part. Being metacognitively challenged by a demanding assignment such as developing an electronic portfolio implies an awareness and knowledge of one's own and other group members' learning style preferences. Virtual team members would have to keep their learning styles in mind when planning for learning, they have to monitor their style, and may have to adapt.

LSF could be combined with the five states of minds York-Barr, Sommers, Ghere, and Montie (2001, p. 51) refer to: Flexibility that "involves thinking outside the box, choosing to look at things from a different perspective," efficacy involving "having an internal locus of control and knowing that you can make a difference," craftsmanship as "a focus on continuous improvement," consciousness as "being aware of your own process of thinking ... contexts or environments around you ... and relationships," and interdependence that "recognizes that you are never working alone." For the purpose of this chapter the focus is on the flexibility of collaborative action learning and electronic portfolio development. Collaborative action learning and electronic portfolio development could be aligned with LSF. It could be considered as aligned "facilitating of e-learning," as adapted from "aligned teaching" (Biggs, 1999).

Action learning is an effective tool for collaborative learning in the e-learning environment, and for promoting deep, holistic learning as proposed by Ramsden (1999), and constructive learning as explicated by Von Glasersfeld (2001). The learner selects and transforms information, constructs hypotheses, and makes decisions relying on cognitive structures to do so. Cognitive structures such as schema, mental models and learning style preferences provide meaning and organization to experiences and allow the individual to go beyond the information given.

Learning entails the capacity to look at problems from a number of different perspectives, being able to analyze, to gather evidence, to synthesize and to think in a flexible and creative way (Ramsden, 1999). These assets apply to all learners across the globe and also in the context of virtual team learning. Ramsden (1999, p. 4) is of the opinion that "learning ... should be about changing the ways in which learners understand, or experience, or conceptualize the world around them" which "includes the concepts and methods that are characteristic of the discipline or profession that they are studying." Such change can be brought about by means of critical reflection.

Critical reflection is an essential part of action learning. Action learning gives shape to self-regulated learning. Therefore, action learning is seen as a valuable tool for promoting constructive learning. Action learning in essence is a learning style flexible way of learning, which is multidimensional. A focus on LSF should be carefully done to the background of this multidimensionality. It forms only one of many components of what Renzulli and Dai (2001) call the "inner environment."

The inner environment becomes a domain of intrapersonal reflection and development (du Toit, 2002). An important point of departure for developing as facilitator of e-learning or action learner is determining one's learning style preference. For this purpose the thinking preference questionnaire (HBDI) of Herrmann (1995) can be used and completed online (Herrmann, 2004). The questionnaire focuses on one's preferred way of learning. One's learning preferences have a direct impact on the way one would prefer to facilitate e-learning, or to learn.

The most appropriate way to learn in the context of virtual teams is to apply the principles of self-regulated or action learning. Typical phases of self-regulated or action learning are planning, implementing, critical reflection and evaluating. Applied to the context of collaborative learning in virtual teams, the first step to be taken is the planning of innovative ways of executing the task at hand. Putting the innovative plan into practice follows this. The next phase is a critical reflection on the experience that includes an assessment of the implementation phase. According to the findings of such an investigation, the virtual team would have to go back to their constructing of meaning and application of learning style flexibility. Accordingly they have to plan for executing similar tasks in future in an innovative way.

New tendencies, such as the focus on continuous assessment, and regarding virtual peer assessment as an integral part of facilitating e-learning and an aid to learning in virtual teams (Miller, Imrie, & Cox, 1998) should be included in virtual teamwork. Based on the principles of LSF facilitators of e-learning should also ensure matching assessment methods with what is expected of learners as the outcome of e-learning in teams. In Miller, Imrie, and Cox (1998), reference is made to the devastating fact that sometimes facilitators report that they want learners to be analytical, critical and creative thinkers, problem-solvers, and independent and autonomous learners. But learners receive a different set of signals from examinations since they demand primarily recall of factual information and lower levels of cognitive processes. It would be the same in the case of e-learning when facilitators expect learners to demonstrate learning style flexibility during virtual teamwork, but do not provide for learning-style flexible assessment.

If the culture of learning to be created is one of deep and self-regulated action learning, and allows for LSF, it is suggested that learners be intentionally involved in online discussions of learning styles and strategies for their intellectual development as well as the quality assurance of the e-learning program (Miller, Imrie, & Cox, 1998).

Developing Social Skills in E-Learning

The role of the facilitator of virtual team learning is by no means merely that of a passive observer, but that of an active partner who facilitates the e-learning process in an LSF way, with the aim of guiding learners towards achieving group goals and learning outcomes.

The role of the facilitator of e-learning could be linked to two types of learning outcomes for virtual learning groups: academic outcomes and developmental outcomes. The latter could be translated in different social skills. The following sequence could be followed to help learners develop relevant social skills:

- Learners receive online instructions and outcomes.
- The facilitator assigns each learner to a virtual learning team. Such a virtual team should as far as possible consist of members with different learning style preferences — representing a heterogeneous group. When virtual team members have the same learning style preference it would be highly likely that they will approach a task or problem to be solved from the same viewpoint. This may result in a mediocre solution to the problem to be solved.
- The facilitator provides needed materials, links or references to such materials, structures online discussions, and assigns each team member a specific role to fulfill in the group, related to the learning task and/or effective group interaction.
- The facilitator virtually explains the learning task to be executed and the collaborative action learning structure.
- The facilitator monitors the functioning of each virtual learning team and intervenes to facilitate the mastery of collaborative skills and assist in academic learning when needed.
- The facilitator evaluates the quality and quantity of each learner's learning and ensures that each group processes how effectively members are working together.

Just as no one is born language proficient, no one is born a skillful collaborative e-learner. Before a child can speak, he/she has to be taught language skills and should be given much opportunity to practice before he/she could be said to have acquired them all. This is the same with social skills — they should be learned and practised, before one can talk of real collaboration.

Virtual learning teams create wonderful opportunities for the acquisition of social skills needed in the workplace. Managing social skills enhances the effectiveness of virtual learning teams.

Team Roles and Social Skills

A useful way to facilitate and practice social skills, is to concentrate on one skill per week only — that one which the learners are most in need of acquiring. Both facilitator and learners should discuss the importance and the appearance of the skill beforehand. A certain role should be associated with that skill and each member of a group should have a turn at the role during the week, while the others fulfill other roles.

The list of virtual team roles in Table 1 can be of help in this regard.

After completing a virtual group discussion or completing any collaborative e-learning task, learners should be given the opportunity to reflect on their own learning as a virtual group. They should reconsider the way in which they completed the task and identify their strengths and weaknesses as group. This should be discussed with the facilitator as a matter of action learning. If the team is heterogeneous in terms of the representation of learning styles the teams'

Table 1. Virtual team member roles matching LSF and social skills (Adapted from Johnson & Johnson, 1992)

Social skill	Corresponding team member role	Quadrant
Encouraging others	Encourager	C
Praising others	Praiser	C
Extending, connecting new knowledge with previous learning and experiences	Elaborator	A, B & D
Celebrating accomplishments	Cheerleader	C
Equalizing participation	Gatekeeper	B
Helping	Coach	C
Asking for help	Question commander	A
Checking for understanding	Checker	A
Staying on task	Taskmaster	B
Recording ideas	Recorder	A & B
Reflecting on group progress	Reflector	C
Not disturbing others	Quiet captain	B
Efficiently distributing materials	Materials monitor/runner	B
Thinking outside the box	Innovator	D

reflection will be enriched. Different team members will approach the online reflection process from a different perspective.

From the discussion on LSF above it can be deducted that virtual team learning in essence is C quadrant learning. Facilitators of e-learning should however realize that virtual team learning could be optimized when the e-learning task expects learners to use all four quadrants. This would mean that learners should include, among others, evidence of the relevant facts they have mastered (A quadrant), evidence of planning how to execute a given task and the sequential execution of the plan (B quadrant), evidence of practicing interpersonal skills (C quadrant), and evidence of innovative problem solving (D quadrant). Developing an electronic portfolio (Cambridge, 2001) complements all of these.

Future Trends

Becoming competent in applying the principles of LSF in e-learning needs continuous improvement of one's e-learning practice. For this purpose action research is a useful tool to monitor one's professional development as facilitator of e-learning. Facilitators of e-learning will have to become more aware of their responsibility to act as co-learners and have to model the skill by demonstrating the monitoring of their learning to e-learners online. This will contribute to creating a culture of collaborative and LSF action learning among learners. On the other hand it will contribute to constructing one's own practice theory as professional facilitator of e-learning.

Future research might focus on the specific application of LSF in the design of curricula for e-learning, the facilitation of e-learning and assessment of e-learners in a mixed method research paradigm (Tashakkori & Teddlie, 2003). It is suggested that quantitative data be gathered by using the HBDI (Herrmann, 2004) for different virtual learning groups in different e-learning contexts and in different fields of specialization. Determining virtual team members' learning styles could be combined with instruments for determining their multiple intelligences, to investigate the relationship between LSF and MI. Longitudinal studies would give evidence of the extent to which promoting LSF in virtual teamwork would influence team members to becoming flexible in learning and problem solving in an independent way.

Conclusion

Our discussion of the LSF theory does not aim to add an additional theory to the existing array of learning style theories. Rather, we propose that facilitators of e-learning are made aware of the fact that in each virtual learning team there will be some combination of preferences for fact-based learning, procedural learning, emotional learning and experimental learning. This will be evident in individual team members and the group as a composite whole. The combination of preferences should be accommodated by the different e-learning tasks that have to be executed. The principles of collaborative virtual learning should be explored to promoting LSF and independent learning.

Realizing the importance of promoting LSF in the context of e-learning would leave no facilitator of e-learning untouched. Even if one were not in favor of MI or LSF one would be sensitized to scientifically substantiate one's viewpoint. One would almost be challenged to prove by means of action research or other scientific approaches that the application of the principles of LSF does not contribute to effective learning in virtual teams in one's authentic context.

References

Andrew, D., Pheiffer, G., Green, M., & Holley, D. (2002). *The uses of learning styles: Beyond the matching hypothesis.* Paper presented at the 7th Annual ELSIN Conference: Learning Styles: Reliability and validity, June 26-28, University of Ghent, Belgium.

Armstrong, T. (1994). *Multiple intelligences in the classroom.* Alexandria, VA: Association for Supervision and Curriculum Development.

Atak, L., & Rankin, J. (2002). A descriptive study of registered nurses' experiences with Web-based learning. *Journal of Advanced Nursing, 40,* 457-465.

Biggs, J. B. (1985). The role of metalearning in study processes. *British Journal of Educational Psychology, 55,* 185-212.

Biggs, J.B. (1999). *Teaching for quality learning at university.* Buckingham: Society for Research into Higher Education & Open University Press.

Biggs, J. (2001). Enhancing learning: A matter of style or approach. In R. J. Sternberg & L. Zhang (Eds.), *Perspectives on thinking, learning, and cognitive styles*. London: Lawrence Erlbaum.

Brandes, D., & Ginnis, P. (1996). *A guide to student-centred learning.* Cheltenham: Stanley Thornes.

Bunderson, C. V. (2004). *The validity of the Herrmann Brian Dominance Instrument.* Retrieved April 28, 2004, from http://www.hbdi.com/hbdi/hbdi_validation_overview.htm

Burge, E. J. (1994). Learning in computer conferenced contexts: The learners' perspective. *Journal of Distance Education, 9*(1), 21-29.

Buzan, T. (1991). *Use both sides of your brain* (3rd edition). New York: Plume Books.

Cambridge, B. L. (Ed.). (2001). *Electronic portfolios: Emerging practices in student, faculty, and institutional learning.* Washington, DC: American Association for Higher Education.

Costantino, M., & Lorenzo, M.N. (1998). *Developing a professional teaching portfolio: A guide for educators.* College of Education, University of Maryland, College Park.

De Boer, A., Steyn, T., & du Toit, P. H. (2001). A whole brain approach to teaching and learning in higher education. *South African Journal of Higher Education, 15*(3), 185-193.

De Verneil, M., & Berge, Z. L. (2000). Going online: Guidelines for faculty in higher education. *International Journal of Education Telecommunications, 6,* 227-242.

du Toit, P. H. (2002). Intrapersonal leadership. In L. Calitz, O. L. Fuglestad, & S. Lillejord (Eds.), *Leadership in education.* Cape Town: Heinemann.

Ellis, D. (1997). *Becoming a master student.* Boston: Houghton Mifflin.

Entwistle, N., McCune, V., & Walker, P. (2001). Conceptions, styles, and approaches within higher education: Analytic abstractions and everyday experience. In R.J. Sternberg & L. Zhang (Eds.), *Perspectives on thinking, learning, and cognitive styles.* London: Lawrence Erlbaum.

Felder, R. (1996, December). Matters of style. *ASEE Prism,* 18-23.

Gardner, H. (1993). *Multiple intelligences: The theory in practice.* New York: Basic Books.

Gazzaniga, M. S. (1998). The split brain revisited. *Science American, 279*(1), 35-39.

Herrmann, N. (1995). *The creative brain* (2nd edition). Kingsport, TN: Quebor Printing Book Group.

Herrmann, N. (1996). *The whole brain business book.* New York: McGraw Hill.

Herrmann, N. (2004). Retrieved April 28, 2004, from http://www.hbdi.com

Johnson, D. W., & Johnson, R. T. (1992). Positive interdependence: Key to effective cooperation. In R. Herz-Lazarowitz & N. Miller (Eds.), *Interaction in cooperative groups.* Cambridge: Cambridge University.

Knowles, M. (1990). *The adult learner—A neglected species* (4th edition). Gulf.

Kolb, D. A. (1984). *Experiential learning.* Englewood Cliffs, NJ: Prentice Hall.

Lumsdaine, M., & Lumsdaine, E. (1995). Thinking preferences of engineering students: Implications for curriculum restructuring. *Journal of Engineering Education, 84*(2), 193-204.

Miller, A. H., Imrie, B. W., & Cox, K. (1998). *Student assessment in higher education: A handbook for assessing performance.* London: Kogan Page.

O'Hara, S., Bourner, T., & Webber, T. (2004). The practice of self-managed action learning. *Action Learning: Research and Practice, 1*(1), 29-42.

Olivier, C. du T. (1998). *How to educate and train outcomes based.* Pretoria, South Africa: J. L. van Schaik.

Ornstein, R. (1997). *The right mind—Making sense of the hemispheres.* New York: Harcourt Brace.

Pesut, D. J. (1990). Creative thinking as a self-regulatory metacognitive process—A model for education, training and further education. *Journal of Creative Behaviour, 24*(2), 105-110.

Ramsden, P. (1999). *Learning to teach in higher education.* London: Routledge.

Renzulli, J. S., & Dai, D. Y. (2001). Abilities, interests, and styles as aptitudes for learning: A person-situation interaction perspective. In R.J. Sternberg & L. Zhang (Eds.), *Perspectives on thinking, learning, and cognitive styles.* London: Lawrence Erlbaum.

South Africa. (1999). *Government Gazette. Norms and standards for educators.* Pretoria: Government Printers.

Sternberg, R. J. (1997). *Thinking styles.* Cambridge: Cambridge University Press.

Sternberg, R. J., & Zhang, L. (Eds.). (2001). *Perspectives on thinking, learning, and cognitive styles.* London: Lawrence Erlbaum.

Swan, K. (2001). Virtual interaction: Design factors affecting student satisfaction and perceived learning in asynchronous online courses. *Distance Education, 22,* 306-331.

Tashakkori, A., & Teddlie, C. (Eds.). (2003). *Handbook of mixed methods in social and behavioral research.* Thousand Oaks, CA: SAGE.

Valcke, M. (2000). *Onderwijskunde as ontwerpwetenschap* [Pedagogy as design science]. Gent: Academia.

Vermunt, J. D. (1995). Process-oriented instruction in learning and thinking strategies. *European Journal of Psychology Education, 10,* 325-339.

Von Glasersfeld, E. (2001). Radical constructivism and teaching. *Prospects, 31,* 161-173.

Wagner, E.D. (1994). In support of a functional definition of interaction. *The American Journal of Distance Education, 8*(2), 6-29.

Woods, R. H., & Baker, J. D. (2004, August). Interaction and immediacy in online learning. *International Review of Research in Open and Distance Learning.* Retrieved September 18, 2004, from http://www.irrodl.org/content/v5.2/woods-baker.html

York-Barr, J., Sommers, W. A., Ghere, G. S., & Montie, J. (2001). *Reflective practice to improve schools: An action guide for educators.* Thousand Oaks, CA: Corwin.

Zuber-Skerritt, O. (2000). A generic model for action learning and research programs within organizations. *Action Learning and Action Research Journal, 5*(1), 41-50.

Chapter III

From WebQuests to Virtual Learning: A Study on Students' Perception of Factors Affecting Design and Development of Online Learning

Robert Zheng
Temple University, USA

Abstract

WebQuest as an Internet-based instructional model has recently been widely adopted in K-16 education. However, its underlying principles and functionality are not well understood, which has resulted in an inconsistency in practice. This chapter investigates the factors that are critical to the design and development of WebQuests from the perspective of students. The four constructs of constructivist problem-solving, social interaction, motivation, and scaffolding were identified as factors critical to WebQuest learning. The identified factors were further studied in a larger context with a focus on virtual teams and virtual learning. Suggestions were made on how to improve the existing practice in virtual team design in light of the factors identified in WebQuest learning.

Introduction

The introduction of the Internet into the educational arena has rapidly changed the way individuals learn and paved the way to widespread collaborative and cooperative learning that was not perceived possible until recent years (Dabbagh & Bannan-Ritland, 2005). Although the Internet has been used by teachers as one of the venues for teaching and learning, it can oftentimes cause confusion and become disorienting for learners. Foshay and Bergeron (2000) pointed out that putting content on a Web page is not a guarantee of learning. There is a big difference between information and instruction. They argued that while the Web may be a great way to distribute information, it does not necessarily follow that one can teach with it. Hopper (2001) expressed concern over the "unchecked zeal" for Internet-based teaching and raised the question of whether distance learners are learning or just distant. The argument hits home the critical issue in online learning; that is, the quality of Internet-based teaching and the benefits that virtual learning can offer its learners as does any type of learning such as face-to-face learning.

WebQuest as an Internet-based instructional model has, in recent years, been widely adopted in K-16 classrooms as an effective way to organize chaotic Internet resources (Patterson & Pipkin, 2001). It has been used across the curricula to improve students' mastery of subject matter, problem solving skills, and skills in collaborative and cooperative learning. Despite its rising popularity, the WebQuest is not well-understood in terms of its functionality and underlying principles. Vidoni and Maddux (2002) noted that WebQuests were sometimes used as "a panacea for all manner of educational ills" (p. 113). Dodge (2001) was concerned with the misuse of WebQuests that "are merely worksheets with URLs" (p. 7). The issues in WebQuest learning and implementation necessitate that more research is needed to study the role of WebQuests and its application in learning, particularly in virtual learning.

This chapter is organized as follows. First, it investigates what and how students think about WebQuests by identifying factors critical to WebQuest learning. Second, it explores ways that the factors identified can be applied to the design of virtual learning and virtual teams.

The Constructs of WebQuest Learning

The WebQuest was originated by Bernie Dodge and Tom March in 1995 and has been used as an Internet-based instructional model with which learners interact with the resources on the Internet, develop small group skills in collaborative learning, and engage in higher level thinking. A WebQuest typically consists of six components: (a) an introduction; (b) a task; (c) a set of information sources; (d) a description of process; (e) an assessment; and, (f) a conclusion. The WebQuest is characterized by what Dodge (2001) called deep learning that involves constructing new knowledge through a critical thinking process. Studies (e.g., Brucklacher & Gimbert, 1999; Dodge, 1995, 2001; March, 2003; Pohan & Mathison, 1998; Vidoni & Maddux, 2002) show that WebQuest learning is supported by four underlying constructs: *critical thinking*, *knowledge application*, *social skills*, and *scaffolding*.

The Construct of Critical Thinking

Critical thinking is an important construct in WebQuest learning. Richard Paul (1995) defines critical thinking as "disciplined, self-directed thinking which exemplifies the perfections of thinking appropriate to a particular mode or domain of thinking" (p. 526). Vidoni and Maddux (2002) identified the theoretical underpinnings of WebQuest learning by comparing the characteristics of WebQuests with the theoretical assumptions of several critical thinking theories including Marzano's Dimensions of Thinking Model and Weinstein's framework of critical thinking. They found that "WebQuests meet all six of Weinstein's key elements in critical thinking and therefore are powerful tools for inspiring critical thinking skills in students" (p. 101). Dodge (2001) stated that one of the purposes of WebQuest learning is to challenge students to think critically so that "the loftier reaches of the brain" do not go unused. In an earlier article, Dodge (1995) emphasized, "The instructional goal of a WebQuest is that a learner would have analyzed a body of knowledge deeply, transformed it in some way, and demonstrated an understanding of the material by creating something that others can respond to, online or off" (p. 10).

The Construct of Knowledge Application

An important component in WebQuest learning is to develop students' ability to apply what they have learned to new learning (Pohan & Mathison, 1998). Dede (2004) described the 21st century skills and knowledge required of learners as "...applying, refining and generalizing [knowledge] ... moving from passive assimilation of information to active construction of knowledge...." (p. 16). According to Dodge (2001), WebQuests require students to go beyond "retelling and mastering factual information... to apply knowledge, engage in problem solving, creativity, design, and judgment" (p. 9). Brucklacher and Gimbert (1999) found that emphasis on knowledge application enables students to better connect with their prior knowledge, understand learning activities and goals, and involve in meaningful, deep learning. Knowledge application as a construct promotes active, constructive learning in WebQuests.

The Construct of Social Skills

Dodge (2001) states that well orchestrated WebQuest learning is "a matter of organizing your learners" (p. 8) and is measured by its effort to create a dynamic learning synergy among learners. The construct of social skills encompasses many key concepts from Johnson and Johnson's (1994) cooperative learning model including positive interdependence, individual and group accountability, and interpersonal and small group skills in learning (Dodge, 2001). Studies found that developing students' social skills such as collaboration, cooperation, and positive interdependence enhances the efficacy of learning "in the quest for knowledge" (Brucklacher & Gimbert, 1999).

The Construct of Scaffolding

Studies show that scaffolding positively affects student achievement (Baylor, 2002; Bereiter & Scardamalia, 1984; Cho & Jonassen, 2002). As an important construct in WebQuest learning, scaffolding helps students achieve better learning results through a structured process. Dodge (2001) mentioned that the role of scaffolding is to "transform what they read into some new form" (p. 58). It facilitates, to some extent, what Mezirow (2000) called transformative learning.

As an Internet-based instructional model the WebQuest is undergirded by the constructs of *critical thinking*, *knowledge application*, *social skills*, and *scaffolding*. Despite the fact that the WebQuest has been widely adopted in K-16 classrooms, issues pertaining to WebQuest learning still exist, and those issues affect the way WebQuest is implemented in schools.

Issues in WebQuest Learning

Different views regarding curriculum, gender, and problem-solving in WebQuest learning exist. First, there are different views regarding the relevancy of WebQuests to curricula. Vidoni et al. (2002) pointed out that many WebQuests seem unrelated to the curricular content of the targeted grade level. They believe that the topics in WebQuests are chosen arbitrarily and not systemically designed. Contrary to Vidoni et al.'s view, educators like Milson and Downey (2001) and Yoder (1999) believe WebQuests are directly relevant to curriculum and support students' learning at all levels. Second, there is a debate on whether WebQuests support individual differences in learning. According to Vidoni et al. (2002), WebQuests "make little allowance for individual differences ... much less differences in learning styles or learning preferences" (p. 114). However, studies by Dott-Doner, Wilmer, Stevens, and Hartmann (2000) showed that students in the WebQuest learning environment have a better chance to bring their potential into full play. They concluded that WebQuest learning "focuses on each individual child, building on the students' strengths to overcome areas of weakness" (p. 155). With regard to the issue of gender differences they found that male students are more likely to play a leading role in the group project in WebQuest learning. Third, although the WebQuest is known for its problem-solving approach and critical thinking development (Dutt-Doner et al., 2000; Pohan & Mathison, 1998), Vidoni et al. (2002) argued that the critical thinking and problem solving skills in WebQuests are too generic and not domain-specific. They suggested that critical thinking skills should be intertwined with domain specific content to "provoke students to think critically about the world" (p. 114). These differing views caused some confusion in WebQuest practice as well as contradictory perceptions about the function and role of WebQuests in teaching and learning. This naturally begs the question: Are WebQuests perceived as meaningful by the teachers as by the students?

The gender issue in technology use, including WebQuests and virtual learning, has become a continuous cause of concern to educators. Forcier and Descy (2005) deplored that "computer use suffers from an inherited gender bias that holds that math and science are not 'feminine things'" (p. 42). This gender bias has deterred many female students from getting involved in computer related learning. However, recent studies showed that female students could become as involved as males in computer literacy and application activities (Forcier & Descy, 2005). Bain, Hess, Jones, and Berelowitz (1999) studied the technological competency of female students in the high-access, integrated program and found that female students exceeded their male counterparts. Their study also found that educational experience could become a determining factor in gender differences in technology as "profoundly altered educational experience enabled women to improve their technological skills beyond the levels of their male counterparts" (p. 7). Nonetheless, the study by Dott-Doner et al. (2000) indicated that girls were more likely to perform a supporting role in WebQuest learning. These contradicting results led to our second question: Would there be a difference in the perception of WebQuest learning based on a student's level of experience and gender? If so, how would this affect WebQuest learning?

Finally, the issue of motivation has frequently surfaced in the WebQuest research literature. Yoder (1999) raised the question of how to use the World Wide Web as a motivating force in classrooms. She asserted that WebQuests had the power to "invigorate a curriculum and enliven a class" (p. 53). Gohagan (1999) called on teachers to pay attention to the affective aspect of WebQuest learning and pointed out that "teaching is anchored in multiple aspects of the teaching environment" (p. 147). Therefore, motivation should become the key component in the design and planning of WebQuest instruction. Whereas the notion of motivation has been addressed in multiple WebQuest related researches, few studies have examined the issue from the perspective of students. Since motivation is a socially constructed concept, its measurement through "logical positivism" has always been a controversial one. McMillan and Schumacher (2001) suggested using a qualitative approach to study socially constructed concepts. Following this line, a third question is raised: Do the constructs identified by quantitative study represent the whole picture of students' perception of WebQuest learning? Would there be any differences between the qualitative approach and quantitative approach in identifying the underlying constructs of WebQuest learning?

Hypotheses

Hypotheses were derived from the above discussions as well as the questions related to each discussion. The following hypotheses form the basis of this study:

- **Hypothesis 1:** There are differences between the theoretical constructs and the constructs as perceived by learners in WebQuest learning.
- **Hypothesis 2:** There would be a difference in the perception of WebQuest learning based on a student's level of experience and gender.
- **Hypothesis 3:** There are differences between the constructs generated by the qualitative study and by the quantitative study.

Methodology

The study took a mixed approach of quantitative and qualitative methods. The quantitative method was used to address the first two hypotheses whereas the qualitative method was employed to address the third hypothesis. The advantage of using two distinctive methods is that they have the potential to bring together unique perspectives and provide insights, hence improving the understanding of the phenomenon under study better than any single method alone.

Quantitative Research

The focus of the quantitative study was to identify factors as perceived by students. A questionnaire was developed based on the four theoretical constructs identified above. A factor analysis was conducted on the data collected.

The Questionnaire

The questionnaire consists of 20 questions with a five-point Likert scale ranging from strongly disagree to strongly agree (strongly disagree = 1, strongly agree = 5). The questions are grouped under the relevant constructs. For example, questions 1-5 are subsumed under the construct of *critical thinking* with an attempt to tap into the concepts of multiple views, multiple solutions and multiple approaches in problem solving. Questions 6-10 are under the construct of *knowledge application* that focuses on the concepts of applying prior knowledge to new learning, knowledge transfer, and so forth. Questions 11-15 are related to the construct of *social skills* that taps into the concepts of interdependence, group accountability, learner interaction, and interpersonal and small group skills. Finally, questions 16-20 are subsumed under the construct of scaffolding that focuses on facilitating problem solving and critical thinking skills (see Appendix A). The questionnaire was carefully reviewed by the instructors. Feedback from each instructor was carefully reviewed and evaluated. Changes were made based upon this feedback to establish the validity of the instrument.

In addition to the questionnaire, some demographic information was also collected for the study. The demographic information includes gender, age, institutions, academic status, and experience pertaining to WebQuest learning. The questionnaire was created as an online form that was hosted on a university server. Participants were asked to sign a consent form and given the URL to complete the survey which took about 40 minutes.

Participants

Two hundred and seven subjects (57 in Fall 2003 and 150 in Spring 2004) participated in this study. Subjects were from one large research university (10%, n = 21), one large teaching university (25%, n = 52), and two private colleges (65%, n = 134). Participants included undergraduate (n = 108) and graduate students (n = 99) enrolled in the Department/College of Education. There were 122 females and 85 males. The range of participants' age is from 18 to 61 (M = 29). Three experience groups emerged as a result of the experience reported by the participants: (a) WebQuests taught by the instructors, (b) WebQuests created by learners, and (c) both.

Participants of the first group (28%, n = 57) reported having used WebQuest that was integrated into the instruction by the instructor. The second group (32%, n = 67) reported having created WebQuests as part of course requirement such as using WebQuests in clinics or student teaching. The last group (40%, n = 83) reported having experienced both. To maintain neutrality in the study, the investigator was not involved in any of the teaching activities. The courses were taught by instructors in the Department/College of Education and the data were collected from students taught by those instructors.

Results

All analyses were performed using SPSS (version 11.5). A Principal Axis Factoring analysis with Varimax orthogonal rotation was performed on the data. Kaiser's eigen value greater than one rule was observed. Selection of items was based on the criterion set by Hair, Anderson, Tatham, and Black (1998) for significant factors (factor loading > .40).

Three interpretable factors with 19 items were extracted, accounting for 55.2 % of the variance. Item 11 was eliminated from the list due to its low loading on all three factors (.268, .360, .329, respectively). The factor analysis rendered the following new constructs: (a) constructivist problem solving, (b) social interaction, and (c) scaffolding. An alpha reliability analysis was performed to determine the internal consistency for the items within each of the three constructs. Reliability scores for constructivist problem-solving, social interaction, and scaffolding were .887, .846, and .825, respectively (See Table 1 of Appendix C).

A 2 x 3 experimental design was used with gender (male and female) and experience group (instructors' use, students' use, and both) as independent variables and factor scores as dependent variables. A MANOVA analysis showed a main effect for gender with no main effect for the experience group. There was a significant difference between males and females in relation to their perception of the WebQuest learning (Wilk's Lambda = 4.216, $p < .01$). A follow-up ANOVA for gender showed that male and female respondents differ significantly in Factor 1 "Constructivist problem solving" ($F(1, 205) = 10.734$, $p < .01$). No gender difference was found for Factor 2 "Social interaction" ($F(1, 205) = 1.759$, $p = .19$) and Factor 3 "Scaffolding" ($F(1, 205) = 2.734$, $p = .10$). No significant difference was found among the experience groups (Wilk's Lambda = 2.114, $p = .051$).

Discussion and Conclusion

The discussion of the findings focuses on the hypotheses of the study.

Hypothesis 1. Hypothesis 1 pertained to differences between the theoretical constructs and the constructs as perceived by students. Results showed that three new constructs — *constructivist problem solving, social interaction, and scaffolding* — were identified. The *construct of constructivist problem* *solving* is related to the following concepts that include facilitating problem solving (loading = .527), facilitating knowledge transfer (loading = .531), facilitating knowledge association (loading = .609), promoting multiple perspectives (loading = .547), developing multiple approaches to problem-solving (loading = .538), and developing multiple solutions to problem-solving (loading = .590) (See Table 1 of Appendix C). This finding is consistent with the literature that a constructivist learner must be: (a) a critical thinker who would examine issues from multiple viewpoints, pose thoughtful, open-ended questions, and (b) an active problem-solver who works on the information and data that are related to his/her schema, who self-initiates the problem and approaches the problem by going from whole to parts (Brooks and Brooks, 1993; Duffy & Jonassen, 1992). The construct of constructivist problem solving indicates a moderately high internal consistency ($\alpha = .887$).

The second factor *social interaction* is closely related to the underlying principles of cooperative learning. It entails the concepts of interpersonal and small group skills (loading = .775), challenging each other's viewpoints (loading = .739), understanding each other's point of view (loading = .617), and promoting interaction between learners (loading = .610) (See Table 1 of Appendix C). The social interaction construct is also consistent with the literature. It aligns with Johnson and Johnson's (1994) theory of cooperative learning theory which defines the cooperative learning as positive interdependence, individual and group accountability, interpersonal and small group skills, and group processing. The social interaction construct shows a moderately high internal consistency ($\alpha = .846$).

The third factor *scaffolding* includes the understanding of what is to be learned (loading = .702), understanding subject content (loading = .689), understanding how to achieve goals (loading = .406), and connecting goals and learning activities (loading = .540) (See Table 1 of Appendix C). Like the previous constructs, the construct of scaffolding is consistent with what has been found in the literature. According to Dodge (2001), scaffolding is a cognitive structure that "helps learners act more skilled than they really are" (p. 58). It facilitates better understanding, bridges prior knowledge to new learning, helps focus on problems, and relates learning activities to goals (Baylor, 2002; Lever-Duffy, McDonald, & Mizell, 2003). The scaffolding construct has a moderately high internal consistency ($\alpha = .825$).

The results showed that there was a conceptual shift between the two groups of constructs. First, the old constructs of *critical thinking* and *knowledge application* were merged to form a new construct called *constructivist problem solving*, which suggests that students believe critical thinking should include knowledge application, whereas under the framework of old theoretical constructs, these two were separated. Second, there was a cross-construct shift, that is, items under a different construct were factored in to form a new construct, and vice versa. For example, the item "Learners develop the ability to challenge each other's point of view" under the construct of *critical thinking* was factored into the new construct called *social interaction*. This seems to suggest that students perceive the social interaction as a process that entails critical thinking. That is, social interaction should include challenging each other's views. Similar findings were made in the construct of *scaffolding* where the item "Scaffolding organizes the way for new learning" was factored out and the item "The task oriented nature of the WebQuest makes it clear what is to be learned" was factored in from a different construct known as *knowledge application*, which again suggests that students believe scaffolding should not be simply a process of providing structured cognitive and academic support. Instead, it should include knowledge application and practices to make learning experience more fruitful. The findings of the study have supported the first hypothesis that there are differences between the theoretical constructs and the constructs perceived by the students.

Hypothesis 2. Hypothesis 2 hypothesized that there would be a difference in the perception of WebQuest learning based on a student's level of experience and gender. Results showed that there was an overall difference in gender regarding learners' perception of WebQuests. However, such difference may not have significant impact in practice due to its small effect size (Effect size = .065) which accounts for only 6% of the variance. Results also showed that there was a gender difference in factor 1. However, no gender differences were found in factor 2 and 3.

One of the possible explanations for "no significant difference" in factor 2 in term of gender differences is that male and female students have equal opportunity to participate in their project which enables them to understand each other's view (item 13 in Table 1 of Appendix C) and to challenge each other's viewpoints (item 2 in Table 1 of Appendix C) on an equal footing regardless of gender. Factor 3 is about scaffolding. It is possible that as a cognitive and academic support, scaffolding is embedded in WebQuests that enables both male and female students to benefit from the scaffolding without any gender preferences. The findings are consistent with the literature that both male and female students can perform equally well in cooperative learning (Forcier & Descy, 2005) and in scaffolding learning (Baylor, 2002).

Surprisingly, no significant difference was found among experience groups (i.e., instructor's use, student's use, and both) in terms of WebQuest perceptions. This suggests that the way the learner gains his/her experience of WebQuest learning, whether it is through his/her instructor, or through one's own creation of WebQuests, or both, does not affect his/her perception of WebQuest learning. In brief, the findings only partially supported hypothesis 2 as there was an overall difference between the genders as well as a difference in Factor 1. However, no significant differences were found in Factor 2 or Factor 3, nor among experience groups.

Qualitative Research

Using grounded theory method the investigator tried to find out if there were differences between the factors derived from quantitative and qualitative approaches in terms of learners' perception of WebQuest learning. Grounded theory, first developed by Glaser and Strauss (1967), is used as an inductive method to analyze the phenomena under study and generate a theory that captures the nuances of the phenomena and explain them with generalized rules and principles (Charmaz, 2000). Grounded theory is operated upon three related concepts: open, axial, and selective coding, each representing a stage in the process of data analysis (Strauss and Corbin, 1998). The open coding is to maximize "opportunities for comparing concepts along their properties for the similarities and differences ... to densify categories, to differentiate among them, and to specify their range of variability" (Strauss et al., 1998, p. 202). The axial coding reassembles the data that are fractured in open coding and builds the subcategories around the axis called the overarching category. Finally, the selective coding is a process of identifying the central phenomenon or central concept under which all other categories can be related, subsumed, and integrated to grow in depth and in explanatory power (Strauss et al., 1998).

The Instrument

The instrument consists of ten questions based on the theoretical constructs identified earlier. To tap into learners' affective aspect in WebQuest learning, a fifth construct called *affective learning* was added (See Appendix B for the questions and their relevant constructs). The instrument was reviewed by a panel of experts in the Department/College of Education. A pilot group was recruited to test the instrument. Feedback from both experts and the pilot group was carefully reviewed. Changes were made based upon the feedback.

Participants

Participants (n = 15) were recruited from an introductory learning and technology graduate course, of which seven were female and eight were male. The average age of the participants was 35 with a range of 25 to 52. Of the 15 participants, ten (67%) were K-12 teachers, three (20%) were full-time graduate students, and two (13%) worked in higher education. The average year of teaching for K-12 teachers is 11 years. All participants had the experience of using WebQuests.

Participants logged onto an asynchronous discussion forum using Blackboard and posted their discussion messages online. The discussion was regulated by the instructor who served as a facilitator for the discussion. The posted messages were collected without student names to preserve the anonymity of participants.

Data Collection and Analysis

The online discussion lasted three weeks. During the three week period, about 260 messages were posted. These messages were collected by the investigator and then coded into a Microsoft Excel database using a random combination of letters and numbers.

Data analysis followed the procedures of open, axial, and selective coding. In the open coding, the researcher tried to identify meaningful units of data, compared and analyzed them line-by-line to discover the relationships among concepts and themes and to generate tentative categories and properties based on relationships. For example, as the key words like "work in group," "share responsibility," and "distribute tasks," were identified and began to form meaningful units of data, the concept of *team work* began to emerge. As concepts of a similar nature continue to emerge, a new category is then generated. For instance, the identification and regrouping of similar concepts like "equal participation," "mutual dependence," "information sharing," etc., led to the creation of a new category called *collaboration* (see Table 2 of

Appendix C). The advantage of the open coding analysis is to group raw data into meaningful units to allow new concepts and categories to emerge.

The categories generated through the open coding are, however, fractured. Dense relationships between the categories must be built so that the logical connection between the categories is shown. Strauss et al. (1998) suggest creating an axis (also called analytic domain) around which the categories are meaningfully grouped. According to Strauss et al. (1998), the axis or analytic domain is characterized by *property* and *dimension*, that is, certain attributes and range of characteristics are associated with a particular analytic domain (Strauss et al., 1998). For instance, the analytic domain *cooperative learning* has three attributes: *collaboration*, *levels of communication*, *role play and responsibility*. Each attribute is defined by a range of characteristics. Take the attribute *collaboration* as an example, its dimension is defined as "From equal participation to mutual dependence, to team work." Seven analytic domains were identified in the axial coding analysis (see Table 3 of Appendix C).

One of the key approaches of the grounded theory method is to identify overarching categories that lead to the discovery of a central idea or phenomenon (Strauss et al., 1998). By carefully comparing, analyzing, and synthesizing the analytic domains and their attributes, the researcher identified four overarching categories. They are: (a) constructivist problem-solving, (b) social interaction, (c) scaffolding, and (d) motivation. Subcategories derived from the relevant analytic domains and attributes were also identified and subsumed under their respective overarching category (see Table 4 of Appendix C).

Finally, the overarching and subcategories were regrouped and integrated into what Strauss (1987) called the organizational scheme or coding paradigm. The basic components of an organizational scheme are central phenomenon, conditions, actions, and outcomes. Figure 1 illustrates the relationships between the central phenomenon "The power of constructivist problem-solving learning" and other categories that are subsumed under the central phenomenon. It also reveals the relationship between the central phenomenon and other conditions. Figure 1 lists three types of conditions: causal, intervening, and contextual. Each condition is related, in a unique way, to the central phenomenon. For example, the causal conditions specify what makes the constructivist problem-solving learning possible, whereas the intervening conditions indicate the factors that may affect constructivist problem-solving learning. And finally, the contextual conditions describe the circumstances in which constructivist problem-solving learning occurs. The strategies and outcomes are determined by the conditions, particularly the intervening and contextual conditions.

Figure 1. Visual diagram illustrating students' perceptional scheme of WebQuest learning

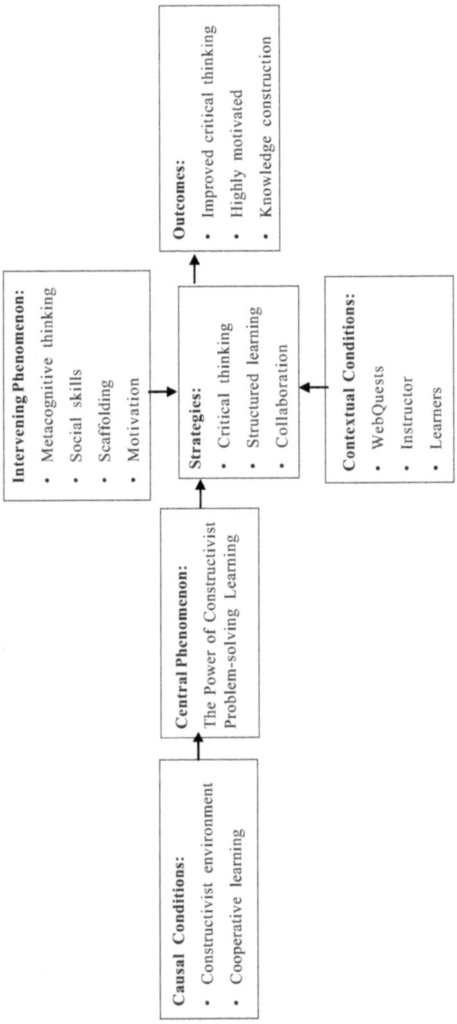

Discussion and Conclusion

The discussion is pivoted on the findings of qualitative study by examining whether the constructs identified in the qualitative study differ from the ones derived from quantitative study. Two important concepts, *analytic domain* and *overarching category*, serve as the focal points of discussion.

Analytic Domain

The pivotal part of the qualitative study was to construct analytic domains that defined the attributes and dimensions of WebQuest learning. Based on open coding, axial coding analysis identified seven analytic domains that consisted of 13 attributes and 16 dimensions. Analyses revealed that several themes emerged from the initial data. One of the themes was constructivist and critical thinking that was characterized by active learning, creativity, levels of higher order thinking, and problem-solving approaches. It seemed that qualitative study revealed a broader range of perceptions perceived by students regarding constructivist and critical thinking in WebQuest learning. For instance, the perceptions as perceived by students ranged from open-ended thinking to knowledge transfer, from multiple perspectives to multiple solutions, and from the ability to discern and compare to synthesize and evaluate, etc. Interestingly, some of the socially constructed concepts such as metacognitive thinking were also integrated into the constructivist and critical thinking categories. For example, several concepts under the metacognitive thinking such as self-selecting strategies fit well into the constructivist and critical thinking conceptual framework. This suggests that students may believe constructivist and critical thinking should include metacognitive thinking as well.

Conversely, concepts relating to critical thinking also appeared under a socially constructed concept—motivation. For example, one of the attributes under motivation called *self-initiation* was defined as self-identifying problems and self-initiating solutions, which suggests that students may believe that the prism of motivation should reflect the dimensions of critical thinking.

Overarching Category

By comparing the constructs derived from qualitative study with the constructs identified in the quantitative study, the investigator found both studies produced similar constructs except for the motivation in the qualitative study. However, a further examination revealed that there were significant differences between the two groups of constructs in terms of the underlying concepts. For example, the construct of constructivist problem-solving in the qualitative study included critical thinking, constructivist learning, and metacognitive thinking whereas the same construct in the quantitative study entails critical thinking and knowledge application. This suggests that the qualitative study may enable students to engage in a deeper thinking than the quantitative study since the Likert-scale questionnaire could limit the scope and depth of what students could express themselves. It is worth noting that students have included the concept of metacognitive thinking in the construct of constructivist problem-solving. Studies (e.g., Baylor, 2002; Jones, Farquhar, & Surry, 1995; Young, 1997) show that metacognitive thinking is related to complex cognitive activities such as problem-solving. In his study Young (1997) pointed out that "metacognitive strategies ... are responsible for governing and overseeing the management of other strategies ... include: planning a problem-solving approach or solution strategy" (p. 38). Obviously, constructs derived from the qualitative study have shown more depth and are therefore valuable information for teachers who are interested in WebQuest construction.

In conclusion, the findings of the qualitative study supported hypothesis 3 that there were differences between the constructs identified by the quantitative study and the qualitative study. The findings suggest that the qualitative study generated more depth and insights in regard to student perceptions about WebQuest learning than did the quantitative study.

General Discussion

Although many studies have been conducted to investigate the theoretical and practical implications of WebQuest in K-16 education, little study has ever been done in terms of its implementation in virtual learning and virtual teams. Because of the dearth of research in this area, this discussion will focus on: (a) the underlying concepts of virtual learning, and (b) how to extrapolate the findings of this study to virtual learning and virtual teams.

The Underlying Concepts of Virtual Learning

Dede (1996) defined virtual learning as "learners immerse themselves in distributed, synthetic environments, becoming avatars (assuming synthetic roles) who vicariously collaborative and learn by doing" (p. 14). It is believed that virtual learning is undergirded by the concepts of creative and critical thinking, collaboration, and motivation (Dede, 2004; Mayrhofer & Back, 2005; Staples & Cameron, 2004). A discussion of these concepts follows:

Creative and Critical Thinking

Commenting on the challenges facing the 21st distributed learning community, Dede (2004) points out that it is essential that the virtual community focuses on "complex skills such as system thinking, creativity and collaboration" (p. 16). He challenges people to unlearn their beliefs, values, and assumptions underlying standard operating practices to become more critical and creative thinkers. Dabbagh et al. (2005) point out that successful online instruction relies heavily on fostering critical and creative thinking skills in learning. Evidently, the concept of creative and critical thinking undergirds what is called virtual learning.

Collaboration

The notion of group interaction and collaboration has been much emphasized in virtual learning (Andriessen & Verburg, 2004; Mayrhofer & Back, 2005). In fact, virtual collaboration modes are used more than ever in today's business world. Mayrhofer et al. (2005) predicted that by 2006 people will spend nearly 70% of their time working collaboratively. According to Ellis, Gibbs, and Rein (1991), the key components of virtual learning collaboration include: (a) a common purpose or goal, (b) interdependence, and (c) sharing information and resources (cited from Mayrhofer et al., 2005). Studies (e.g., Wang & Newlin, 2001) showed that social skills such as collaboration are highly correlated with students' achievement in virtual learning.

Motivation

The distributed nature of virtual learning poses difficulties in controlling variables such as attitude and motivation. Dabbagh et al. (2005) noted that interpersonal issues are crucial for synchronous and asynchronous online learning. They suggest that online instructors "need to model openness, warmth, and expressions of feelings and self-disclosure to help create a trusting learning environment" (p. 73). Staples et al. (2004) found that design task issues are correlated with motivation. A case in point is that a process variable, caring for others in the group, is found to be significantly related to training motivation (Colquitt, LePine, & Noe, 2000, cited from Staples et al., 2004).

In short, the three concepts of *creative and critical thinking*, *collaboration*, and *motivation* are believed to support virtual learning. The following is an examination of the factors identified in WebQuest study and how they can be incorporated into the design and development of virtual teams.

Extrapolating WebQuest Learning to Virtual Teams

This part of the discussion focuses on how the factors identified in WebQuests can be extrapolated to virtual learning. Suggestions will be made with regard to the design and development of virtual teams.

This study indicates that although both WebQuests and virtual learning are undergirded by similar concepts, that is, both emphasize *creative and critical thinking*, *collaboration*, and *motivation*, there are fundamental differences between the two. Understanding these differences can help us better apply the WebQuest instructional model to virtual learning. First, despite the fact that critical thinking skills are accentuated in virtual learning, the findings of this study showed that WebQuests emphasize constructivist and metacognitive thinking along with critical thinking. Since virtual teams consist of people with different learning styles and cognitive styles, teaching people to understand their abilities, strengths and weaknesses can make learning more meaningful, thus conducive to critical and creative thinking. Second, simply by incorporating collaboration into virtual teams does not necessarily guarantee efficacy of learning. The concept of collaboration should be examined in a larger context, that is, it should be placed in a set of related concepts to examine its function more properly. The findings of this study revealed that the concept of collaboration is closely associated with other concepts relating to social interaction skills such as levels of communication, role and responsibility. Thus, for members of a virtual team to collaborate effectively, they need to understand and learn other related skills such as determining appropriate level(s) of communication (e.g., synchronous vs. asynchronous; partners vs. small groups, etc.) and the role and responsibility of collaboration (e.g., individual accountability, interdependence, etc.). Third, motivation is considered as an important concept both in WebQuest and virtual learning. However, research on motivation in virtual learning is limited. So far, little in-depth qualitative study has been done on the topic. The findings of this study identified two key concepts under motivation: empowerment and self-initiation. It is assumed that members in virtual teams become motivated if they are empowered to control what they learn and become self-initiated in identifying problems and finding the solutions. Based on the above discussion, the investigator would like to advance several suggestions regarding the existing practice in virtual learning and virtual teams:

1. It is suggested that the existing design of virtual teams emphasize cultivating constructivist and critical thinking skills along with metacognitive thinking so that learners become more active and creative in learning.
2. It is suggested that the existing design of virtual teams emphasize developing collaborative skills in a larger context so that learners acquire other socially related skills such as levels of communication, role and responsibility.
3. It is suggested that the existing design of virtual teams emphasize motivation in virtual learning through empowerment and self-initiation.

Conclusion

As an increasing number of schools, including higher education institutions, are turning to the Internet to deliver courses to students both at a distance and on campus (National Center for Education Statistics, 2004), it becomes critically important to understand the variables that define the success of a virtual learning environment. This study attempts to identify factors that are critical to WebQuest learning as perceived by learners. Both quantitative and qualitative methods were employed to reveal the depth and breadth of the issues under study. The results indicate that factors of *constructivist problem solving*, *social interaction*, *scaffolding*, and *motivation* are critical to a successful WebQuest learning.

The factors identified in this study have significant ramifications for the design and development of virtual learning and virtual teams. By identifying the underlying concepts of virtual learning and comparing them with factors identified in WebQuest learning, the author found that there is some room for improvement of the existing practice in virtual team design. This study is a preliminary step towards a systematic study of factors in virtual learning. Future research should include an investigation of teachers' perceptions and practices in virtual learning so as to better understand the variables that critically define the success of virtual learning and virtual teams.

Acknowledgment

The author would like to acknowledge the insightful comments of the anonymous reviewers who suggested changes, raised caveats, and caused him to focus on the emphasis of the book considerably. The author would also like to thank Bradd Stucky, Sue Staddort, Matt McAlack, and Michael Menchaca for their assistance in collecting the quantitative data. Finally, special thanks go to Dr. Joseph DuCette who patiently proofread as well as made insightful comments on the manuscript.

References

Andriessen, J. H. E., & Verburg, R. M. (2004). A model for the analysis of virtual teams. In S. H. Godar & S. P. Ferris (Eds.), *Virtual and collaborative teams: Process, technologies, and practice* (pp. 269-278). Hershey, PA: Idea Group Publishing.

Bain, A., Hess, P. T., Jones, G., & Berelowitz, C. (1999). Gender differences and computer competency: The effects of a high access computer program on the computer competence of young women. *International Journal of Educational Technology, 1*(1). Retrieved January 18, 2005, from http://smi.curtin.edu.au/ijet/v1n1/bain/index.html

Baylor, A. (2002). Expanding preservice teachers' metacognitive awareness of instructional planning through pedagogical agents. *Educational Technology Research and Development, 50*(2), 5-22.

Bereiter, C., & Scardamalia, M. (1984). Teachability of reflective processes in written composition. *Cognitive Science, 180*(8), 173-190.

Brooks, J. G., & Brooks, M. G. (1993). *In search of understanding: The case for constructivist classroom.* Alexandria, VA: ASCD.

Brucklacher, B., & Gimbert, B. (1999). Role-playing software and WebQuests: What's possible with cooperative learning and computers. *Computers in the Schools, 15*(2), 37-48.

Charmaz, K. (2000). Grounded theory: Objectivist and constructivist methods. In N. K. Denin & Y. S. Lincoln (Eds.), *Handbook of qualitative research* (2nd ed., pp. 509-535). Thousand Oaks, CA: Sage.

Cho, K., & Jonassen, D. (2002). The effects of argumentation scaffolds on argumentation and problem solving. *Educational Technology Research and Development, 50*(3), 5-22.

Dabbagh, N., & Bannan-Ritland, B. (2005). *Online learning: Concepts, strategies, and application.* Upper Saddle River, NJ: Pearson, Merrill/Prentice Hall.

Dede, C. (1996). Emerging technologies and distributed learning. *American Journal of Distance Education, 10*(2), 4-36.

Dede, C. (2004). Enabling distributed learning communities via emerging technologies—Part one. *T.H.E. Journal, 32*(2), 12-22.

Dodge, B. (1995). WebQuests: A technique for Internet-based learning. *Distance Educator, 1*(2), 10-13.

Dodge, B. (2001). FOCUS: Five rules for writing a great WebQuest. *Learning and Leading with Technology, 28*(8), 6-9, 58.

Dott-Doner, K., Wilmer, M., Stevens, C., & Hartmann, L. (2000). Actively engaging learners in interdisciplinary curriculum through the integration of technology. *Computers in the Schools, 16*(3-4), 151-166.

Duffy, T. M., & Jonassen, D. H. (Eds.). (1992). *Constructivism and the technology of instruction: A conversation.* Hillsdale, NJ: Lawrence Erlbaum.

Forcier, R. C., & Descy, D.E. (2005). *The computer as an educational tool: Productivity and problem solving* (4th ed.). Upper Saddle River, NJ: Pearson-Merrill/Prentice Hall.

Foshay, R., & Bergeron, C. (2000). Web-based education: A reality check. *TechTrends, 44*(5), 16-19.

Glaser, B. G., & Strauss, A. L. (1967). *The discovery of grounded theory: Strategies for qualitative research.* Chicago, IL: Aldine.

Gohagan, D. (1999). Computer-facilitated instructional strategies for education: Designing WebQuests. *Journal of Technology in Human Services, 16*(2-3), 145-159.

Hair, J., Anderson, R., Tatham, R., & Black, W. (1998). *Multivariate data analysis* (5th ed.). Upper Saddle River, NJ: Prentice Hall.

Hopper, K. (2001). Is the Internet a classroom? *TechTrends, 45*(5), 35-43.

Johnson, D. W., & Johnson, R. T. (1994). *Leading the cooperative school* (2nd ed.). Edina, MN: Interaction Book.

Jones, M. G., Farquhar, J. D., & Surry, D. W. (1995). Using metacognitive theories to design user interfaces for computer-based learning. *Educational Technology, 35*(4), 12-14.

Lever-Duffy, J., McDonald, J. B., & Mizell, A. P. (2003). *Teaching and learning with technology*. Boston: Allyn and Bacon.

March, T. (2003). The learning power of WebQuests. *Educational Leadership, 61*(4), 42-48.

Mayrhofer, D., & Back, A. (2005). Workplace e-collaboration in practice: Practical guidelines for implementing e-collaboration in organizations. In M. W. L. Fong (Ed.), *E-collaborations and virtual organizations* (pp. 29-60). Hershey, PA: IRM Press.

McMillan, J. H., & Schumacher, S. (2001). *Research in education: A conceptual introduction* (5th ed.). New York: Addison Wesley Longman.

Mezirow, J. (2000). Learning to think like an adult: Core concepts of transformation theory. In J. Mezirow (Ed.), *Learning as transformation: Critical perspectives on a theory in progress* (pp. 3-33). San Francisco: Jossey-Bass.

Milson, A. J., & Downey, P. (2001). WebQuest: Using Internet resources for cooperative inquiry. *Social Education, 65*(3), 144-146.

National Center for Education Statistics. (NCES). *Distance Education at Degree-Granting Postsecondary Institutions: 2000–2001*. Retrieved September 10, 2004, from http://nces.ed.gov/surveys/peqis/publications/2003017/

Patterson, N., & Pipkin, G. (2001). Guiding readers to new understandings through electronic text. *Voices from the Middle, 8*(4), 64-66.

Paul, R. (1995). *Critical thinking: How to prepare students for a rapidly changing world*. Santa Rosa, CA: Foundation for Critical Thinking.

Pohan, C., & Mathison, C. (1998). WebQuests: The potential of Internet-based instruction for global education. *Social Studies Review, 37*(2), 91-93.

Staples, D. S., & Cameron, A. F. (2004). Creating positive attitudes in virtual team members. In S. H. Godar & S. P. Ferris (Eds.), *Virtual and collaborative teams: Process, technologies, and practice* (pp. 76-98). Hershey, PA: Idea Group Publishing.

Strauss, A. (1987). *Qualitative analysis for social scientists*. Cambridge, UK: University of Cambridge Press.

Strauss, A., & Corbin, J. (1998). *Basics of qualitative research: Techniques and procedures for developing grounded theory* (2nd ed.). Thousand Oaks, CA: Sage.

Vidoni, K. L & Maddux, C. D. (2002). WebQuests: Can they be used to improve critical thinking skills in students? *Computers in the Schools, 19*(1-2), 101-17.

Wang, A., & Newlin, M. (2001). Online lectures: Benefits for the virtual classroom. *T.H.E. Journal, 29*(1), 17-22.

Yoder, M. B. (1999). The student WebQuest: A productive and thought-provoking use of the Internet. *Learning and Leading with Technology, 26*(7), 6-9, 52-53.

Young, A. C. (1997). Higher-order learning and thinking: What is it and how is it taught? *Educational Technology, 37*(4), 38-41.

Appendix A

WebQuest Questionnaire

Please select the answer that you believe most appropriate to each of the situation in WebQuest environment.

1	2	3	4	5
Strongly Disagree	Disagree	Neutral	Agree	Strongly Agree

Construct 1: Critical Thinking

1. In WebQuest learning, learners are able to examine the problem from multiple lenses.
2. In WebQuest learning, learners develop the ability to challenge each other's point of view
3. WebQuest learning facilitates learners to arrive at a conclusion by assembling the various evidences though reasoning.
4. Learners are able to propose a solution with more than one approach.
5. Learners are able to solve the problem with more than one solution.

Construct 2: Knowledge Application

6. WebQuests enable learners to effectively use the information to solve problems.
7. In a WebQuest learning environment, the knowledge gained from one problem solving situation can be transferred to another situation.
8. The task oriented nature of the WebQuest makes it clear what is to be learned.
9. In a WebQuest learning environment, learners are able to pull knowledge from different fields to solve problems.
10. The structured nature of WebQuests facilitates retrieval of prior knowledge to new learning.

Construct 3: Social Skills

11. Collaboration among learners in WebQuests learning promotes positive interdependence.
12. WebQuests learning promotes accountability among learners.
13. Learners gain a better understanding of each other's point of view in a WebQuest learning environment.
14. WebQuests promotes interaction between learners.
15. Learners develop better interpersonal and small group skills in a WebQuest learning environment.

Construct 4: Scaffold Learning

16. Scaffolding in WebQuest learning facilitates the understanding of the subject content.
17. Scaffolding organizes the way for new learning.
18. Scaffolding enables learners to focus on problems.
19. In a WebQuest learning environment, scaffolding enables learners to connect between their learning activities and goals.
20. In a WebQuest learning environment, scaffolding enables learners to better understand how to achieve their goals.

Appendix B

Online Discussion Questions

Construct 1: Critical Thinking

1. To what extent do WebQuests facilitate learners' constructivist learning?
2. What are the critical thinking skills learners may develop in WebQuest learning?

Construct 2: Knowledge Application

3. Comment on "WebQuests enable learners to pull knowledge from different fields to solve problem."
4. In what way do WebQuests help learners apply knowledge to new learning?

Construct 3: Social Skills

5. What are the social skills learners may develop in WebQuest learning?
6. To what extent does cooperative learning promote social interaction and the understanding from other people's view?

Construct 4: Scaffolding

7. What are the benefits of scaffolding in WebQuest learning?
8. To what extent does the structured nature of WebQuest learning (scaffolding) influence students' learning?

Construct 5: Affective Learning

9. What are the benefits that learners gain cognitively and psychologically from WebQuest learning?
10. What are some of the challenges (both emotionally and academically) that learners may have in WebQuest learning?

Appendix C

Table 1. Rotated factor loading and eigenvalues for three factors

		Factors		
Item No.	**Questions**	**Factor 1**	**Factor 2**	**Factor 3**
1.	Learners are able to examine the problem from multiple lenses.	.547		
2.	Learners develop the ability to challenge each other's point of view.		.739	
3.	Learners arrive at a conclusion by assembling the various evidences through reasoning.	.514		

Table 1. (continued)

		Factors		
Item No.	**Questions**	**Factor 1**	**Factor 2**	**Factor 3**
4.	Learners are able to propose a solution with more than one approach.	.583		
5.	Learners are able to solve the problem with more than one solution.	.590		
6.	Learners are able to use the information collected to solve problems.	.527		
7.	The knowledge gained from one problem solving situation can be transferred to another one.	.531		
8.	The task oriented nature of the WebQuest makes it clear what is to be learned.			.702
9.	Learners are able to pull knowledge from different fields to solve problems.	.609		
10.	WebQuests facilitate retrieval of prior knowledge to learning.	.442		
11.	Cooperation among learners in WebQuest promotes positives interdependence.	-	-	-
12.	Learners become accountable for their group work.	.494		
13.	Learners gain a better understanding of each other's point of view.		.617	
14.	WebQuests promote interaction between learners.		.610	
15.	Learners develop better interpersonal and small group skills.		.755	
16.	Scaffolding facilitates the understanding of the subject content.		.689	
17.	Scaffolding organizes the way for new learning.		.401	
18.	Scaffolding enables learners to focus on problems.			.424
19.	Scaffolding enables learners to connect between their learning activities and goals.			.540
20.	Scaffolding enables learners to better understand how to achieve their goals.			.406
Eigenvalue		8.42	1.50	1.11
% of variance		42.1	7.51	5.57
Cronbach alpha		.887	.846	.825

Note. Extraction Method: Principal Axis Factoring. Rotation Method: Varimax with Kaiser Normalization.

Table 2. Open coding analysis based on raw data

Category	Emerging Concepts / Themes
Active Learning	Authentic learning; knowledge association; open-ended thinking; connecting prior knowledge to new learning; transferring knowledge to other domains
Collaboration	Equal participation; distributed tasks; information sharing; mutual dependence; mutual respect; team work
Communication	Communicating with partners; small group discussion; synchronous and asynchronous discussion
Creativity	Thinking from multiple perspectives; finding multiple solutions to problems; approaching issues in non-conventional ways
Guided Tasks	Structuring critical thinking process; organizing learning tasks; connecting learning activities to goals and objectives
Higher Order Training	Comparing, discerning, analyzing , synthesizing, evaluating information
Instructional Template	Pre-designed learning tasks; organized learning; structured learning procedures
Learner Responsibility	Individual accountability; positive interdependence
Learning Empowerment	Learner control; self reliance; self confidence
Problem Solving	Identifying problems; proposing multiple solutions; proposing multiple approaches
Role Play	Exploring different viewpoints; tackling assigned roles; thinking from other's viewpoint
Self-awareness	Understanding one's strength and weakness; aware of one's cognitive and learning styles
Self-initiation	Actively identifying problems; using of resources efficiently; searching information; initiating solutions
Strategic Learner	Learning how to learn; self-selecting learning strategies

Table 3. Axial coding analysis based on open coding

Analytical Domains *Properties*	**Dimensions**
Constructivist	
Active Learning	From knowledge association, open-ended thinking to transferring knowledge to other domains
Creativity	From thinking from multiple perspectives to finding multiple solutions to problems
Cooperative Learning	
Levels of Communication	From synchronous to asynchronous; from partners to small group
Collaboration	From equal participation to mutual dependence, to team work
Role Play and Responsibility	From exploring different viewpoints to thinking from other's viewpoint; from individual accountability to positive interdependence
Critical Thinking	
Levels of Higher Order Thinking	From discerning, comparing information to synthesizing, evaluating information
Problem Solving Approaches	Multiple approaches to one solution; multiple solutions with one approach
Learning Support	
Guided Tasks	From organizing learning tasks to structuring critical thinking process
Metacognitive Thinking	
Self-awareness	From understanding one's strength and weakness to becoming aware of one's cognitive and learning styles
Strategic Learner	From learning how to learn to self-selecting learning strategies
Motivation	
Empowerment	From self confident to learner control
Self-initiation	From identifying problems to self-initiating solutions
Structured Learning	
Instructional Templates	From WebQuest templates to organized tasks and activities

Table 4. Overarching categories and subcategories derived from axial coding

Overarching Categories	Subcategories
Constructivist Problem-Solving Learning	Critical thinking Constructivist learning Metacognitive thinking
Social Interaction	Cooperative learning Collaboration Communication
Scaffolding	Structured learning Learning support
Motivation	Empowerment Self-initiating

Chapter IV

Team Effectiveness in Virtual Environments: An Ecological Approach

Pnina Shachaf
Indiana University, USA

Noriko Hara
Indiana University, USA

Abstract

This chapter attempts to address the need for more research on virtual team effectiveness and outlines an ecological theoretical framework that is applicable to virtual learning environments (VLE). Prior empirical studies on virtual team effectiveness used frameworks of traditional team effectiveness and mainly followed Hackman's normative model (input-process-output). We propose an ecological approach for virtual team effectiveness that accounts for team boundaries management, technology use, and external environment in VLE, properties which were previously either nonexistent or contextual. The ecological framework suggests that three components — external environment, internal environment, and boundary management — reciprocally interact with effectiveness. The significance of the proposed framework is a holistic perspective that takes into account the complexity of the external and internal environment of the team. Furthermore, we address the needs for new pedagogical approaches in VLE.

Introduction

As a result of globalization and advances in information and communication technologies, the increased use of virtual teams (VT) in both education and business has become prominent (Weiss, Nolan, & Trifonas, in press). VTs are "group[s] of people who work interdependently with a shared purpose across space, time, and organization boundaries using technology" (Lipnack & Stamps, 2000, p. 18). The need for more theoretical and empirical research on virtual team effectiveness (VTE) (e.g., DeSanctis & Poole, 1997; Furst, Blackburn, & Rosen, 1999) attracted several empirical studies (e.g., Vickery, Clark, & Carlson, 1999; Anderson, 2000; Lurey & Raisinghani, 2001). Most of these studies on VTE were conducted under the systems approach using Hackman's normative model (input-process-output) for traditional team effectiveness (Hackman & Oldham, 1980).

Previous studies of VTE emerged from the body of knowledge on traditional (face-to-face) teams (Hackman & Oldaham, 1980; Shea & Guzzo, 1987; Pearce & Ravlin, 1987; Sundstrom, DeMuese, & Futrell, 1990; Cohen & Bailey, 1997) and from theoretical perspectives on the interplay between information technology (IT) and organizations (Orlikowski, 1992; DeSanctis & Poole, 1994; Kling, McKim, & King, 2003). In this chapter we will capture the complexity of work groups and IT under a framework that manifests environmental aspects (social, cultural, organizational, and technological) and propose an ecological approach that would be relevant to teaching and learning with virtual teams. This theoretical framework is delineated from synthesizing, adopting, and modifying theories from other fields and levels of analysis. Specifically, we are influenced by several ecological theories, such as ecological psychology at the individual level (Barker, 1968; Bronfenbrenner, 1979;

Wicker, 1979) and group level (Sundstrom et al., 1990), as well as theories on IT and organizations, such as media richness theory (Lengel & Daft, 1988), and a social action framework (Ngwenyama & Lyytinen, 1997).

While many universities offer education via online environments (Dutton & Loader, 2002), it is becoming crucial to understand VTE for teaching and learning. Some MBA programs (e.g., Kelly Direct Online Program at Indiana University, Ohio University Without Boundaries) organize their online courses around team-based environments, and students are required to work in VT. In order to work effectively in VT, students and especially instructors need to become aware of all the components that influence VTE. This chapter proposes ecological approach to VTE and indicates its implications for online learning.

The main reason for selecting an ecological framework for VTE is because it stresses the critical role of the environment through a reciprocal interdependency between internal processes and the external environment. It was previously suggested that internal and external environments influence VTE (Lurey & Raisinghani, 2001), and that an ecological approach helps us understand VTs.

Before we outline the ecological framework components, several assumptions should be stressed (Wicker, 1979):

1. A VT organism cannot be considered to exist or act in isolation. Every VT organism is linked with other organisms in a complex network of relationships.
2. All VT organisms are affected by forces inside themselves, such as leadership, team norms, technology use, and process losses (e.g., conflict management), as well as by external forces of other organisms, such as team competitors, the instructors, and the VLE technology.
3. VTs adapt and act in a way that achieves balanced and harmonious working relationships with their environment, distinguishing between features that are appropriate for their needs and those that are not.

Virtual Team Effectiveness

The research on virtual teams is in its infancy and has a variety of foci. Researchers are making efforts to determine how virtuality impacts team effectiveness (Dube & Pare, 2004; Furst, Blackburn, & Rosen, 1999; Martins, Gilson, & Maynard, 2004; Pauleen, 2003). Furst, Blackburn, and Rosen (1999) suggest that the lack of research on VTE is partially a result of the newness of VTs and partially a result of the underlying assumption that the existing knowledge of traditional team effectiveness is applicable in the virtual environment. They proposed a research agenda on VTE based on Hackman's normative model (Furst, Blackburn, & Rosen, 1999). Likewise, Martins, Gilson, and Maynard (2004) recently reviewed the body of knowledge on virtual teams, and also followed Hackman's normative model for team effectiveness. They suggest future research directions that focus on virtual teams.

A recent claim was made that a virtual team "can be more productive if they stay separated and do all their collaborating virtually" (Majchrzak, Malhotra, Stamps, & Lipnack, 2004, p.131). A few studies have made an effort to compare performance of traditional and virtual teams and to identify factors that are involved in virtual team effectiveness (Dennis & Wixon, 2002; May & Carter, 2001; McDonough et al., 2001; Vickery, Clark, & Carlson, 1999). May and Carter (2001) found that team effectiveness and efficiency are higher for virtual teams compared to traditional teams but that the level of satisfaction is lower. Dennis and Wixon (2002) in their meta-analysis of group support systems use examined 61 articles and compared the performance of face-to-face (FTF) vs. distributed virtual teams. They reported that "FTF use of GSS [group support systems] improves decision quality and the number of ideas relative to the control groups working without GSS, however, FTF GSS use requires more time and lower process satisfaction. In contrast, distributed teams made worse decisions than the control groups working without GSS" (p.245). Decision quality is lower for virtual teams, but the number of ideas generated is not different.

Greater management challenges are associated with lower performance for the three types of teams in a study of new product development teams: collocated, global, and virtual. According to a survey of 103 individuals, conducted by McDonough et al. (2001), global team performance is lower than the performance of virtual or collocated teams. The global teams also face greater behavioral and project management challenges than the virtual teams. The results suggest that project management challenges are more a function of geographical distance than of cultural or language differences. However, no relationship is evident between behavioral challenges and team performance.

Another study involved 273 individuals from 84 teams and focused on performance (Vickery, Clark, & Carlson, 1999). The researchers found that stronger virtual positions perform better in complex rather than simple task situations. Furthermore, they suggest that the organizational structure of the parent organization of team members affects the allegiance structure and the control climate of the virtual team. This, in turn, affects the strength of the virtual position.

A survey, completed by 67 participants from 12 teams in 8 companies, involved a questionnaire based on a framework for virtual team effectiveness developed by Lurey and Raisinghani (2001). The framework includes three main factors that are expected to have a direct effect on team effectiveness. These factors are: internal group dynamics (job characteristics, selection procedure, team member relations, team process, internal team leadership); external support mechanisms (education system, reward system, executive leadership style, tools and technologies, communication patterns); and design process. The outcome measures of effectiveness were performance and satisfaction. Correlations among the predictor variables and performance and satisfaction were significant at the 0.01 for all variables except for tools and technology, which was significant at 0.05.

Ecological Framework

The proposed ecological framework consists of three components that are critical to VTE: external environment, internal environment, and boundaries. Compared to Hackman's normative model (Hackman & Oldham, 1980), our framework is more holistic and emphasizes continuing dynamic process, disregarding chronological sequence. The components are reciprocal and interdependent among themselves (Figure 1).

External Environment

The external environment is a critical component for VTE. Following Bronfenbrenner (1979), we suggest that VT behavior is embedded in a setting that could be categorized into four levels: microsystem, mesosystem, exosystem, and macrosystem (Figure 2).

The microsystem is the immediate setting in which the team experiences its own activities, roles, and interdependency, within a specific setting (e.g., the VT

Figure 1. Ecological framework for virtual team effectiveness

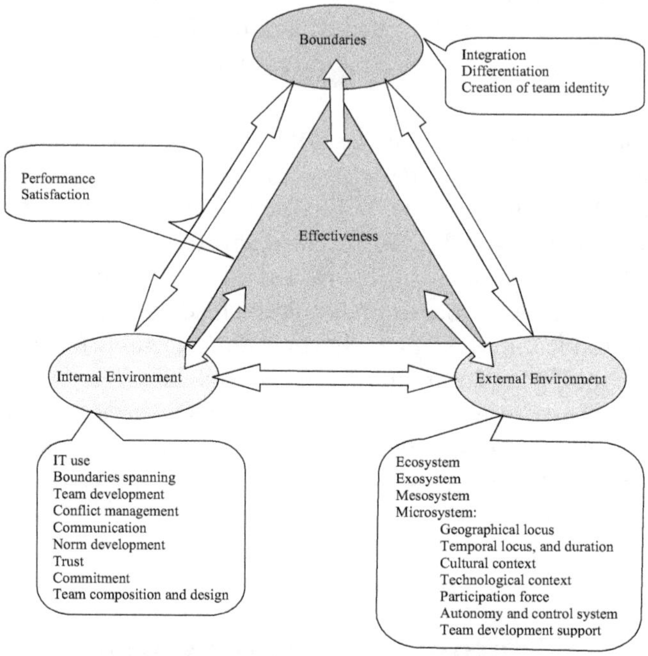

Figure 2. External environment

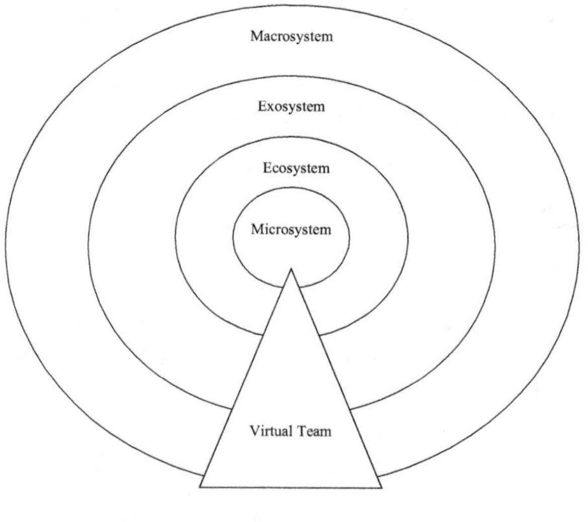

physical and digital space, their role setting, assignments, and participation requirements). In virtual learning environments (VLE), it is equivalent to pedagogy that instructors incorporate. The mesosystem refers to the relationships between two or more of the settings in which the team participates. The network of teams (virtual and collocated) and organizations that team members act within are a system of microsystems making up a mesosystem. In VLE, it refers to the course. The exosystem refers to one or more settings that the team is not involved in as an active participant, but in which events occur that affect, or are affected by, what happens in the setting of the VT (for example, in this case, curriculum). The macrosystem refers to consistencies among the lower level systems, at the level of culture or subculture, such as department, school, and university. The macrosystem also refers to the general environment—the legal, political, social and cultural environments.

In this chapter, among the four levels of environments, we mainly elaborate on the microsystem because it has an immediate impact on the VTE. VT behavior and its effectiveness are embedded within specific the setting of the team's microsystem. This context is a critical component of team effectiveness (Hackman & Oldham, 1980; Pearce & Ravlin, 1987; Shea & Guzzo, 1987; Sundstrom et al., 1990) and is composed of seven dimensions. These seven dimensions are derived from factors that were proposed by other frameworks for traditional team effectiveness and in particular from the Sundstrom et al. (1987) ecological approach to traditional teams. In addition, Barker's (1968) ecological approach influenced us to include additional factors, which are relevant to virtual teams, and have not been included in the Sundstrom et al. (1987) framework. The following paragraphs describe these seven dimensions.

Geographical locus (Barker, 1968) is the physical setting of the VT. Space is a critical component of identity and boundary maintenance (Sundstrom et al., 1990). The VT's physical space is used only for temporary co-location (e.g., during face-to-face meetings) or not used at all for teams who never meet. However, the VT uses a digital space to substitute for the lack of physical space. Any courseware (e.g., Blackboard and WebCT) has a shared digital space for students to share files and have team online discussions. Instructors who teach online courses should take advantage of such functions available through courseware.

Temporal locus and duration (Barker, 1968) are the team life-cycle and the pace and length of member interactions within the team. VT development and life-cycle are temporal (Vickery, Clark, & Carlson, 1999) and members share work time based on the shared digital space. Although online courses are also organized temporally, some online programs structure the curriculum so that student cohorts stay together throughout the program.

Cultural contexts (Shea & Guzzo, 1987; Sundstrom et al., 1990) are the cultures surrounding the team at three levels: professional, organizational, and national culture (Schein, 1992; Hofstede, 1991). For example, the culture would affect team norm development, communication, decision making, and performance evaluation (Furst, Blackburn, & Rosen, 1999). As online learning offers flexibility and convenience, many working professionals enroll in online courses. Consequently the students in online courses tend to be nontraditional with diverse backgrounds. Moreover, online courses offered by American universities attract students from all over the world. The instructors and students in VLE need to be sensitive to cultural diversity.

Technological context refers to "task technology," which is the technology used for performing the task (Hackman & Oldham, 1980, Shea & Guzzo, 1987; Sundstrom et al., 1990), to media channels and to telecommunication infrastructure. The infrastructure should be taken into consideration in terms of team effectiveness. It is evident that administrators of distance education programs should pay attention to which subject-matters can be properly taught in VTE. For example, highly technical content is rather difficult to teach and learn in online environments (e.g., Hara & Kling, 2000) because students need to deal with both technologies as means as well as subject matter. Additionally, VT might have to deal with diverse configurations and regulations which exist in different places (e.g., several organizations, several countries).

Participation forces (Barker, 1968) are the environmental factors that motivate team members to be part of the VT. The rationale for participation in a VT could be intrinsic, for example, to volunteer (e.g., open source community) or to work under a specific organizational reward system, which involves extrinsic motivation (Hackman & Oldham, 1980; Pearce & Ravlin, 1987; Shea & Guzzo, 1987; Sundstrom et al., 1990. Students in VLE seldom have the choice of participation in teams due to the fact that this is part of the course requirements. However, students vary in their motivation for participation. Participation forces are relevant to retention rates in online learning. Studies (e.g., Irizarry, 2002) show that students who are self-motivated and have high self-efficacy tend to stay with online courses. In addition, student achievement level, ability to conceptualize, interest in the topic, and other factors which are relevant to team success in the traditional face-to-face learning environment, define their participation and contribution to the virtual team. Finally, the weight of the grade assigned by the instructor to the virtual team assignment in any particular course (reward) will define the level of participation of student in the VLE.

Autonomy and control system are the degree of independence a VT has to conduct its task (Shea & Guzzo, 1987; Pearce & Ravlin, 1987; Sundstrom et al., 1990). For example, high team autonomy means that the team could make decisions in regard to members' roles, without approval from instructors. Instructors make decisions about how much autonomy students have in VLE.

Team development support is the training and consultation the instructors and higher education institutions provide to support teamwork (Hackman & Oldham, 1980; Pearce & Ravlin, 1987; Sundstrom et al., 1990) and performance evaluation (Sundstrom et al., 1990). Studies that focused attention on VT facilitation (Montoya-Weiss, Massey, & Song, 2001; Pauleen & Yoong, 2001; Warkentin & Beranek, 1999) stressed the importance of team building training. Institutions providing online courses should pay particular attention to this kind of training.

To summarize, in this section, we described four levels of VT's external environment: microsystem, mesosystem, exosystem, and macrosystem, in which the VTs are embedded. A specific elaboration and emphasis of the components of microsystems was further described because these components are more critical success factors for VTs. Among these factors are geographical locus; temporal locus and duration; cultural context; technological infrastructure; organizational support mechanism; autonomy and control mechanism; and forces of participation.

Boundaries Management

The second component of the ecological framework is boundary management. The ecological approach emphasizes the issue of creating and maintaining boundaries (Sundstrom et al., 1990). Group boundaries (physical and psychological) determine who is in the group (Alderfer, 1977). A VT is defined as a team by the boundaries that are formed and maintained over time. These boundaries become critical components of VT viability. Experimental studies of traditional teams and VTs do not stress this aspect (Sundstrom et al., 1990) because team boundaries are predefined, and that is the case for many VLE. Studies on real VTs in an organizational setting suggest that boundary creation and maintenance are critical (Pawar & Sharifi, 1997; Robey, Khoo, & Powers, 2000; May & Carter, 2001; Sole & Edmondson, 2001). Boundary management differentiates the team from its environment, so that it will have its unique identity. At the same time, boundary management integrates the team with its environment to avoid isolation. Three components of boundary management will be further described: differentiation, integration (Sundstrom et al., 1990), and the creation of team identity.

Differentiation refers to the specialization, interdependence, and autonomy of the team. VTE depends on the ability of the team to differentiate its members from others, in order to conduct meetings and share information (Sundstrom et al., 1990). Both for traditional and virtual teams the task and team resources (e.g., members, time, and space — even temporarily physical co-location) are critical for differentiation. However, in VT, the physical limitations make this process more complex, and the differentiation is based also on the shared digital space of the team.

Integration refers to the ties of the VT with its immediate organizational environment and to other teams. Integration refers to the team's relationships with peers and instructors, which are not part of the VT. To facilitate the process of integration, many online programs offer face-to-face orientations as well as summer sessions. Research (see e.g., Barbian, 2002) also suggests that blended online learning (i.e., combining face-to-face and virtual learning) produces best learning outcomes.

Creation of team identity is crucial to the performance of VTs. Physical territories reinforce group boundaries and identities (Sundstrom et al., 1990). The lack of physical territories was attributed to the de-individuation process of computer-mediated groups (Lea & Spears, 1991). In order to overcome this drawback, VT members rely on shared electronic space for the creation of team identity. This electronic shared space is devoted only to the members of the team and enables them to share experience.

In summary, VT creates and maintains permeable "virtual boundaries," which are not defined by functional or geographical aspects, but are instead based on a temporal task or project. The shared digital space creates and maintains boundaries. This shared digital space and the temporal physical collocation of team members help the team to mange its boundaries and identities. Differentiation and integration should be balanced. For example, too much differentiation inhibits integration, and vice versa.

Internal Environment

The third component in the proposed ecological framework is the internal environment. Within the internal environment, the following factors for team effectiveness have been discussed in the literature as process or contextual variables: team composition and design (Hackman & Oldham, 1980; Pearce & Ravlin, 1987), communication (Javenpaa & Liedner, 1999; Pearce & Ravlin, 1987), team development (Sundstrom et al., 1990), conflict management (Montoya-Weiss et al., 2001), leadership (Lurey & Raisinghani, 2001), norms (Sundstrom et al., 1990), commitment (Hackman & Oldham, 1980; Pearce & Ravlin, 1987), and trust (Javenpaa & Liedner, 1999). We suggest two additional components that influence VTE: technology use (Ngwenyama, & Lyytinen, 1997; Lengel & Daft, 1988) and internal boundary spanning (Wenger, 1998). Unlike other authors (Sundstrom et al., 1990), we propose to differentiate task technology and information and communication technology (ICT) and consider technology use not only as a contextual factor, but also as an internal factor, specifically by using a social action framework (Ngwenyama & Lyytinen, 1997).

The technology that the VT uses to achieve its tasks should support team social actions. The focus of the social action framework for analyzing groupware (Ngwenyama & Lyytinen, 1997) is the use of IT for communication and creation/use of knowledge among VT members. They suggest the following four social action categories in groupware: instrumental, communicative, discursive, and strategic. Instrumental action focuses on end products by controlling, manipulating, and transforming physical artifacts, such as providing concrete explanations for assignments, distributing readings, and making links to library databases. Communicative action supports creating and maintaining shared understanding among members and is facilitated by computer-mediated communication (CMC). Discursive action specifies and evaluates goals and objectives as well as achieving a consensus on shared values and norms, for example, through the use of a voting system or anonymous contributions to course online discussion forums. Strategic action influences the group behavior to achieve common goals, such as access restrictions to the shared digital space. During the process of work, each of these social actions uses technology, appropriating different functions of courseware.

In addition, the other internal component critical to VTE is internal boundary spanning. We suggest that not only external boundary management, in the traditional sense, but also internal boundary spanning should be discussed as part of the VTE ecological framework. Heterogeneous VTs incorporate multiple boundaries. Individuals from different geographical locations, organizations, nations, and professions traditionally have boundaries that differentiate each group from others. Watson-Manheim, Crowston, and Chudoba (2002) defined virtual work as work that spans discontinuities of temporal work location, geographic work location, group membership, organizational affiliation, and cultural background. Therefore, in VTs, these discontinuities create a need for the internal process of boundary spanning, as students in VLE come from diverse backgrounds. In a heterogeneous VT, these boundaries are integrated internally within the team through the process of boundary spanning.

Several types of boundary spanning are embedded in heterogeneous VT (Lipnack & Stamps, 2000). The first type of boundary spanning occurs on geographical dispersion, where team members do not share the same physical space. The second type of boundary spanning occurs based on cross-functional membership of professionals using several languages, backgrounds, and cultures. The third is of organizational affiliation manifesting inter-organizational relationships, organizational cultures, and power interdependencies of the team members' parent organization. This dimension is relevant only to the rare examples of collaborative courses among several institutions. The educational culture, rules and procedures, vary among institutions. The fourth is based on international diversity of languages, cultures, and religions. The final type of boundary spanning is time zones of team members who are working in different parts of the globe. Not all types of boundary spanning, except for geographical dispersion, may occur in individual VTs. The boundary spanning process occurs either through a broker or boundary object (Wenger, 1998). Brokers are team members who introduce new knowledge and practices into the VT while boundary objects are artifacts within a VT digital space (e.g., new literature).

The next sections will describe other components of our ecological framework internal environment as emerged from previous studies on virtual teams. This involves an outline of the findings of studies that focus on team processes, such as trust, leadership, commitment, conflict management, and communication.

Communication among team members is one of the process predictors of team effectiveness. Effective communication is attributed to effective teams. Communication impacts satisfaction and performance, helps overcome process losses, and strengthens process gains. Communication among global virtual team (GVT) members is more complex due to the fact that it is mediated by computers and involves cross-cultural communication. Therefore, effective communication is even more critical for success in the virtual setting. For that reason, several studies focus attention on the virtual team communication process (e.g., Jarvenpaa & Leidner, 1999; Maznevski & Choduba, 2000; Pauleen & Yoong, 2001a; Pawar & Sharifi, 1997; Robey, Khoo, & Powers, 2000).

Communication among virtual team members has been examined within virtual teams and also in comparison with collocated teams. Scholars stress that effective GVTs fit their communication patterns to the task and keep a strict pace of face-to-face meetings (Pawar & Sharifi, 1997; Maznevski & Choduba, 2000). In addition, they suggest that temporal collocation and face-to-face meetings among virtual team members increase communication effectiveness and information sharing (Sole & Edmondson, 2002). Pauleen and Yoong (2001a) found that some electronic communication channels are more effective than others in building online relationships. In their study, e-mail was the basic channel for communication but was used primarily for information sharing and not for relationship building, which was primarily supported by telephone exchange. The participants (facilitators of virtual teams) in this study used chat (ICQ) to set up opportunities for informal, spontaneous communication between facilitators and team members. As several scholars stress, however, informal communication is minimal among virtual team members (Pawar & Sharifi, 1997; Carletta et al., 2000; Robey, Khoo, & Powers, 2000). According to Carletta et al. (2000), if meetings are kept small and informal, interactivity and sociability improve, scheduling delays decrease, and opportunities for members of lower status to raise their own concerns are created. In research by Massey et al. (2001), significant differences occurred in the perception of task technology fit between virtual team members from the US, Asia, and Europe. Team members perceived communication, particularly media choice, as a strategic activity that had to be planned (Suchan & Hayzak, 2001).

Categorization of communication incidents are performed in several studies, using various categorization schemas. Maznevski and Choduba (2000) distinguish among communication incidents based on objectives: information gathering, problem solving, idea generating, and comprehensive decision-making. Categories of communication behavior of virtual teams using a synchronous virtual room (Qureshi, 2000) include providing information, seeking information, requesting action, confirming action, seeking consensus, stating a problem, stating a solution, notifying of the occurrence of an event, making a decision, volunteering assistance, raising funds, seeking funds, providing funds, and providing humor. The first two, providing information and seeking information, were the most frequently observed behaviors in this case study. Robey et al. (2000) categorized communication differently, sorting it into three types: communication for cultural understanding, task-related communication, and socio-emotional communication.

Cramton (2001) explored 13 virtual teams' difficulties in maintaining "mutual knowledge" and described the consequences of failure to do so. She identified five types of problems constituting failures of mutual knowledge: failure to communicate and retain contextual information, unevenly distributed information, difficulty communicating and understanding the salience of information, differences in speed of access to information, and difficulty interpreting the meaning of silence. These difficulties were associated with episodes of conflict, frustration or confusion in the teams.

Trust in traditional teams was an important component, but in virtual teams, it is an even more important quality (Lipnack & Stamps, 1997). GVT members have to trust other people, share purposes and rewards, and trust their information channels, and GVT members have only their shared trust in one another to guarantee the success of their joint work (Lipnack & Stamps, 2000). This is not only a theoretical claim, but also it is evident in empirical study results (Buckley, 2000), which find that trust accounts for a quarter of the variance observed in virtual team effectiveness. Morris, Marshall and Rainer (2002) found that trust and user satisfaction with the IT used explained 31% of the variance in job satisfaction of virtual team members.

The factors identified as sources of trust in the traditional FTF context were examined in a study of the virtual team setting by Jarvenpaa et al. (1998). They reported that team members act as if trust is present from the first interaction. Explicitly, GVTs experience "swift trust," which is temporal and very fragile (Jarvenpaa & Leidner, 1999). The concept of swift trust was developed to describe trust in temporary teams, which form and function around a common temporal task. Swift trust might be imported to the virtual teams but is more likely to be created via the communication behaviors of group members during the first interaction they experience together. Furthermore, task communications are crucial, while social communication that complements the task may strengthen trust in the teams. Response behavior and verbalizations of member commitment are also critical for trust development (Jarvenpaa & Leidner, 1999). Jarvenpaa, Shaw, and Staples (2004) suggest that the impact of trust on global virtual teams is different in different situations (context). Furthermore, training can increase the level of trustworthiness and trust among team members, and encourage team members to be open and frank in expressing their feelings and ideas (Beranek, 2000; Warkentin & Beranek, 1999). Training enables virtual teams to develop trust faster than do teams with no training as well as to increase levels of trustworthiness.

Kanawattanachai and Yoo (2002) examined the dynamic nature of trust and its changing patterns with 38 teams in a simulation game. They focused on cognitive-based trust, which is based on elements such as competence, reliability, and professionalism, and on affective-based trust, which is based on elements such as caring and emotional connection to each other. The study compared both affective-based and cognitive-based trust between high- and low-performing teams over time. They found that both high- and low-performing teams started with similar levels of trust in both cognitive and affective dimensions. Unlike the low-performing teams, better development and maintenance of trust level throughout the project life were attributed to the high-performing teams.

Commitment to a virtual team influences satisfaction and performance and, moreover, findings suggest that commitment to the virtual team can be manipulated (Powell, 2000). Furthermore, this study found no significant relationship between commitment to the virtual team and task competence, personality, and others' commitments. Training can improve not only communication, but also increase the commitment of team members to the team's goals and objectives (Warkentin & Beranek, 1999; Beranek, 2000).

Leadership is another important factor for team effectiveness in traditional collocated teams. Leaders in GVTs face challenges that are different from the traditional FTF environment (Oakley, 1998; Switzer, 2000). Leaders' aggressiveness and assertiveness, for example, are directed by cultural norms (O'Hara-Davereaux & Johnsen, 1994). As a result, the GVT leader must develop a style that will fit the cultural composition of its team members and optimize the cultural differences (Oakley, 1998; O'Hara-Davereaux & Johnsen, 1994). Lurey and Raisinghani (2001) suggest that leadership style is related to virtual team effectiveness only moderately. Switzer (2000) found no differences in leadership profiles between the virtual and FTF group leaders. Hara, Bonk, and Angeli (2000) found that discussion leaders influence cognitive and metacognitive depth of students' online discussions.

Leadership is the main focus of Kayworth and Leidner's study (2001) of 13 GVTs comprised of students from the USA, Mexico, and France. The goal of their study is to identify the factors that contribute to effective leadership in a virtual team environment. Their quantitative analysis reflects that a significant predictor of leadership effectiveness in the virtual environment is the mentoring capability of the leader. Furthermore, effective leadership is associated with team members' perceptions of communication effectiveness, communication satisfaction, and the ability of the leader to establish role clarity among team members. Importantly, their qualitative analysis is consistent with the literature on face-to face teams (Kayworth & Leidner, 2001). All of this research suggests four dimensions of effective virtual team leadership: (1) Communication (the leader provides continuous feedback, engages in regular and prompt communication, and clarifies tasks); (2) Understanding (the leader is sensitive to schedules of members, appreciates their opinions and suggestions, cares about member's problems, gets to know them, and expresses a personal interest in them); (3) Role clarity (the leader clearly defines responsibilities of all members, exercises authority, and mentors virtual team members); and (4) Leadership attitude (the leader is assertive yet not too "bossy," caring, relates to members at their own levels, and maintains a consistent attitude over the life of the project).

Majchrzak et al. (2000b) conclude that in the virtual team, the decision-making shifts from hierarchical in nature to more participative due to the adoption of technology. The leader's role becomes more ambiguous in the virtual team in that the leader is not the information gatekeeper but rather a negotiator and facilitator. The leader of this team complained that, "I've never seen a rocket designed by committee before" (Majchrzak et al., 2000b, p. 588). The same type of change in the position and roles of the leader of a virtual team is evident in the case study of a virtual team in the automotive industry (May, Carter, & Joyner, 2000). The researchers stress that the use of groupware and adoption of it by the virtual team enabled more delegation of responsibilities down to team members. In addition, the uncertainty that members of virtual teams face creates the need for a rotating leadership strategy in order to avoid dependence on any particular member (Jarvenpaa et al., 1998; Johnson, Suriya, Won Yoon, Barrett, & La Fluer, 2002).

Another impact on virtual team effectiveness is managerial control. Piccoli and Ives (2003) indicate that the managerial behavior control mechanism used has a negative effect on individual psychological outcomes and has no effect on team performance and team member viability. Therefore, different managerial solutions (from the traditional control mechanisms) should be implemented in order to increase virtual team performance (McDonough et al., 2001; Piccoli & Ives, 2003).

Conflict management behavior in GVTs is the focus of a study by Montoya-Weiss et al. (2001) that also examines the effect of temporal coordination intervention on team effectiveness. Based on the five conflict-handling modes rooted in the research on face-to face teams — avoidance, accommodation, competition, collaboration, and compromise — they have generated hypotheses with regard to the effect of each of these behaviors on virtual teams. Accommodation and compromise behaviors generated different effects than were expected based on the traditional team literature. Accommodation had no significant effect on performance of virtual teams, and compromise behavior had a significant negative effect on performance of virtual teams. One of the explanations for the minimal effect of accommodation behavior could be that "no matter how much an individual may express accommodation; the team does not experience it" (Montoya-Weiss et al., 2001, p. 1257). The significant negative effect of compromise behavior can be explained as follows: "It may be that compromise behavior was manifested as 'cutting and pasting' content in order to develop a middle of the road, representative team document" (Montoya-Weiss et al., 2001, p. 1259).

The final factor in the internal environment is norms development. Norms development is explored in a study by Malhotra, Majchrzak, Carman, and Lott (2001). They stress that one of the managerial challenges for a virtual team is coordinating norms: "Communication protocols about what gets communicated to whom, when, and how, can be established at the outset and aid team success" (Malhotra et al., 2001, p. 233). The set of norms and behaviors that helps the team communicate about their task in the virtual setting is the focus of a study involving engineers by Majchrzak et al. (1999, 2000a). The authors report on norm development and adaptation of inter-organizational virtual teams using collaborative technology that focuses on knowledge sharing and reuse. At the kickoff team meeting, this team set up a coordination protocol that included 11 formal norms prepared in advance by a subgroup of the teams and modified during the first meeting. Many of these norms were later called into question, and the need for new practices and norms was evident. During the team's first working period, 15 modified norms were set up, which were replaced with nine norms after the first team's technical review, a process which facilitated the knowledge-sharing process in this team. It is clear that effective communication protocols are difficult to define *a priori*, as during the team development, team norms change as well (Malhotra et al., 2001). The team in this case study adopted a practice of democratic participation and encouraged the use of "common language" metaphors. Since in virtual teams one cannot assume that members bring shared understanding to the team through common affiliation with one organization or profession, shared understanding must be created (Malhotra et al., 2001).

In this section, we described several unique components of the internal environment in our framework: technology use and boundary spanning. These factors and other internal factors were recognized by other researchers to support VTE. In the following section, we further discuss effectiveness.

Effectiveness

Effectiveness has been the focus of several frameworks for traditional teams as well as VTs. Effectiveness could refer to whether the team has accomplished its assigned tasks (Shea & Guzzo, 1987). Another approach embraces socio-emotional consequences of group action, such as member satisfaction and attraction to the group as elements of effectiveness (Hackman, 1987). Many researchers agree that effectiveness includes more than performance (Hackman, 1987; Pearce & Ravlin, 1987; Sundstrom et al., 1990).

Beyond these two more traditional effectiveness measures (performance and satisfaction), an effective virtual team creates and maintains a shared digital space during a team life-cycle. This shared electronic space could be preserved for future use by the organization and other teams (Furst, Blackborn, & Rosen, 1999).

Future Trends

In the online learning environments, internal environments gain more attention than other components (boundaries and external environments) in the past. For example, dealing with various technological configurations was found as a major setback in a study of a Web-based distance education course (Hara & Kling, 2000). This issue was embedded within external environment and was not anticipated as a problem. In addition, how the external environments, such as participation forces and autonomy and control systems, influence learning environments is discussed thoroughly in Kling and Courtright's work (2004). Moreover, teachers who traditionally assume the role of leaders become more like facilitators in online learning environments (Wallace, 2003). This new role of instructors affects their communication strategies, norm development, and eventually trust among students. Our wish is that the ecological model, which was originally developed for virtual teams in organizational setting (Shachaf & Hara, 2002), will help understand VTE in instructional settings as well.

Another emerging trend in online learning is the emphasis on building learning community (Barab, Gray, & Kling, 2004). Instructors can facilitate developing a sense of belonging to the learning community through peer-to-peer learning occurred in VLE. One strategy is to put emphasis on social aspects of students' interactions. Learning is social (Lave, 1988; Vygotsky, 1978). Instructors could provide a virtual space called "coffee table" where students can engage in social discussions, such as hobbies and other interests. As the corporate world show keen interests in building communities of practice both online and face-to-face (Wenger, McDermott, & Snyder, 2002), instructors should consider providing learning community for students.

Conclusion

In this chapter, we proposed an ecological framework to understand VTE. This framework consists of three components: external environment, internal environment, and boundaries. We proposed reciprocal interdependency among the three components and VTE, by stressing the effects of components on VTE, and vice versa, the effects of VTE on the three components. The significance of the proposed framework is threefold. First, we internalized technology, which is traditionally a contextual variable in team effectiveness models, and stressed its roles and impacts as a part of internal environment on VTE. Second, boundary management, as well as boundary spanning effects, was explained in relation to VTE, whereas most traditional frameworks tend to ignore this aspect. Third, we expanded on the factors of the external environment of VT as they relate to virtual learning team effectiveness. Specifically, we delineated the factors of the microsystem. Evidently, further empirical study to validate this framework is yet to be done both in business and instructional settings. We do hope that this framework will inform other researchers' studies to consider environmental aspects and not only examine this phenomenon under closed systems perspectives when studying VTE.

References

Alderfer, C. P. (1977). Improving organizational communication through long-term inter-group intervention. *Journal of Applied Behavioral Science, 13,* 193-210.

Anderson, W. N. (2000). *Cultural values and communication mode: A study of culturally homogeneous and culturally heterogeneous groups.* Unpublished doctoral dissertation, Rutgers State University of New Jersey, Newark.

Barab, S., Gray, J., & Kling, R. (Eds.). (2004). *Building online communities in the service of learning.* Cambridge: Cambridge University Press.

Barbian, J. (2002). Here's proof. *Online Learning Magazine, 6*(6), 27-31.

Barker, R. G. (1968). *Ecological psychology: Concepts and methods for studying the environment of human behavior*. Stanford, CA: Stanford University Press.

Beranek, P. M. (2000, January 4-7). The impacts of relational and trust development training on virtual teams: An exploratory investigation. *Proceedings of 33 Hawaii International Conference on System Sciences,* Maui, Hawaii. Retrieved March 10, 2003, from www.computer.org/proceedings/hicss/ 0493/04931/04931020.pdf

Bronfenbrenner, U. (1979). *The ecology of human development: Experiments by nature and design*. Cambridge, MA: Harvard University.

Carletta, J., Anderson, A. H., & McEwan, R. (2000). The effects of multimedia communication technology on non-collocated teams: A case study. *Ergonomics*, *4*(8), 1237-1251.

Cohen, S. G., & Bailey, D. E. (1997). What makes teams work: Group effectiveness research from the shop floor to the executive suite. *Journal of Management, 23*(3), 239-291.

Cramton, C. D. (2001). The mutual knowledge problem and its consequences for dispersed collaboration. *Organization Science*, *12*(3), 346-371.

Davidow, W. H., & Malone, M. S. (1992). *The virtual organization.* New York: Harper Collins.

Dennis, A. R., & Wixom, B. H. (2001-2002). Investigating the moderators of the group support system use with meta-analysis. *Journal of Management Information Systems, 18*(3), 235-257.

DeSanctis G., & Poole, M. S. (1994). Capturing the complexity in advanced technology use: Adaptive structuration theory. *Organization Science, 5*(2), 1994.

DeSanctis, G., & Poole, M. S. (1997). Transition in teamwork in new organizational forms. *Advances in Group Processes, 14*, 157-176.

Dube, L., & Pare, G. (2001). Global virtual teams. *Communications of the ACM, 44*(12), 71-73.

Dutton, W. H., & Loader, B. D. (Eds.). (2002). *Digital Academe: The new media and institutions of higher education and learning*. London: Routledge.

Furst, S., Blackburn, R., & Rosen, B. (1999). Virtual team effectiveness: A proposed research agenda. *Information Systems Journal, 9*, 249-269.

Gibson, C. B., & Cohen, S. G. (2003). *Virtual teams that work creating conditions for virtual team effectiveness*. San Francisco: Jossey-Bass.

Hackman, J. R. (1987). The design of work teams. In J. Lorsch (Ed.), *Handbook of organizational behavior* (pp. 315-342). Englewood Cliffs, NJ: Prentice-Hall.

Hackman, J. R., & Oldham, G. R. (1980). *Work redesign.* Reading, MA: Addison-Wesley.

Hara, N., Bonk, C. J., & Angeli, C. (2000). Content analysis of on-line discussion in an applied educational psychology course. *Instructional Science, 28*, 115-152.

Hara, N., & Kling, R. (2000). Students' distress with a web-based distance education course. *Information, Communication and Society, 3*(4), 557-579.

Hofstede, G. H. (1991). *Cultures and organizations: Software of the mind.* London: McGraw-Hill.

Irizarry, R. (2002). Self-efficacy & motivation effects on online psychology student retention. *United States Distance Learning Association Journal, 16*(12). Retrieved January 22, 2005, from http://www.usdla.org/html/journal/DEC02_Issue/article07.html

Jarvenpaa, S. L., Knoll, K., & Leidner, D. E. (1998). Is anybody out there? Antecedents of trust in global virtual teams. *Journal of Management Information Systems, 14*(4), 29-64.

Jarvenpaa, S. L., & Liedner, D. E. (1999). Communication and trust in global virtual teams. *Organization Science, 10*(6), 791-815.

Jarvenpaa, S. L., Shaw, T. R., & Staples, D. S. (2004). Toward contextualized theories of trust: The role of trust in global virtual teams. *Information Systems Research, 15*(3), 250-267.

Johnson, S. D., Suriya, C., Won Yoon, S., Berrett, J. V., & La Fleur, J. (2002). Team development and group processes of virtual learning teams. *Computers and Education, 39*(4), 379-393.

Kanawattanachai, P., & Yoo, Y. (2002). Dynamic nature of trust in virtual teams. *Sprouts: Working papers on information environments, systems and organizations*, Vol. 2. Retrieved March 10, 2003, from http://weatherhead.cwru.edu/sprouts/2002/020204.pdf

Kayworth, T. R., & Leidner, D. E. (2001). Leadership effectiveness in global virtual teams. *Journal of Management Information Systems, 18*(3), 7-40.

Kling, R., McKim, G., & King, A. (2003). A bit more to IT: Scientific Communication forums as socio-technical interaction networks. *Journal of American Society for Information Science & Technology, 54*(1), 47-67.

Kling, R., & Courtright, C. (2004). Group behavior and learning in electronic forums: A socio-technical approach. In S. A. Barab, R. Kling, & J. H. Gray (Eds.), *Designing for virtual communities in the service of learning* (pp. 91-119). Cambridge: Cambridge University.

Lave, J. (1988). *Cognition in practice: Mind, mathematics and culture in everyday life.* Cambridge: Cambridge University Press.

Lea, M., & Spears, R. (1991). Computer-mediated communication, de-individuation, and group decision-making. *International Journal of Man Machine Studies, 34*, 283-301.

Lee, A. S. (1994). Electronic mail as a medium for rich communication: An empirical investigation using hermeneutic interpretation. *MIS Quarterly, 18*(2), 143-157.

Lipnack, J., & Stamps, J. (1997). *Virtual teams: Reaching across space, time and organizations with technology*. New York: John Wiley.

Lipnack, J., & Stamps, J. (2000). *Virtual teams: People working across boundaries with technology* (2nd ed.). New York: John Wiley.

Lurey, J. M., & Raisinghani, M. S. (2001). An empirical study of best practices in virtual teams. *Information & Management, 38*(8), 523-544.

Majchrzak, A., Malhotra, A., Stamps, J., & Lipnack, J. (2004). Can absence make a team grow stronger? *Harvard Business Review, 82*(5), 131-137.

Majchrzak, A., Rice, R. E., King, N., Malhotra, A., & Ba, S. (1999). *Development and adaptation of inter-organizational virtual team norms using collaborative technology.* Retrieved March, 10, 2003, from http://www.cogtech.org/CT99/Rice1.htm

Majchrzak, A., Rice, R. E., King, N., Malhotra, A., & Ba, S. (2000a). Computer-mediated inter-organizational knowledge-sharing: Insights from a virtual team innovating using a collaborative tool. *Information Resources Management Journal, 13*(1), 44-53.

Majchrzak, A., Rice, R. E., Malhotra, A., King, N., & Ba, S. (2000b). Technology adaptation: the case of a computer-supported inter-organizational virtual team. *MIS Quarterly, 24*(4), 569-600.

Malhotra, A., Majchrzak, A., Carman, R., & Lott, V. (2001). Radical innovation without collocation: A case study at Boeing-Rocketdyne. *MIS Quarterly, 25*(2), 229-249.

Martins, L. L., Gilson, L. L., & Maynard, M. T. (2004). Virtual teams: What do we know and where do we go from here? *Journal of Management, 30*(6), 805-835.

Massey, A. P., Hung, C. Y., Montoya-Weiss, M., & Ramesh, V. (2001, September 30-October 3). When culture and style aren't about clothes: Perceptions of task-technology "fit" in GVTs. *Proceedings of GROUP '01*, Boudler, CO (pp. 207-213).

May, A., Carter, C., & Joyner, S. (2000). Virtual teams working in the European automotive industry: User requirements and a case study approach. *Human Factors and Ergonomics in manufacturing, 10*(3), 273-289.

May, A., & Carter, C. (2001). A case study of virtual team working in the European automotive industry. *International Journal of Industrial Ergonomics, 27*(3), 171-186.

Maznevski, M. L., & Chudoba, K. M. (2000). Bridging space over time: Global virtual team dynamics and effectiveness. *Organization Science, 11*(5), 473-492.

McDonough, E. F., Kahn, K. B., & Barczak, G. (2001). An investigation of the use of global, virtual, and collocated new product development teams. *Journal of Product Innovation Management, 18*(2), 110-120.

Montoya-Weiss, M. M., Massey, A. P., & Song, M. (2001). Getting it together: temporal coordination and conflict management in global virtual teams. *Academy of Management Journal, 44*(6), 1251-1262.

Morris, S. A., Marshall, T. E., & Rainer, R. K. (2002). Impact of user satisfaction and trust on virtual team members. *Information Resources Management Journal, 15*(2), 22-30.

Ngwenyama, O. K., & Lyytinen, K. (1997). Groupware environments as action constitutive resources: A social action framework for analyzing groupware technologies. *Computer Supported Cooperative Work: The Journal of Collaborative Computing, 6*(1), 71-93.

Oakley, J. G. (1998). Leadership processes in virtual teams and organizations. *The Journal of Leadership Studies, 5*(3), 3-17.

O'Hara-Devereux, M., & Johansen, R. (1994). *Global work—Bridging distance, culture and time*. San Francisco: Jossey-Bass.

Orlikowski, W. J. (1992). The duality of technology: Rethinking the concept of technology in organizations. *Organization Science, 3*(3), 398-427.

Pauleen, D. J. (2003). Lessons learned crossing boundaries in an ICT-supported distributed team. *Journal of Global Information Management, 11*(4), 1-19.

Pauleen, D. F., & Yoong, P. (2001). Relationship building and the use of ICT in boundary-crossing virtual teams: A facilitator's perspective. *Journal of Information Technology, 16*(4), 205-220.

Pawar, K. S., & Sharifi, S. (1997) Physical or virtual team collocation: Does it matter? *International Journal of Production Economics, 52*(3), 283-290.

Pearce, J. A. I., & Ravlin, E. C. (1987). The design and activation of self regulating work groups. *Human Relations, 40*(11), 751-760.

Piccoli, G., & Ives, B. (2003). Trust and the unintended effects of behavior control in virtual teams. *MIS Quarterly, 27*(3), 365-395.

Powell, A. L. (2000). *Antecedence and outcomes of team commitment in a global, virtual environment*. Unpublished doctoral dissertation, Indiana University, Bloomington.

Qureshi, S. (1998). Supporting a network way of working in an electronic social space. *Group Decision and Negotiation, 7*(5), 399-416.

Qureshi, S., & Vogel, D. (2001). Adaptiveness in virtual teams: Organisational challenges and research directions. *Group Decision and Negotiation, 10*(1), 27-46.

Robey, D., Khoo, H., & Powers, C. (2000). Situated learning in cross-functional virtual teams. *IEEE Transactions on Professional Communications, 43*, 51-66 and *Technical Communication, 47*(1), 51-66. (Joint Special Issue).

Schein, E. H. (1992). *Organizational culture and leadership* (2nd ed.) San Francisco: Jossey-Bass.

Shachaf, P., & Hara, N. (2002). Ecological approach to virtual team effectiveness. *Proceedings of Americas Conference on Information Systems 8* (pp. 1814-1819).

Shea, G. P., & Guzzo R. A. (1987). Groups as human resources. *Research in Personnel and Human Resources Management, 5,* 323-356.

Sole, D. L., & Edmondson, A. C. (2001, June). Situated knowledge and learning in dispersed teams. *Proceedings of 4th International Conference on Organizational Learning and Knowledge Management*, London, Canada, (HBS #01-068).

Sundstrom, E., DeMuese, K. P., & Futrell D. (1990). Work teams: Applications and effectiveness. *The American Psychologist, 45*(2), 120-133.

Suchan, J., & Hayzak, G. (2001). The Communication Characteristics of Virtual Teams: A Case Study. *IEEE Transactions on Professional Communication, 44*(3), 174-186.

Switzer, J. S. (2000). *Virtual teams: Profiles of successful leaders*. Unpublished doctoral dissertation, Pepperdine University, California.

Vickery, C. M., Clark, T. D., & Carlson, J. R. (1999). Virtual positions: An examination of structure and performance in ad hoc workgroups. *Information Systems Journal, 9*(4), 291-312.

Vygotsky, L. S. (1978). *Mind in society*. Cambridge, MA: Harvard University.

Wallace, R. M. (2003). Online learning in higher education: A review of research on interactions among teachers and students. *Education, Communication, & Information, 3*(2), 241-280.

Walsham, G. (2002). Cross-cultural software production and use: A structurational analysis. *MIS Quarterly, 26*(4), 359-380.

Warkentin, M. E., & Beranek, P. M. (1999). Training to improve virtual team communication. *Information Systems Journal, 9*(4), 271-289.

Wicker, A.W. (1979). *An introduction to ecological psychology*. Belmont, CA: Wadsworth.

Wenger, E. (1998). *Communities of practice: Learning, meaning, and identity*. Cambridge, UK: Cambridge University.

Wenger, E., McDermott, R., & Snyder, W. M. (2002). *Cultivating communities of practice*. Boston: Harvard Business School.

Wong, S., & Burton, R. M. (2000). Virtual teams: What are their characteristics, and impact on team performance? *Computational & Mathematical Organization Theory, 6*, 339-360.

Watson-Manheim, M. B., Crowston, K., & Chudoba, K. M. (2002, January). A new perspective on "virtual": Analyzing discontinuities in the work environment. *Proceedings of HICSS-2002*, Kona, Hawaii.

Weiss, J., Nolan, J., & Trifonas, P. (Eds.) (in press). *International Handbook of Virtual Learning Environments*. Kluwer Academic.

Section II

Strategies for Effective Teaching and Learning in Virtual Teams

Chapter V

Learning in a Geographically Dispersed Context:

Building a Community of Learning in Dispersed Space

Rashmi H. Assudani*
Xavier University, USA

Abstract

The use of the Internet to deliver management education has increased dramatically over the last decade. Academic institutions and business organizations are harnessing technological advances to enable Web-based learning for individuals who are geographically dispersed across different physical locations. One source of learning for such individuals is their interaction with their dispersed peers. However, it is challenging for dispersed individuals to interact with each other and to learn from each other because of a lack of common context among them. This chapter aims to explore the conditions that are conducive to ferment learning in a dispersed setting. The findings demonstrate that dispersed learning is a socio-technical process. The chapter concludes with implications for Web-enabled institutions to develop competencies to build a community of learning in dispersed space.

Introduction

In the field of management education, the use of the Internet to deliver management education has increased dramatically over the last decade (Alavi & Leidner, 2001). Technological tools such as shared knowledge repositories and chat rooms create an opportunity for fostering collaboration and are employed to help build knowledge infrastructure among geographically dispersed[1] individuals. Although such tools enable the access to the knowledge of dispersed[2] individuals, it remains a challenge to appropriate this knowledge for generating new learning through electronic forms of communication. In the context of delivering education through the Web, this raises concerns for the dispersed individuals to learn from each other.

Research in the area of Web-enabled education is limited and has so far looked at the technological and pedagogical characteristics that influence Web-based learning (Arbaugh & Durray, 2001; Leidner & Jarvenpaa, 1993; 1995). This research has contributed much to our understanding and has yielded very interesting insights in advancing the theoretical base and in offering practical implications for Web-enabled learning. However, the academic literature provides little understanding of how dispersed individuals effectively collaborate and learn from *each other* virtually[3]. The research on dispersed collaboration and knowledge management is young and the domain is still being mapped out (Susman & Majzrchak, 2003).

This ethnographic research aims to examine how dispersed individuals learn from each other in a Web-enabled setting. The first section of the chapter reviews the knowledge-based view of the firm and dispersed collaboration literatures to guide this work. The perspectives from these literatures suggest why learning in a dispersed setting may be problematic. This section builds the context for my research question, which I examine with an in-depth ethnographic study. The findings suggest that certain conditions are conducive to fostering Web-enabled learning. I then discuss the implications of these findings on the Web-enabled educational institutions: such institutions need competencies to build a community of learning among dispersed learners.

Literature Review

Questions related to the essence of knowledge have intrigued and preoccupied many of the world's greatest thinkers, from Plato to Popper. A review of the *knowledge-based view of the firm* literature permits one to discern that exchange of knowledge among individuals is integral to create new knowledge which may appear in the form of new learning, new processes or new products (Grant, 1996; Kogut & Zander, 1992; Nahapiet & Ghoshal, 1998; Nonaka, 1994). In this respect, the process of knowledge exchange is a necessary precursor to generate learning for the individuals. Knowledge exchange is defined as the (perceived) contribution of one's knowledge to others and the (perceived) acquisition of others' knowledge by the individual(s) that produces new actionable insights for the individual(s) (Faraj & Wasko, 2001). Research has demonstrated that this process is influenced by the social (Szulanski, 1996), cognitive (Cohen & Levinthal, 1990; Weick & Roberts, 1993), and organizational (Kim & Mauborgne, 1998) factors.

In addition to these factors, another stream of literature that has offered thought-provoking insights suggests that the process of knowledge exchange is also influenced by the physical factors within which the individuals are situated. This perspective (Brown & Duguid, 1991; Lave & Wenger, 1990) emphasizes that the collective and situated nature of knowledge contributes to the learning process in several ways. For example, Lave and Wenger (1990) point out that people will approach a problem differently when they act in different settings because each setting tends to evoke certain kinds of appropriate modes of thought and action. Tyre and von Hippel (1997) demonstrate that the physical settings and the artifacts influence the efficacy of new learning by shaping the cognition of individuals in that particular context (Madhavan & Grover, 1998). In other words, an important component of what individuals know is determined by the physical locations they are situated in. Thus, individuals who are situated in different physical locations are likely to be working with different contextual[4] knowledge (Gluesing et al., 2003) and this impedes the ease of exchanging knowledge among them. In essence, this stream of research has offered evidence that the incommensurability of the physical location may hinder the generation of new learning across (departmental, firm, geographic, cultural) boundaries. This perspective therefore questions the currently popular assumptions about conducting knowledge work through dispersed arrangements. For example, the results from Tyre and von Hippel's study (1997) force them "to question some currently popular assumptions about the power of electronic media to link 'knowledge workers' within or across organizations. Existing electronic media are limited because they are decontextualized" (p. 81). Further, Madhavan, and Grover (1998) also demonstrate that "such virtual teams may not be the best vehicles for new product development" (p. 10). Their model suggests that being in the same information rich location enables knowledge creation.

In addition to the knowledge-based view of the firm that calls into question certain aspects of the received management wisdom about conducting knowledge work through dispersed arrangements, the review of the literature on *dispersed collaboration* has also started to provide evidence for reasons that have the potential to impede dispersed collaboration. The review cites at least three reasons why dispersed individuals may not have a common context, thus making collaboration problematic.

One such reason is the *incommensurable categorization schemes* (Duimering & Wensley, 2001) among them. The logic here is that the objective environment (physical space), within which an individual is situated, shapes the subjective environment (cognition) of that individual. The objective environment shapes the way an individual categorizes and therefore individuals dispersed across different physical locations are likely to be working with different categorization schemes. In other words, dispersed individuals are situated in different objective and subjective contexts, and the process of learning among them requires an exchange of knowledge across multiple contexts and this is difficult to accomplish through electronic forms of communication.

Geographic distances have the potential to impede *mutual knowledge* generation among dispersed individuals (Cramton, 2001). Mutual knowledge is referred to more broadly as "common knowledge" and the usage of "common ground" suggests how deeply engrained physical co-presence and shared physical setting may be to establishing shared understanding and affiliation. Such knowledge is generated by firsthand experience with individuals, through interaction, and on the basis of social categorizations that are applied to people. Also, such knowledge is critical in facilitating cohesion and collaboration. Dispersed individuals may not have a common context for working together since the opportunities to develop such knowledge are limited, implying that cohesion and collaboration among them may be difficult.

Another reason why dispersed individuals may not have a common context for working together is a gap in knowing the expertise of their dispersed peers. *Transactive memory system* (TMS) is the meta-knowledge of who knows what in the team (Wegner et al., 1991). For dispersed individuals, it is difficult to develop TMS about their peers (Yoo & Kanawattachai, 2001) since there is less opportunity for them to participate in common training experiences (Griffith & Neale, 2001). Also, no physical markers that may identify their diversity of perspectives and expertise are visible.

Taken together, the perspectives from both knowledge-based view of the firm and dispersed collaboration literature suggest that a lack of a common context is likely to exist among dispersed individuals. Since a common context is conducive to successfully exchanging knowledge (Kostova, 1999; Lam, 1997), a lack of such a context limits this possibility and therefore limits the possibility of learning among them. Despite these warnings, we continue to witness a steep increase in dispersed knowledge work (Cohen & Mankin, 1999; Rae, 1998). For example, academic evidence points to a rapid increase in the use of dispersed teams for conducting tasks such as new product development (McDonough et al., 2001). Evidence from the popular press also suggests that Web-casts are gaining momentum (*USA Today*, September 2002) and distance learning's popularity is taking a big jump (CNN, July 2003).

Since research in this area is in its nascent stages, further research is needed to examine these complexities. Conducting a field study in a real-life context would reveal insights into how dispersed individuals learn from each other. This study thus seeks to address the basic, but important, research question, "How do dispersed individuals learn from each other?" In doing so, the research question seeks to identify the conditions that foster learning in a Web-enabled setting.

Method

I undertook two exploratory case studies to address the research question posed above. The study design was open-ended to allow unforeseen themes to emerge. Case study methodology (Yin, 1984) was well suited to my goal of conducting research in an area where relatively little empirical data exists. I conducted ethnographic field studies on two teams of dispersed learners[5] to examine how these learners learned from each other through Web-enabled mechanisms.

Site

The site for these case studies was an educational institution based in eastern Canada that offers distance education for MBA and the eMBA (executive MBA) programs. The institution does not offer any traditional classroom-based classes to supplement the distance education classes. The learners, therefore, go through these programs from their own geographic locations. The institution provides the voice-over IP (VoIP) technology that enables the dispersed learners to communicate with each other. This technology has voice and text messaging capability. The institution also provides a messaging board where learners can generate threaded discussions. Other than this, learners have the freedom to make their own arrangements to use other types of technology such as MSN messaging, Webex, telephones, e-mails, and face-to-face (FTF) meetings.

Teams

The context of the study was a course in a Web-enabled eMBA program in which two teams of dispersed learners were enrolled. Most members of these teams had prior experience of working together with each other in the same team. Only one member on each team was new. The first team, called Team A, had six members who were dispersed (2-3-1) as follows: two in Ottawa, Ontario (Canada), three in Montreal, Quebec (Canada) and one in Dallas, Texas (USA). The Canadian team members had a prior history of working together on multiple occasions over the past two years of the program. Also, the Canadian team members were about two hours away from each other (this is the time that it takes to traverse the distance between Ottawa and Montreal by road). Paula, the team member from USA, was a new addition to this team. The second team, called Team B, had four members who were dispersed (2-1-1) as follows: two in Toronto, Ontario (Canada), one in Ottawa, Ontario (Canada), and one in Fredericton, New Brunswick (Canada). Three of these four team members had had a working relationship over the past two years and Erin (who was based in Toronto) was a new addition to the team.

Task

This was a capstone strategy course for the eMBA learners and was the last course for the eMBA learners before they graduated. For this course, learners were putting into practice what they had learned over the last two years of their eMBA program. This course was atypical since lectures by the instructor were not required. The instructor's role was to facilitate the teams, if required. Other than this, the instructor's role was to grade the usefulness of the project findings for the firm that the team was analyzing. This course, however, required interactions among the learners.

The team task was to conduct a field project to build a turnaround strategy for the firm for which it was responsible. This was a new task for each team. The teams approached the firms in a consulting role. Such a task is less predictable, requires creativity, demands interdependencies among team members and uncertainty of the task is high because of a variety of information that may be required to conduct this task. Team members need reciprocal workflow arrangements to collaborate with each other, and the task thus could be defined as a non routine task (Daft & Macintosh, 1981; Perrow, 1967). The duration for the project work for both teams was 10 weeks. The project findings were graded by the instructor and by the CEO of the client firm.

A Pittsburgh-based firm (USA), TAG, for which the team was conducting the consulting assignment, was engaged in the electrical contracting business. TAG has traditionally been growing by offering franchises in North America. However, the franchising was reaching its saturation point. TAG wished to find various options to continue the corporate growth at TAG once the franchise markets in North America became saturated. The task for Team A team was to find and evaluate these various options and to present the best option to the management at TAG. The team used electronic forms of communication (VoIP, Webex, e-mails, MSN messaging and threaded discussions) to "meet" each other. Over the course of the project, some learners also met FTF. The first FTF meeting happened in Montreal with four of the six team members. The other FTF meeting happened in Ottawa with three of the six learners who met with a representative from TAG. The third team meeting happened in Ottawa with four of the six learners meeting in person while the other two learners communicated with the team over the phone. Besides this, collocated team members (two in Ottawa and three in Montreal) often had FTF meetings with each other. Paula was the only learner who could not attend any of the FTF team meetings.

A Toronto-based firm (Canada), SANG, for which Team B was conducting the consulting assignment, was a product-based company that delivered technology-based equipment. SANG had recently moved from being a private to a public company. Before going public in 2002, they had a slow growth. However, despite the slow growth, the company was profitable. Since going public, there had been an increase in costs and SANG was also suffering from declining sales. The major objectives for SANG were thus to increase sales and raise additional equity capital/sell more shares. The task for the SANG team was to decipher different strategies for SANG to become profitable. The team used teleconferences (Webex), e-mails, and MSN messaging as the modes for communicating to "meet" each other. Learners barely exercised dyadic conversations and all conversations were made transparent by circulating agenda of the meetings prior to the team meetings and by circulating minutes of the meetings after the team meetings. Three of the four learners visited SANG in Toronto just at the beginning of the project. Buddy (from Fredericton) attended this meeting remotely through a teleconference. Other than this, neither the team nor the collocated learners met each other FTF.

Design

I obtained the informed consent of the learners before I started to collect data. I relied upon multiple methods of data collection, which included: (a) participant observation during team meetings, (b) team documents (presentations, reports, etc.) sent through e-mails or posted on threaded discussions, and (c) semi-structured interviews that were conducted with each team member at the completion of the project (each team member therefore served as a respondent). This triangulation of various data collection techniques provided multiple perspectives on issues, and allowed for cross-checking of existing and emerging concepts (Eisenhardt, 1989).

Data Sources

Observation and participation. During these 10 weeks, I "observed" the meetings that the team conducted using multiple forms of electronic communication such as VoIP, Webex teleconferences and MSN messaging. The duration of these meetings lasted between 20 and 90 minutes. I had access to transcripts of all such meetings. I did not, however, have access to the FTF team interactions. Wherever possible, I was able to teleconference into these FTF meetings. After the meeting had transpired, I also made every effort to get the content of these meetings from the attendee(s).

Project documentation. I had access to the documentation that learners circulated either through the e-mails or posted on the threaded discussion. These shared electronic repositories provided an effective means for cross-checking informants' retrospective reports and observed behavior.

Interviews. At the end of the project work, I interviewed the learners individually. Interviews, which lasted between 45 and 60 minutes, were conducted before learners received their feedback from the instructor and the firm. Because there was no research base on which to formulate closed-ended items, I used open-ended interview questions (and observations). Such open-ended questions are useful in allowing unforeseen themes to emerge. The interviews focused on the details of the project, the history of the learner teams, use of technology, perceived knowledge that the individual learners contributed and acquired and the challenges that the team faced in accomplishing the task. I also asked probes that asked the learners to extend their analyses.

Measures

For measuring new knowledge generation in the form of learning, I looked for instances that conveyed the perceived acquisition or perceived contribution of knowledge among the learners in the team. I further looked for instances that conveyed the conditions that favored such a learning to take place.

Data Analysis

I made field notes[6] during the course of the case studies. I taped all the team meetings and the interviews and transcribed the data. I closely read these transcripts, the project documentation and the field notes. I content analyzed and coded the data using the guidelines suggested in Miles and Huberman (1994). I made every effort to analyze the data to "move from a shapeless data spaghetti towards some kind of theoretical understanding that does not betray the richness, dynamism and complexity of the data but that is potentially useful to others" (Langley, 1999, p. 694). I analyzed the data through an inductive process to identify the key elements integral to the process of dispersed learning. I thus relied on narratives to organize the events and used multiple sources of evidence such as the interview protocol and observations (Miles & Huberman, 1994). Using such an in-depth study that examined the interactions within these teams of dispersed learners permitted me to refine the understanding of the complexities of dispersed learning.

Results

A closer look at the findings from the field studies allows us to move from a discussion of how dispersed learners situate a knowledge Web[7] in a virtual space. Since knowledge is distributed across time and space, dispersed learning is a comprehensible activity so far as the "character of the dispersed team is appreciated as a discursive practice: a form of life, a community in which individuals come to share an unarticulated background of common understandings" (Tsoukas, 1996, p. 23). Interactions with the dispersed learners are instrumental in serving as "bricoleurs" – interactions pull an order and the "community of interaction" plays a critical role in situating a knowledge Web (Nonaka, 1994). The findings suggest that conditions such as the use of multiple technologies, familiarity among dispersed learners owing to their prior interaction, and conscious attempts by them to exhibit their virtual presence on the team help in bridging the geographic distance among them. These facilitated the acquisition and contribution of knowledge and were therefore conducive to build a virtual community of learners.

Use of Multiple Technologies

The findings demonstrate that dispersed learners used multiple technologies to stay connected and to bridge the geographic distance. Use of multiple technologies such as VoIP, Webex, MSN messaging, threaded discussions, and e-mails made sure that everyone was on the same page. Textual messages such as MSN messaging, threaded discussions, and e-mails were useful for documentation.

The context of the task determined the type of communication mode that they used. To build a shared interpretive context, learners relied on technology that allowed a high level of discursive interaction such as brainstorming and storytelling. For example, VoIP and teleconferences provided high levels of interactivity and *"if we wanted interaction or brainstorming, or if we wanted a discussion, then we would meet up on the voice-over IP."* I also found that for both teams face-to-face (FTF) communication was critical for deliberating on the differences and for developing shared systems of meaning among them. Learners "*used multiple technologies to stay connected... MSN chat, threaded discussions, vClass, etc. However, dispersed work requires that we meet at least once face-to-face. When you have people together, you can exchange ideas and you can move forward. It's easier to establish groundwork when you meet face-to-face.*" For example, geographically proximal learners from Team A met each other FTF, and the team (except for Paula) met each other once during the mid-point of the project. Such a meeting was the turning point in this team since "*there was too much conflict in the direction. Until the direction was set, people had to argue. It was a lot easier to get-together and finalize it. And it was important to meet face-to-face.*" Unlike the dispersed teams in the real-life business world, the learner teams lacked resources such as financial support for conducting the FTF meetings. However, the Canadian learners who were at accessible distances used their personal resources to organize such meetings. Paula was the most physically distant from the rest and the learners felt that "*the drawback for her was that everyone was in Canada.*" She could not physically attend these meetings and *"these were some of the things that hurt."* This affected the contribution she could make to the team and she said that, *"I could have contributed more if I had been able to just get into the room one time."* For Team B, learners met FTF once at the initiation of the project. Other than this, learners did not feel the need to co-locate. The initial meeting put everyone on the same page "*and put us all on the same wavelength. In the 2 and a ½ hours that we were there, everybody heard the same information.*"

Familiarity

Another possible mechanism that may compensate for distance and enable dispersed learners to learn from each other is some level of familiarity. The findings from these field studies demonstrate that a history of interactions helped in generating familiarity and in fostering durable networks among them.

Learners were familiar with each other *"just by working together a lot and the team's past helped in understanding what people are good at and what we expected from each other. And this is what didn't help Paula."* In the dispersed team of familiars, such a history of shared interactions was important to the development of transactive memory system. Over time, team members had built an understanding of their partners' domains of expertise and *"they all knew who had strengths in certain areas ... if you keep the same team from the beginning to the end of the program, you all know what each other's strengths are, you know who is going to do what, who can ride, and who can't, etc."*

The findings also show that familiarity with each other had the potential to create mutual knowledge among dispersed learners. A history of prior interactions had built an understanding *"about how each of us worked, about who is more structured, about each other's technological constraints, and also about each other's quirks. It's funny because after a while you recognize voices, and you know who is more verbose and who is more quiet."* For example, learners in Team B who had worked together in the past (Dig, Crane, & Buddy) knew that each one used a high-speed Internet connection. They knew that Dig checked his e-mails once in the morning and once in the evening, and was logged on MSN messenger every evening. They were aware that Crane's responsibilities at the office demanded a lot of out-station travel. Buddy had family commitments and Dig and Crane knew that Buddy preferred to have team meetings much later in the evening. Familiar learners also had information such as alternate e-mail addresses and alternate communication channels to reach their distant partners. This facilitated the communication and knowledge exchange was therefore eased among such learners.

However, shared "history" of interactions, as it implies, is a time-bound process. Learners who were new to the team *"didn't have a lot of time to build relationships with the rest of the team"* and this affected their involvement in the team. In other words, their contribution of knowledge and their motivation to participate in team meetings was influenced by their perception of their integration (or not) in the team.

Conscious Attempts to Exhibit the Virtual Presence

Other than familiarity, exhibiting "virtual" presence by communicating their contextual conditions to the other team members and simply by reaching out to each other also facilitated in bridging the geographic distance. Such actions influenced the perceived integration (or not) of learners in the dispersed team and therefore facilitdate acquisition and contribution of knowledge among them: *"In a virtual team it's even more important to be present as much as possible when the team meets because you don't have that contact outside those meeting spaces. You might be meeting your team once a week and if you are not visually present at that point, it is more noted than if you are in an office environment where your presence is always there regardless of whether you are going into a meeting or not."*

Dispersed learners who proactively reached out to each other by facilitating conversations were able to integrate with each other, particularly with new learners. For example, learners in Team B were prompt in reaching out to each other—during an early exchange of information, they discussed their respective expertise and schedules for the next 10 weeks. They *"identified upfront and very quickly what people's schedules were and identified days and times that made sense to get together."* These conscious attempts were useful to generate mutual knowledge particularly with Erin (who was a new addition to the team). Early on, they learnt that he used dial-up for an internet connection instead of a high-speed Internet connection. They also learnt that in addition to this course, Erin was also enrolled in another course in the same semester and therefore knew the time pressures Erin would be facing in this semester. Familiarity with each other's context reduces conflict and frustration in a dispersed team and promotes integration in dispersed team (Cramton, 2001). This learner team was therefore well-integrated, generating an active participation from all in the team.

Team A took no such proactive measures, particularly with the new learner (Paula). While the learners knew the expertise and context of other familiar learners, they remained unaware about Paula's expertise and her context. *"Clearly they had worked together before and they all knew each other's strengths. I (Paula) felt the team knew each other well and so they were off and running. I really didn't get a chance to understand each team member's backgrounds. The team assigned me operations which I totally, not knowing the industry at all, was very uncomfortable with. I asked to change it to IT, for which I have 28 years of experience."* Team members remained unaware about Paula's office schedules and her technological constraints. Her job sometimes demanded extra hours at the last-minute. She was unable to log into the VoIP sessions due to firewall issues at her office. However, while she was logged on to the computer at her office, her MSN buddy would pop up on her team members' computer screens. *"I (Paula) was online at home, but I wasn't. I was online at my office. My computer (at the office) is not always set up to get into the VoIP. But you could see me on the MSN always."* Since Paula did not communicate this context, this unrecognized context left the team members wondering why Paula could not attend the pre-scheduled VoIP meetings while they could see that she was logged onto the computer. Team members attributed this absence to her "irresponsive behavior" and this developed deep "fault lines" (Lau & Murninghan, 1998) in the team. Such resentment escalated to a point that they eventually worked as if Paula never existed. While they recognized that "*her work would have added a lot of value and the team members would have learnt a lot,*" they did not pull in her contributions *"because of the tardiness of her delivery, because of her (unaccounted for) absence and because the team didn't know what to expect of her.*" They felt that if Paula was more involved in the team and if she had showed up and discussed with them her reasons why she couldn't make it to the meetings — perhaps a simple e-mail — then they would've been more tolerant of her absence and would have pulled in her contributions.

Discussion

Implications of the Study

The findings from this qualitative ethnographic study resonate the previous findings in the literature: learning ferments and finds effervescence in a "social community" (Kogut & Zander, 1992). Harnessing learning-in-working requires conceiving the dispersed team as a community (Brown & Duguid, 1991). It is through the dynamic interactions in such a community that new configurations of the knowledge net emerge by creating new meanings. The challenge for a team of dispersed learners lies in generating such a community in a virtual space. For learners to be satisfied with the Web-enabled type of education medium, it is important that they "feel" a sense of communion as in a traditional class. Thus, institutions that provide Web-enabled education require competencies and strategies for yielding a virtual community of learning for them.

One way of doing this is to provide dispersed learners with multiple technologies such as VoIP, Webex, MSN messaging, e-mails, and threaded discussions to stay connected with each other. The findings from this study reaffirm the ubiquitous recommendation in the literature that dispersed teams need to, at least occasionally, meet face-to-face (Maznevski & Chudoba, 2000). While this offers practical and managerial implications for business organization, it poses a constraint for Web-enabled institutions that span geographical, cultural, and temporal boundaries. Arranging face-to-face meetings among learners dispersed across these various boundaries requires a lot of resources, and this may not actually be a feasible option for Web-enabled institutions. In such institutions it may be useful to build teams with (at least some) geographically proximal learners. Such an arrangement may facilitate in conducting face-to-face meetings and in ensuring integration among them. This has implications on the enrollment patterns in a Web-enabled institution — such institutions could strive to strategically enroll at least a few learners from geographically proximal locations.

Web-enabled institutions also require technological and social competencies to generate familiarity among the dispersed learners. Familiarity emerged as a factor that mitigated the psychological feeling of geographic distance. The links between individuals in a dispersed unit may be less tangible and more social and psychological in nature (Wiesenfeld et al., 1999). This implies that it is not only important to recognize the geographic distance between individuals, but also how these individuals "feel" the distance between themselves by virtue of their familiarity with each other. Web-enabled institutions could develop social and technological competencies to allow personal rapport building among all learners in the dispersed class. It is crucial for the dispersed learners to stay connected to their fellow students so they could have access to a wider knowledge base and enhanced learning.

Finally, consistent communication to exhibit virtual presence is critical to establish and to maintain a communion among dispersed learners. "Silence is not golden," and conscious attempts to make your own context transparent to the rest of the dispersed team is necessary for integrating with the team. The process of learning is eased when learners have close social interaction ties. An obvious implication is that it is important to train learners with competencies, such as self-efficacy, to stay connected. Staples et al. (1999) used the self-efficacy theory to explain the functioning of virtual workers. They empirically demonstrated that the judgments of the virtual workers in their own self — also called the self-efficacy judgments — have considerable impact on their performance. These judgments depend upon the experience and training of these individuals in conducting remote work, information technology capabilities that these individuals rely upon and the absence of computer anxiety of these individuals. Thus, the greater the self-efficacy of a virtual worker, the greater is his or her propensity to share and exchange knowledge virtually. In order to ensure sustained learning among dispersed learners, Web-enabled institutions need to train and equip them with competencies to conduct dispersed work.

Future Trends

Does geographic distance matter for Web-enabled learning? This study suggests that social and technological competencies build a virtual community among dispersed learners and such a communion has the potential to diminish the influence of geographic distance. Future research should continue to determine other factors that have the potential to moderate the effects of geographic distance. For example, research may be conducted to examine what kinds of socialization mechanisms may be employed to minimize the influence of geographic distance. The findings from such research have the potential to suggest that how the dispersed individuals "feel" the distance between themselves may be as important as the geographic distance between them. This study had teams with learners dispersed across North America. Future research may be conducted with teams which have learners dispersed across different parts of the globe. Such research has the potential to suggest whether other factors, such as cultural and temporal, have the potential to exacerbate or diminish the influence of geographic distance.

The teams in this study were self-managing and did not have a designated leader. The instructor for the course was not an active participant or an active facilitator for the dispersed teams. The role of the instructor was largely to watch from the periphery how learners worked together and to judge them on the final product. The findings from this study may in fact differ if such dispersed teams have a designated leader who acts like a moderator or a facilitator. Future research could be designed to examine whether designating a leader has the potential to exacerbate or diminish the influence of geographic distance.

Limitations of the Study

This was an exploratory study and suffers from the limitation of the sampling frame. The generalizability of the findings may thus be limited. Further research is needed to examine the results of this study. More ethnographic studies with teams of dispersed learners in different types of institutions and conducting different types of tasks will be useful.

Conclusion

Learning emanates from multiple sources, one of which is learning from each other. The challenge to learn from each other in a Web-enabled institution arises especially because dispersed learners do not share contextual knowledge with each other by virtue of the geographic distance among them. Web-enabled learning is a socio-technical process — while the technological infrastructure provides the dispersed learners with tools to access knowledge dispersed across multiple physical locations, the social process of generating familiarity and of exhibiting your virtual presence is integral to the appropriation of dispersed knowledge for generating new learning. Such a process is vital to build a community of learning in the dispersed space. Building the socio-technical competencies for enabling such a virtual community will be critical to the success of Web-enabled educational institutions as also to the learning for the learners enrolled in such institutions.

References

Alavi, M., & Leidner, D. E. (2001). Research commentary: Technology-mediated learning — A call for greater depth and breadth of research. *Information Systems Research, 12*(1), 1-10.

Arbaugh, J. B., & Durray, R. (2001). Class section size, perceived classroom characteristics, instructor experience, and student learning and satisfaction with web-based courses: A study and comparison of two on-line MBA programs. In D. Nagao (Ed.), *Academy of Management Best Paper Proceedings*. MED A1-A6.

Brown, J. S., & Duguid, P. (1991). Organizational learning and communities of practice: Towards a unified view of working, learning and innovation. *Organization Science, 2,* 40-57.

Cohen, W., & Levinthal, D. (1990). Absorptive Capacity: A new perspective on learning and innovation. *Administrative Science Quarterly, 35,* 128-152.

Cohen, S. G., & Mankin, D. (1999). Collaboration in the virtual organization. *Journal of Organizational Behavior, 6,* 105-120.

Cramton, C. D. (2001). The mutual knowledge problem and its consequences for dispersed collaboration. *Organization Science, 12*(3), 346-371.

Duimering, P.R., & Wensley, A. K. P. (2001). *Knowledge transfer between organizational contexts.* Paper presented at 2001 Academy of Management Meeting, Organizational Communication and Information Systems Division, Washington, DC

Faraj, S., & Wasko, M. M. (2001). *The web of knowledge: An investigation of knowledge exchange in networks of practice.* Paper presented at the annual meeting of the Academy of Management, Washington, DC.

Gluesing, et al. (2003). The development of global virtual teams. In S. Cohen & C. Gibson (Eds.), *Virtual teams that work: Creating conditions for virtual team effectiveness.* San Francisco: Jossey-Bass.

Grant, R. M. (1996). Prospering in dynamically competitive environments: Organizational capability as knowledge integration. *Organization Science, 7*(4), 375-387.

Griffith, T. L., & Neale, M. A. (2001). Information processing in traditional, hybrid and virtual teams: From nascent knowledge to transactive memory. *Research in Organizational Behavior, 23,* 379-421.

Kim C. W., & Mauborgne, R. (1998). Procedural justice, strategic decision making and the knowledge economy. *Strategic Management Journal, 19,* 323-338.

Kogut, B., & Zander, U. (1992). Knowledge of the firm, combinative capabilities, and the replication of technology. *Organization Science, 3*(3), 383-397.

Kostova, T. (1999). Transnational transfer of strategic organizational practices: A contextual perspective. *Academy of Management Review, 24*(2), 308-324.

Lam, A. (1997). Embedded firms, embedded knowledge: Problems of collaboration and knowledge transfer in global co-operative ventures. *Organization Studies, 18*(6), 973-96.

Langley, A. (1999). Strategies for theorizing from process data. *Academy of Management Review, 24*(4), 691-710.

Lau, D.C., & Murninghan, K. (1998). Demographic diversity and faultlines: The compositional dynamics of organizational groups. *Academy of Management Review, 23*(2), 325-340.

Lave, J., & Wenger, E. (1990). *Situated Learning: Legitimate Peripheral Participation.* Cambridge: Cambridge University.

Leidner, D. E., & Jarvenpaa, S. L. (1993). The information age confronts education: Case studies on electronic classrooms. *Information Systems Research, 4,* 24-54.

Leidner, D. E., & Jarvenpaa, S. L. (1995). The use of information technology to enhance management school education: A theoretical view. *MIS Quarterly, 19,* 265-291.

Madhavan, R., & Grover, R. (1998). From embedded knowledge to embodied knowledge: New product development as knowledge management. *Journal of Marketing, 62,* 1-12.

Maznevski, M. L., & Chudoba, K. M. (2000). Bridging space over time: Global virtual team dynamics and effectiveness. *Organization Science, 11*(5), 473-492.

McDonough, E. F. Kahn, K. B., & Barczak, G. (2001). An investigation of the use of global, virtual and co-located new product development teams. *Journal of Product Innovation Management, 18,* 110-120.

Miles, M. B., & Huberman, A. M. (1994). *An expanded source-book of qualitative data analysis* (2nd edition). Sage

Nahapiet, J., & Ghoshal, S. (1998). Social Capital, Intellectual Capital and the Organizational Advantage. *Academy of Management Review, 23*(2), 242-266.

Nonaka, I. (1994). A dynamic theory of knowledge creation. *Organization Science, 5*(1), 14-37.

Rae, L. (1998). Knowledge sharing and the virtual organization: Meeting 21st century challenges. *Thunderbird International Review, 40*(5), 525-540.

Staples, D. S., Hulland, J. S., & Higgins, C. A. (1999). A Self-Efficacy Theory Explanation for the Management of Remote Workers in Virtual Organizations. *Organization Science, 10*(6), 758-776.

Susman, G. I., & Majchzrak, A. (2003). Research issues in knowledge management and virtual collaboration in new product development: An introductory essay. *Journal of Engineering and Technology Management, 20,* 1-5.

Szulanski, G. (1996, Winter). Exploring internal stickiness: Impediments to the transfer of best practice within the firm. *Strategic Management Journal,* 17, 27-43.

Tsoukas, H. (1996). The firm as a distributed knowledge system: A constructionist approach. *Strategic Management Journal, 17,* 11-25.

Tyre, M. J., & von Hippel, E. (1997). The situated nature of learning in organizations. *Organization Science, 8,* 71-83.

Wasko, M. M., & Faraj, S. (1999). *Webs of knowledge: An examination of knowledge types and knowledge flows in an electronic community of practice.* Paper presented at the Academy of Management Meeting, Chicago.

Wegner, D. M., Erber, E., & Raymond, P. (1991). Transactive memory in close relationship. *Journal of Personality and social psychology, 61,* 923-929.

Weick, K., & Roberts, K. (1993). Collective mind in organizations: Heedful inter-relating on flight decks. *Administrative Science Quarterly, 38*(3), 357-381.

Wiesenfeld, B., Raghuram, S., & Garud, R. (1999). Communication patterns as determinants of organizational identification in a virtual organization. *Organization Science, 10*(6), 777-790.

Yin, R. K. (1984). *Case study research: Design and methods (applied social research methods series, Vol. 5).* Beverly Hills, CA: Sage.

Yoo, Y., & Kanawattanachai, P. (2001). Developments of transactive memory systems and collective mind in virtual teams. *The International Journal of Organizational Analysis, 9*(2), 187-208.

Endnotes

* I would like to acknowledge the support of my dissertation supervisor, Professor Jan Jorgensen, McGill University. I would also like to thank

Prof. David Large, University of Ottawa, for helping organize the site for data collection. This research was conducted during my doctoral dissertation at the Faculty of Management, McGill University. An earlier version of this paper was presented at the Academy of Management Meeting, 2003 in Seattle, Washington in the Management, Education & Development (MED) division. Correspondence concerning this article should be addressed to Dr. Rashmi H. Assudani (assudanir@xavier.edu) at Williams College of Business, Department of Management & Entrepreneurship, Xavier University, Cincinnati, OH, 45207.

1 Geographically dispersed teams are groups of people with a common purpose who carry out interdependent tasks across locations and time, using technology to communicate much more than they use face-to-face meetings (adapted from Lipnack & Stamps, 1997; Maznevski & Chudoba, 2000).

2 The term "dispersed" implies geographically dispersed.

3 Virtual team is a group of people who interact through interdependent tasks guided by common purpose and who work across space, time and organizational boundaries with links strengthened by webs of communication technologies (Lipnack & Stamps, 1997). Comparing this definition with that of dispersed teams, I treat the terms "virtual" and "dispersed" as synonymous.

4 Context is defined as a way of life and work in a specific geographic area with its own set of business conditions, cultural assumptions and unique history (adapted from Gluesing et al., 2003).

5 I use the term "learners" for the students enrolled in a management education program.

6 Field notes are an on-going commentary on what is happening in the research.

7 The metaphorical symbol of "web" has been used in previous organizational research. For example, Geertz (1973) suggested that culture could be construed as a web that individuals comprising the culture spin around themselves. Wasko and Faraj (1999) describe the loosely linked individuals linked in an online community as constituting webs of knowledge. I use the notion of knowledge web in a similar spirit to suggest the patterned interaction and links that dispersed team members create and situate among themselves.

Chapter VI

Virtual Study Groups:
A Challenging Centerpiece for "Working Adult" Management Education

Gregory B. Northcraft
University of Illinois, USA

Terri L. Griffith
Santa Clara University, USA

Mark A. Fuller
Washington State University, USA

Abstract

Groups and teams are critical to modern organizations, and consequently management education has incorporated groups as a centerpiece of both content (the study of group process) and process (the use of study groups and group projects). Unfortunately, working-adult educational programs appear to have yet to take an important final step — acknowledging that study groups often interact virtually and then providing support for virtual study group interaction. We provide both theory and data concerning the use of study groups as virtual teams. We believe that there are important benefits to be gained when study groups make educated decisions about the design and process of their virtual interaction.

Introduction

Groups and teams have emerged as a central building block of modern global commerce (Devine, Clayton, Philips, Dunford, & Melner, 1999), with as many as 80% of Fortune 500 companies having a majority of their employees involved in work teams of one sort or another (Cohen & Bailey, 1997). The reliance of modern business organizations on teams reflects a growing understanding that the interaction opportunities provided by group settings offer advantages for both organizations and their employees. Teams provide a vehicle for employee inclusiveness that enhances organizational effectiveness (Griffith & Neale, 2001). As Lawler (1999, p. 18) emphatically noted, "The results are in: teams are more popular in the United States workplace, and employee involvement (EI) leads to better business performance."

In concert with this apparent shift of emphasis in business to teams has been a corresponding emergence of teams as a centerpiece of cooperative education (e.g., Chen, Donahue, & Klimoski, 2004; Michaelson, Jones, & Watson, 1993; Schmuck & Schmuck, 1997). Stunkel (1998) identified an increasing use of teams and groups as one of the predominant trends in higher education. Teams have proven to be an excellent vehicle for accomplishing interactive, cooperative instruction (Lengnick-Hall & Sanders, 1997). Research has shown that students learn most effectively when working in groups, where they can verbalize their thoughts, challenge the ideas of others, and collaborate to achieve group solutions to problems (Deutsch, 1962; Johnson & Johnson, 1989, 1994).

In this chapter we focus on a particular use of teams in higher educational settings—the study group. In particular, we focus on the likely effects of study groups that meet virtually, and present some empirical evidence concerning the effects of virtual study group interaction patterns on study group effectiveness. We close with some recommendations about how to manage instruction design in order to maximize the benefits of virtual study groups.

What Study Groups Have to Offer

Study groups have become a centerpiece of graduate management education, such as MBA and Executive MBA programs (Baldwin, Bedell, & Johnson, 1997; Byrne, 1995). The emphasis on study group interaction in such programs reflects three critical benefits that the use of study groups brings to the table.

Intellectual Cross-Pollination

When study groups are appropriately strategically composed (e.g., when study group members have different backgrounds and thus distinct strengths), the diversity of skills and background experience represented in the study group can allow stronger students in one discipline to share their strengths and thus help the study group's weaker students in that discipline. Further, when the study group changes its focus to a new discipline, those same students can switch roles, allowing a previously "weak student" to lead and facilitate group learning. In this way, study groups provide the opportunity for diversity (Schneider & Northcraft, 1999) that can be leveraged for learning opportunities far beyond what students could get from personal contact with a professor. In effect, study groups co-opt students into taking responsibility for "co-producing" the education product (Lengnick-Hall & Saunders, 1997).

Group Dynamics/Leadership Skills

Study groups also provide students invaluable experience in learning how to manage groups effectively. Stevens and Campion (1994) have identified conflict resolution, collaborative problem-solving, communication, goal setting and performance management, and planning and task coordination all as critical competencies needed for a team — and a study group — to run effectively and efficiently. Study groups provide a setting in which these competencies can be rehearsed, refined, and routinized into students' skill sets. O'Neil, Allerd, and Baker (1997) note that these are skills highly prized by potential employers.

Social Networking

Study groups also provide an arena in which invaluable social networking can take place (Baldwin et al., 1997). Students cultivate strong relationships under the interdependence of study groups. Just as those relationships co-opt students into co-producing the educational product at school, they also represent a critical storehouse of potential information (different experiences and perspectives) for students to draw upon after graduation. The development of strong social network contacts during school can help ensure that learning (from each other!) continues to take place long after students have forgotten the names of their courses and their professors.

Study Groups in "Wording Adult" Management Education Programs

The three primary benefits of study groups outlined above — intellectual cross-pollination, group dynamics/leadership skills, and social networking — seem to represent a particularly important component of "working adult" management educational programs (e.g., part-time MBA and Executive MBA programs). In such programs, professorial contact hours are limited and study group work is intended to leverage that professorial contact. In terms of the three benefits of study groups outlined above, these students bring more to the table. They have more experience to draw upon — both in terms of the course content and in terms of their own past group dynamics/leadership experiences. In many cases these students also already have well-developed social networks of their own, which makes social networking with them even more "value-added."

Paradoxically, although study group-focused learning provides the most promise for working-adult students, it may also pose the most challenges. Study groups in full-time programs — such as a regular full-time MBA — probably meet face-to-face. For their working-adult counterparts, face-to-face meetings may seem an out-of-reach luxury. Rather, such groups are more likely to meet virtually.

Study Groups as Virtual Teams

Study groups become virtual teams when their primary means of interaction is not face-to-face (Lipnack and Stamps, 1997). As noted by Stunkel (1998), another of the trends in higher education is an increasing reliance on technology, and it is technology that makes it increasingly possible for teams to "meet" (interact) without being face-to-face (Griffith & Neale, 2001)—for example, using conference calls or Web-meetings (e.g., using Microsoft Netmeeting).

As Griffith and Neale (2001) note, there is a range of technologies used by virtual groups. These technologies vary by the level of communication and documentation support they provide. At the low end, one can imagine virtual groups using traditional mail in the same way that "correspondence chess" was played in the 1900s. More reasonably, our experience suggests that most student groups make heavy use of conference calls for their synchronous meetings, supplemented by e-mail for asynchronous coordination and document transfer. More adventuresome groups will make use of shared file servers (generally free ones, such as Yahoo! Groups). It is rare to find study groups using more sophisticated tools like those provided by WebEx, Groove, or Facilitate.com. Regardless of the particular technology adopted, groups will need to consider their own experience with the technology, each other, and the task as they make choices about how to meet and what technologies to employ (Carlson & Zmud, 1999).

Study groups can be intentionally arranged to encourage face-to-face meetings. For example, in the University of Illinois Executive MBA program, study groups historically have been formed on the basis of geographic proximity (for example, all the enrolled students from Bloomington, Illinois may form one study group) precisely to facilitate regular face-to-face study group meetings by minimizing the amount of travel required to meet between formal class sessions.

Unfortunately, the intention of arranging study groups to be physically proximal (and thus allow face-to-face meetings) may underestimate the primacy of convenience to very busy working adults. Lengnick-Hall and Sanders (1997, p. 1363), in their study of empowered student learning systems noted that, "...as more students find they must balance family and work demands and expectations with their student roles, the issue of expediency and convenience becomes increasingly important." Even when programs organize study groups geographically to facilitate face-to-face meetings, in reality students may still meet virtually because virtual meetings — no matter what the intervening distance — are easier to arrange than face-to-face meetings. If technology makes it possible for a student to be "at home" with the family while also meeting with a study group (e.g., via conference call or Web-meeting), the opportunity to be two places at once may prove too attractive for a working adult to pass up.

Composing study groups on the basis of geographic proximity to encourage face-to-face interaction may be ill-advised in any event. Geographically proximal students may come from the same employer (or share some regional culture biases), thereby limiting the potential for intellectual cross-pollination and social networking with individuals from other companies and even other industries. As one University of Illinois Executive MBA student put it, "I didn't join this program to socially network with other people from my own company!"

Composing study groups on the basis of geographic proximity to encourage face-to-face interaction may also limit the potential for intellectual cross-pollination and social networking by limiting the number of students with which a student can cross-pollinate and socially network during the program. For example, University of Illinois Executive MBA students occasionally have suggested that study groups be "rotated" (that is, reformed) at the conclusion of every two-month, two-course module. Rotation would increase the probability that every student in the program will have the opportunity to be in a study group — and thereby to intellectually cross-pollinate and socially network — with every other student in the program. To the extent that study groups offer intellectual and social networking value, rotating study groups seems to be the recipe for maximizing these values. Such a strategy, however, demands that geographic proximity *not* be allowed to drive study group composition. If instead study group composition is driven by the potential benefits of diversity, this diversity may be best achieved by having study groups meet virtually — so that location (geographic proximity of study group members) is not a consideration. If study groups meet virtually, however, are there unintended consequences?

The Limits of Meeting Virtually

If the point of study groups is to enhance intellectual cross-pollination, foster the development of group dynamics/leadership skills, and to develop social network connections, it seems significant that virtual interaction probably threatens the accomplishment of two of these objectives. Rockmann and

Northcraft (2005, p. 11) note that, "...the dispersion of team members across space and time can interrupt communication and erode any sense of group-ness or identity within a virtual team." Thus, virtual study groups may not accomplish strong intellectual cross-pollination because of disrupted information sharing, and may not develop strong social network connections because of degraded attachment among study group members. Further, both of these problems might be particularly likely to occur when convenience considerations drive study groups to "meet" asynchronously (for example, using round-robin e-mail to revise a group project write-up).

Disrupted information sharing. A primary characteristic of virtual interaction is the substitution of some form of technology-mediated communication (e.g., telephone, e-mail, Web-conferencing) for face-to-face interaction. McGrath and Hollingshead (1994) found that computer-mediated groups tend to have fewer interactions and less information exchange among members than face-to-face groups (Ramsower, 1985; Richter & Meshulam, 1993). Virtual team members can exchange verbal information as efficiently as a face-to-face team, but their ability to handle nonverbal exchange is severely limited, which can contribute to increased misunderstanding among members (Warkentin, Sayeed, & Hightower, 1997). Hewitt and Scardamalia (1998, p. 87) note that, "While online discourse may promote equality, it is arguably less conducive to maintaining an optimal level of conflict.... Without the real-time, aural and visual cues of face-to-face discourse (smiles, nods, 'uh-huh,' and so forth), it becomes difficult for writers to know how their statements are being interpreted. 'Grounding a conversation'.... is a difficult task across media that lack co-presence, visibility, audibility, and simultaneity..." In another study, face-to-face teams were also found to have better internal leadership and coordination than virtual teams (Burke & Chidambaram, 1999). Finally, research has demonstrated that virtuality may encourage individuals to be less open in their communication (Alge, Wiethoff, & Klein, 2003; Hollingshead, 1996). In all of these cases, meeting virtually may contribute to a disruption of effective information sharing among study group members.

Degraded attachment. Virtual interaction may also prove less likely to create the relationships required to foster valuable social network connections. Face-to-face contact has been found to be a primary driver of relationship development (Festinger, Schachter, & Back, 1950). Not surprisingly then, telecommuting research has found that telecommuters develop less organizational commitment (Kinsman, 1987), and experience increased feelings of isolation (Chapman, Sheehy, Heywood, Dooley, & Collins, 1995; Huws,

1993; Solomon & Templer, 1993). Virtual interaction may exacerbate feelings that others are not doing their share of the work (e.g., Broad, 1981) since their work is not as visible and is more difficult to verify (Graetz, Boyle, Kimble, Thompson, & Garloch, 1998). This inability to verify can decrease trust (Alge et al., 2003; Hollingshead, 1996), which is critical to the development of strong long-term relationships (Jarvenpaa, Knoll, & Leidner, 1998).

Finally, virtual communication may hamper the development of transactive memory within the group (Griffith, Sawyer, & Neale, 2003). Transactive memory is the capacity of group members to know who in a group knows what — that is, where (in which person) particular information expertise resides within the group (Wegner, 1987). This has implications for both the short-term and long-term value of study groups. In the short-term, effective co-production seems less likely to occur if study group members do not know where to turn to find the information they need. In the long-term, social network connections are only of value to the extent that study group members know what value (informationally) each individual in the network brings to the table.

The bottom line is that virtual interaction in study groups may lessen the effectiveness of the behavioral integration (Hambrick, 1994) required for effective intellectual cross-pollination and educational co-production. In addition, virtual interaction may also reduce the social integration (Smith, Smith, Olian, Sims, O'Bannon, & Scully, 1994) that provides the foundation for strong social network connections.

The Real Issue with Virtual Study Groups

The real issue with study groups may be not that virtual interaction is less effective than non-virtual interaction. Instead the real problem may be that study groups that interact virtually may be unlikely to interact with all members on an equal communication footing, and thereby may jeopardize the potential benefits of study group interaction. Virtual study group members may interact with one another in markedly different ways, and these different forms of interaction may influence the benefits that each member takes from the study group.

Johnson, Suriya, Yoon, Berrett, and LaFleur (2002) define virtual team interaction as interaction that is "geographically unrestricted." It is worth noting that this definition doesn't mean face-to-face interaction among virtual study group members isn't possible or even prevalent, just that it is *only one of many* possible options for interacting with other study group members. Griffith, Mannix, and Neale (2003) similarly note that virtual teams often contain a mixture of co-located and virtual members, such that virtuality represents a continuum rather than a dichotomy (Griffith & Neale, 2001). These comments raise the specter of "hybrid" virtual study groups. A hybrid virtual study group could be one in which the study group meets completely (all members) face-to-face sometimes, and meets completely (all members) virtually (synchronously or asynchronously) at others. However, a hybrid study group could also be one in which only some members are co-located during study group meetings, so that study group members might simultaneously communicate with some study group members face-to-face and some virtually.

Three distinct dispersion configurations of study groups are illustrated in Figure 1: traditional, hybrid, and pure virtual. The x-axis represents the percentage of work that the group does with its members distributed across time or space. The y-axis represents the level of technological support used by the team. Technological support (either electronic or otherwise) is largely about communication, but also includes documentation, and/or decision support capability. The z-axis represents the distribution of the physical locations occupied by the group members. As noted earlier, this dimension brings into play the tension between convenience and diversity. Purely virtual groups take up the plane depicted on the far right, regardless of the level/type of technological support they use. Purely face-to-face (traditional) groups form the other extreme and

Figure 1. Adapted from Griffith, Sawyer, and Neale (2003)

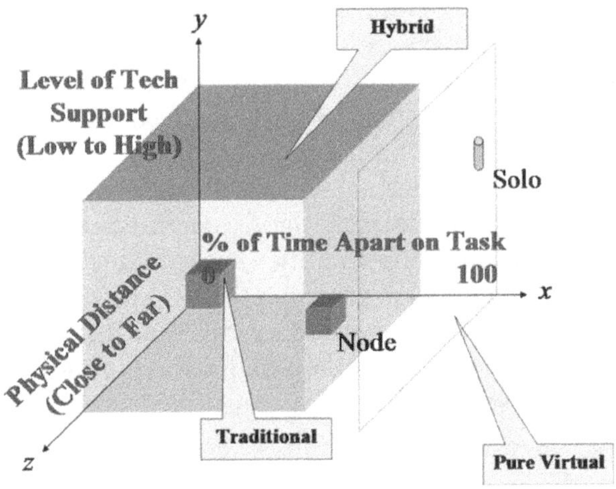

are depicted as the cube at the origin of the graph. Purely face-to-face groups do *all* of their work face-to-face and are expected to be rare, at best.

Between these two "pure" forms of study groups lies the problem: virtualness may vary not only *across* groups (some study groups utilize more face-to-face interaction than others) but also *within* groups (some study group members utilize more face-to-face interaction than others). When virtualness varies within a study group, it creates a non-level communication playing field. That means the connections among some study group members will be disrupted and degraded through the use of virtual interaction, while the connections among other study group members (those interacting face-to-face) will not be disrupted and degraded. This non-level communication playing field in turn raises the specter of subgroups, fault lines, and the marginalization of some study group members.

Virtual groups whose virtuality varies across group members are not uncommon. For example, Griffith, Mannix, and Neale (2003) studied teams at a large enterprise software firm. The 28 teams they studied ranged from fully co-located (13 teams) to an eight-person team with seven locations—and everything in between. Majchrzak, Rice, Malhotra, King, and Ba (2000, p. 574) provide another example: "Virtual team members were geographically distributed: two members were located in different ends of the same building, three other members were each one mile away in different buildings; one member of a second organization was located 100 miles away; and two members of the third organization were located 1,000 miles away in different buildings."

Prior research provides a variety of insights concerning the likely effects of subgroups created when some study group members are co-located and some are not. For example, in-group bias—social competition and discrimination against out-groups and favoritism towards the in-group (Mugny, Sanchez-Mazas, Roux, & Perez, 1991)—may play a key role. Intergroup communication can be affected if in-group bias distorts effective information sharing and mutual influence (Lee & Ottati, 1993). Recent work specifically focused on subgroups in distributed teams suggests the types of issues that may arise. Cramton (2002, p. 203) notes that, "there seems to be a tendency for dispersed teams to develop sub-group identities based on location." Members of a software engineering organization studied by Armstrong and Cole (2002) considered co-located team members as "us" and distant team members as "them." Distributed groups may be prone to develop cliques based on where they work, thereby splitting the group into multiple factions (Armstrong & Cole, 2002; Cramton, 2001; Hinds & Bailey, 2003).

As these examples illustrate, the geographical distribution of members of a group creates a possible "fault line" within the group (Rockmann, Pratt, & Northcraft, 2004). A fault line is a characteristic (for example, location) that segregates a team into subgroups. Lau and Murnighan (1998) note that fault lines can be particularly divisive when subgroup boundaries converge (Brewer & Campbell, 1976). For example, if a distant study group member is also the only female in the group, fault lines may lead subgroups to "marginalize" other group members—for example, to ignore them—and marginalization thereby contributes directly to decreases in the synergistic value of having a study group in the first place.

When fault lines "marginalize" group members, those group members are likely to have less access to important resources (Brass, 1992)—such as the information and support of other group members—which may compromise their effectiveness as members of the group. Armstrong and Cole (2002) and Cramton (2001) describe how polarized subgroups in the distributed teams they studied withheld information from each other. Similarly, Kramer and Brewer (1984) and Earley and Mosakowski (2000) report that subgroup differentiation interferes with cooperative group behavior. Finally, Cramton (2002) noted that attributions made about non-co-located team members may be harshly inaccurate in ways that polarize a group by strengthening identifications only with co-located others.

From a social network perspective, face-to-face contact is likely to influence the strength of social network ties (Byrne, 1961), such that differential virtuality within a study group will mean that more social capital is created among some study group members than among others. In turn, the strength of network ties can also influence the quality of information shared among study group members. For example, Cross and Sproull (2004) found that individuals with weak ties were more likely to simply share solutions to problems, while individuals with stronger ties were more likely to engage in deeper forms of problem reformulation.

In the end, these concerns all suggest that disrupted information sharing and degraded social networking effectiveness may not be the most important—and certainly not the only—challenge faced by virtual study groups. Virtual study groups must also be concerned with the effects of marginalizing study group members when disrupted information sharing and degraded networking effectiveness operate differentially among members within a study group.

An Empirical Investigation of Study Group Dispersion Patterns

Given the problems that meeting virtually poses for study groups, Hewitt and Scardamalia (1998, p. 81) note that, "The challenge is to identify the kinds of distributions [of students and student cognitions] that are educationally effective, and then to search for ways that they can play a more central role in day-to-day classroom activities." To borrow from Rock and Pratt (2002), if differences in virtuality within study groups cause problems because they create fault lines, it is critical to understand the effects of different student dispersion patterns when study groups meet.

What follows is the summary of an empirical investigation of different representative types of study group dispersion patterns. Twenty-eight female and 40 male undergraduates at a major university participated in exchange for course extra-credit. Single-sex groups of four were randomly assigned to one of the four dispersion configurations. Communication was face-to-face or via speakerphone, as required by the configuration. We chose this design to provide a solid foundation for the study of information transfer in virtual groups. Conference calls and face-to-face interaction provide the most basic communication choices that groups might employ. (Below, we will put conference calls in context with more complex communication dynamics and options.)

Each participant's materials included: (a) information about three faculty candidates to be considered for a job in the Business School's Business Communication Department and (b) two paper-and-pencil questionnaires (which provided the dependent measures for the study). The faculty candidate information was provided in the form of a hidden-profile task (Stasser & Stewart, 1992) roughly based on the scenario presented in Cruz, Henningsen, and Williams (1996). Each participant played the role of a professor on a recruiting committee and received three unique letters of recommendation—one for each candidate. Each letter of recommendation provided one piece of unique information (received only by that participant) regarding the candidate, as well as six pieces of common information (received by all participants). Two remaining pieces of common information were provided in the form of Equal Employment Opportunity Commission (EEOC) reporting documents for each candidate.

Each participant's unique information focused on one dimension across all three candidates. For example, the letters of recommendation provided to

Professor White included information about the three candidates' teaching excellence (the unique information provided to Professor White), as well as information about the eight common dimensions. The instructions noted that each of the 12 (eight common and four unique) dimensions were equally important to the hiring decision. Table 1 shows how the information was distributed and scored. The hidden profile nature of this information distribution requires that all participants effectively share their unique information with the group in order for the group's deliberations to reach an appropriate conclusion.

The key design features of the dispersion patterns in the study were *nodes* and *solos*. A node occurs where multiple members of a study group are co-located (i.e., meeting face-to-face). A solo occurs where one member of the study group is not co-located with any other member of the study group (i.e., is alone). Thus, a completely face-to-face group consists of one node, while a completely virtual group consists of four solos. The other possibilities are multiple nodes, or a mixture of nodes and solos. (Figure 1 depicts one node and one solo.)

Our empirical investigation focused on four different group dispersion configurations: (1) four members completely face-to-face (4Node), (2) four solo members, none co-located—completely virtual (4Solo), (3) two nodes of two members each (2-2Node), and (3) one node of three members with one solo (3Node/1Solo). These different dispersion patterns were chosen to represent the most prototypical ways that study groups might meet.

Table 1. Information distribution and qualification content

		FACULTY CANDIDATE		
QUALIFICATION DIMENSION	Who Held Information	John	Sally	Edna
Excellent teacher	Prof. White	1	0	0
Able to teach a diverse set of courses	Everyone	0	1	.5
Record of producing a large quantity research	Everyone	0	1	1
Quality Research	Prof. Green	1	0	0
Willing to engage in internal service activities	Prof. Red	1	0	0
Willing to engage in external service activities	Everyone	0	1	1
Strong educational preparation	Prof. Blue	1	0	0
Considerable college teaching experience	Everyone	1	.5	1
Woman	Everyone	0	1	1
Minority	Everyone	1	1	0
Unable to offer a large salary	Everyone	1	0	1
Likely to stay with the department for a substantial period of time	Everyone	0	1	1
Total Score for Candidate:		7	6.5	6.5

John equal to 1 indicates that information shows John to be qualified on that dimension. Zero means not qualified and 0.5 is partially qualified.

As noted above, communication for these groups was via conference call in the non-co-located settings. We have found that conference calls are a modal way for virtual teams to work when synchronous communication is possible. These calls are often augmented with use of instant messaging (allowing for subgroups to carry on parallel conversations), e-mail or other methods of sharing documents, and (in rare cases) video. This study thus provides a base-line for consideration of more sophisticated virtual communication scenarios.

Figure 2 provides a conceptual model of the effects of different study group dispersion configurations. The effects of nodes and solos in study group dispersion configurations hinge on two issues: Member Salience and Information Acquisition Urgency. These two dynamics are expected to be key to understanding study group performance given any current or future technical environment. The measured effects in the study were information integration (which reflects the study group goal of intellectual cross-pollination) and social integration (which reflects the study group goal of social networking).

Member Salience

Starbuck and Milliken (1988, p. 60) noted that, "noticing may be at least as important as sensemaking.... If events are noticed, people make sense of them; and if events are not noticed, they are not available for sensemaking." This has direct bearing on the understanding of team dispersion configurations and information flow dynamics. All other things being equal, fellow study group members who are co-located are more likely to be noticed than fellow study group members who are not.

Physical contact has been shown to be a primary determinant of liking (Zajonc, 1968) and friendship development (Festinger et al., 1950), and effective research and development interactions (Allen, 1977). In the context of teams with nodes and solos, this means that all study group members are not created equal. The physical presence of others influences an individual's perception of salient social categories (Ashforth & Mael, 1989; Hogg & Turner, 1984; Turner, 1985). The specific operationalization of these effects is that non-co-located members may fall, "'off people's radar screens' and [be] ignored even during telephone and videoconferences" (Armstrong & Cole, 2002, pp. 170-171). This leads to a first testable proposition:

Proposition 1: Co-located group members are more salient to one another than are non-co-located group members.

Proposition 1 was supported. Our measure of salience was whom participants mentioned first when asked to list the other group members. Co-located study group members were 29% more salient than non-co-located members ($t = 3.6$, $p < .001$).

The next question is whether salience matters to study group effectiveness. For this, we focused on the role salience plays in the likelihood that a participant's unique information is integrated into the other group members' understanding of the problem.

Proposition 2: Higher member salience will result in greater integration of available unique information.

Proposition 2 was also supported. Other members' salience was a significant predictor of a participant's ability to recall the unique information held by all group members ($F_{(1,66)} = 3.99, p < .05$). Scores could range from 0 to 12 given that there were three pieces of unique information for each participant. The mean was 5.68 correct ($SD = 1.44$). See Figure 3 for the overall results by condition.

Information Acquisition Urgency

As depicted in Figure 2, study group dispersion configuration may also create a sense of urgency regarding the acquisition of other group members' attention and unique information—keeping fellow study group members engaged in the discussion. Teams have been shown to adaptively structure their interactions (DeSanctis, Poole, & Dickson, 2000)—they may pick different processes or technologies given their situation. Teams with dispersion configurations that reduce member salience may also increase urgency to acquire information.

Urgency is likely a function of the study group's dispersion configuration—for example, a function of the presence of solos in the group. Individuals in completely face-to-face settings probably will feel the least urgency to keep fellow group members in the discussion, since they are all co-located. How-

Figure 2. Conceptual model

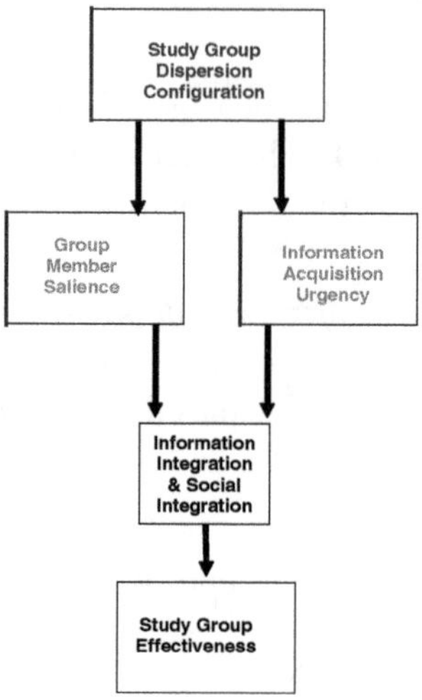

Figure 3.

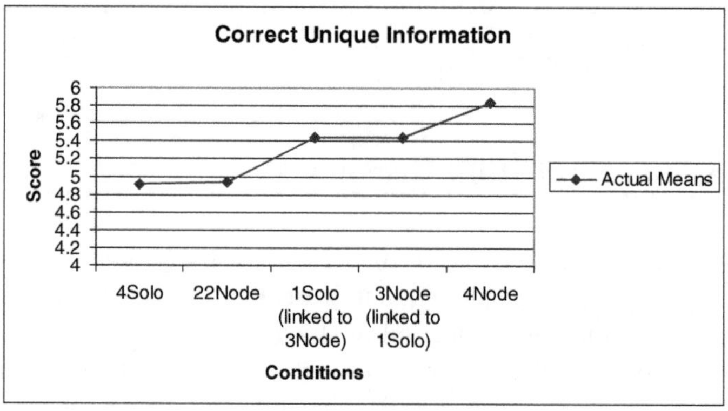

ever, dispersion configurations that create multiple subgroups (in this setting, the 2-2Nodes) may prove equally complacent. All group members are co-located with someone (no solos). Each study group member has another study group member to work with, and no one has to be concerned that anyone is cut off from the study group.

In contrast, when all study group members are solos (4Solo), there may be lots of urgency. When everyone is known to be on their own (not co-located with anyone else), there is a level playing field, and everyone probably feels some responsibility for getting everyone involved and any unique information shared. Ironically, groups with a combination of nodes and solos (3Node/1Solo) may also experience a strong sense of urgency. In this configuration, the solos are known to be in a compromised situation. The solos know that they need to break into the face-to-face node, and the face-to-face node realizes that there are solos who are conspicuous in their absence. This leads to a third testable proposition:

Proposition 3: An individual's urgency to gather information from others is a function of the number of group members not co-located with that individual, and the number of solos in the study group.

Urgency was measured by a two-item scale ("How important was it for you to hear the comments from the other group members?" and "How essential did you think it was for you to have access to the other group member's information?"—measured on a five-point rating scale, 1=Not at all, 5 = Extremely Hard). Proposition 3 was supported ($F_{(3, 63)} = 3.34, p < .02$).

The urgency displayed by a group member may also have an affect on the ability of the other group members to integrate that person's information. The dynamic of striving to collect information may push a reciprocal effort from the other group members. This leads to a final proposition:

Proposition 4: An individual's urgency to gather information from others influences the likelihood that his/her unique information is known to other study group members.

We tested this last proposition by using each participant's own urgency score as the predictor for whether or not that participant's unique information was known by their fellow group members. This final proposition also was supported ($F_{(1,202)} = 5.26, p < .02$).

General Discussion and Conclusions

The goal of this chapter has been to provide a theoretical perspective on the use of virtual study groups, and to detail an initial empirical investigation into the effects of different virtual study group dispersion configurations. What seems clear from our discussion is that virtual study groups provide a high-potential design element in working adult education programs, but one whose value could easily be compromised by the mismanagement of study group interaction patterns.

One of the first things educational program designers need to appreciate is that different study group interaction patterns and environments will have implications for what students are likely to take away from the program itself. Study groups are an effective method for enhancing collaborative student learning by increasing idea exchange and drawing on other team members' discipline-specific strengths. These interactions can also foster the development of skills related to managing group dynamics, as well as leading teams. Finally, study groups give students the benefit of developing social networks—relationships that will likely continue adding value well after the formal educational experience has ended.

Virtual study groups can also serve to help students meet these same goals, and virtual interaction is particularly attractive for very busy working adults, who themselves have an ever increasing familiarity with technology that can facilitate study group interactions. While in the past geographic considerations may have necessarily played a large role in study group composition, Internet-based collaboration tools now allow for the formation of virtual study groups whose members represent a broad diversity of geographic locations and business backgrounds.

While such virtual study groups have benefits, the use of such groups creates some special considerations that educational program designers need to consider. As noted in this chapter, information sharing in virtual study groups may be disrupted relative to face-to-face arrangements. Such disrupted information exchange runs counter to the goal of collaborative learning through effective idea exchange—an advantage typically associated with group work. In addition, virtual teamwork may degrade attachment among members, which again runs counter to the social network development benefits that many students seek. Finally, such study groups may also function less efficiently because members may have more difficulty assessing the skills and knowledge of other group members.

So what conclusions should we draw regarding the dispersion configurations of study groups in educational settings? Specifically, how should working-adult educational programs design study groups in support of the classroom experience? Our empirical investigation points to the importance of understanding that differential virtuality within a study group may create fault lines and subgroups that can disrupt information flow and degrade the social networking potential of study groups. We believe these results are telling regardless of the particular technology used. All groups make decisions regarding the types of technologies they will use to interact, the aspects of the technologies that will be appropriated, and the interplay between group dynamics and technology use (e.g., DeSanctis et al., 2000).

Study group training done early in any "working adult" curriculum should plant the seed that there are serious consequences to the interaction routines a study group establishes. Just as study groups make decisions about whether or not to use video versus conference calling, they also need to make decisions about how they will structure study group interaction, and given a structure, how the team will be managed. What follows are four results that can form the basis of such training and better inform study group decision-making.

First, students need to know that co-located group members are more salient to one another than are non-co-located group members. This most basic of our findings can be captured in the maxim, "out of sight, out of mind"—rather than "absence makes the heart grow fonder." To manage this problem we offer two suggestions—work in a face-to-face configuration when feasible, but also develop group processes that raise the salience of each group member when face-to-face interaction is not possible. For example, explicitly put each member on the agenda. Use a conferencing system that shows each person's location, time zone, and so forth. Some groups use systems displaying pictures or avatars to personalize the communication. More facilitation-focused tools could be used to keep the "pulse" of the team— perhaps by an anonymous display of engagement, or the level of participation by group members in discussion threads and the like.

Second, groups need to understand that the payoff of higher group member salience is greater integration of available information. In our research, group members were better able to integrate the information of more salient others. Encourage study groups to carefully weigh the costs/benefits of working apart. Groups need to make educated decisions about their task and interaction routine choices and then adapt their process as needed (as noted above).

Third, an individual's urgency to gather information from other group members is a function of the number of group members not co-located with that individual and the number of solo group members. This seems to result in an interesting effect whereby working face-to-face with those you can (creating multiple co-located subgroups) may be a bad idea. This common practice (for example those on the north side of town meeting face-to-face to conference call with those on the south side of town, or those at the Singapore office meeting face-to-face to conference call with those in the German office) resulted in low integration in our study. Our results suggest that dispersion configurations composed only of nodes result in a form of information-sharing complacency. The results from dispersion configurations with at least one solo (for example, the 3Node/1Solo configuration in our study) keep urgency high enough to overcome what could be complacency on the part of the node members.

Finally, a study group member's own urgency influences the likelihood that her/his information is integrated into the study group's outcome. One person can make a difference. Group members who understand that they need to work to gain access to information—whether they are solos or members of nodes—positively influence the likelihood that their information is heard. Systems that allow individuals to "break" into on-going conversations to signal their urgency add value to more virtual groups. Some computer conferencing systems allow users to virtually "raise your hand." Some teleconferencing groups manage this more socially; group members understand that a tapping noise on the microphone is akin to raising your hand. The key is for the group to understand that urgency to contribute is important, and that methods for signaling urgency need to be developed for whatever communication tools are in use.

These recommendations all point to the importance of study group training and orientation in order for virtual study groups to succeed. Almost all graduate management degree programs emphasize the importance of groups, and some even provide separate team building or training (in support of study groups and group project work) beyond that covered in the organization behavior content areas. There seems to remain, however, a gap between what programs desire with respect to groupwork, and how those same programs train people in groupwork—particularly *virtual* groupwork. Most orientation programs are face-to-face, even when the overall program is considered to be virtual or "global." For example, one distributed MBA program we are familiar with opens with a brief reading period where the students prepare for the first face-to-face session. During the face-to-face session there are a variety of orientation programs, including discussions of groupwork. Though some of the discussion focuses on effective practices for working in distributed study groups, none of the experiential training is conducted in a virtual environment.

This seems a critical mismatch. Moreland (2000) found that team training needs to be on task and with team members to be effective. This suggests that effective study group training—and effective group content education—needs to include a virtual component. Study groups should not be trained to work in face-to-face settings when they will be working in virtual environments. We should be helping them understand the implications of their choices regarding how they do their study group work. While researchers have found virtual interaction to be disruptive, they have also found that experience can help overcome the limitations of meeting virtually (e.g., Burke, Aytes, & Chidambaram, 2001; Chidambaram, 1996). As Hoag, Jayakar, and Erickson (2003, p. 379) noted, under the right circumstances, "...there may be no significant difference in the way individuals perceive online or face-to-face team interaction." Those "right circumstances" almost certainly include getting study groups far down the virtual groupwork learning curve as quickly as possible, so that by the time they need to be on task together they have expanded both their understanding of and capacity to interact richly, even when interacting virtually (Carlson & Zmud, 1999).

If virtual study groups have the drawbacks we have discussed, should programs catering to busy working-adults encourage their use? We believe the answer is yes. The potential benefits of such study groups are great. Increased study group diversity allowed by the possibility of virtual interaction should increase learning, social networks, and group dynamics and leadership skills, but only if study groups are assisted in overcoming the problems we have identified here.

References

Alge, B. J., Wiethoff, C., & Klein, H. J. (2003). When does the medium matter? Knowledge-building experiences and opportunities in decision-making teams. *Organizational Behavior and Human Decision Processes, 91*, 26-37.

Allen, T. J. (1977). *Managing the flow of technology, technology transfer and the dissemination of technological information with the R&D organization*. Cambridge: MIT Press.

Armstrong, D. J., & Cole, P. (2002). Managing distances and differences in geographically distributed work groups. In P. J. Hinds & S. Kiesler (Eds.), *Distributed work* (pp. 167-186). Cambridge: MIT

Ashforth, B. E., & Mael, F. (1989). Social identity theory and the organization. *Academy of Management Review, 14,* 20-39.

Baldwin, T. T., Bedell, M. D., & Johnson, J. L. (1997). The social fabric of a team-based MBA program: Network effects on student satisfaction and performance. *Academy of Management Journal, 40,* 1369-1397

Brass, D. J. (1992). Power in organizations: A social network perspective. In G. Moore and J. A. Whitt (Eds.), *Research in politics and society* (pp. 295-323). Greenwich, CT: JAI.

Brewer, M. B., & Campbell, D. T. (1976). *Ethnocentrism and intergroup attitudes: East African evidence*. New York: Halstead Press (Sage).

Broad, W. J. (1981). The publishing game: Getting more for less. *Science, 211,* 1137-1138.

Burke, K., Aytes, K., & Chidambaram, L. (2001). Media effects on the development of cohesion and process satisfaction in computer-supported workgroups: An analysis from two longitudinal studies. *Information Technology and People, 14,* 122-141.

Burke, K., & Chidambaram, L. (1999). How much bandwidth is enough? A longitudinal examination of media characteristics and group outcomes. *MIS Quarterly, 23,* 557-579.

Byrne, D. (1961). The influence of propinquity and opportunities for interaction on classroom relationships, *Human Relations*, *14*, 63-69.

Byrne, J. A. (1995) Business Week guide to the best business schools. *Business Week.* New York: McGraw-Hill.

Carlson, J. R., & Zmud, R. W. (1999) Channel expansion theory and the experiential nature of media richness perceptions. *Academy of Management Journal, 42,* 153-170.

Chapman, A. J., Sheehy, N. P., Heywood, S., Dooley, B., & Collins, S. C. (1995). The organizational implications of teleworking. In I. T. Robertson (Ed.), *International review of industrial and organizational psychology*, (Vol. 10, pp. 229-248). Chichester, UK: John Wiley.

Chen, G., Donahue, L. M., & Klimoski, R. J. (2004). Training undergraduates to work in organizational teams. *Academy of Management Learning and Education, 3*, 27-40.

Chidambaram, L. (1996). Relational development in computer-supported groups. *MIS Quarterly, 20,* 143-165.

Cohen S. G., & Bailey D.E. (1997). What makes teams work: Group effectiveness research from the shop floor to the executive suite. *Journal of Management, 23,* 239-290.

Cramton, C. D. (2001). The mutual knowledge problem and its consequences for dispersed collaboration. *Organization Science, 12,* 346-371.

Cramton, C. D. (2002). Attribution in distributed work groups. In P. Hinds & S. Kiesler (Eds.), *Distributed work* (pp. 191-212). Cambridge: MIT Press.

Cross, R., & Sproull, L. (2004). More than an answer: Information relationships for actionable knowledge, *Organization Science, 15,* 446-462.

Cruz, M. G., Henningsen, D. D., & Williams, M. L. M. (1996). *Normative influence in the absence of groups? Consequences for decisions, task difficulty, task attractiveness, decision quality, and conformity.* Retrieved December 28, 2002, from http://www.public.asu.edu/~corman/infosys/papers/cruz.pdf

DeSanctis, G., Poole, M. S., & Dickson, G. W. (2000). Teams and technology: Interactions over time. In M. A. Neale, E. A. Mannix, & T. L. Griffith (Eds.), *Research on managing groups and teams: Technology* (Vol. 3). Stamford, CT: JAI.

Deutsch, M. (1962). Cooperation and trust: Some theoretical notes. In M. R. Jones (Ed.), *Nebraska Symposium on motivation* (pp. 275-319). Lincoln, NE: University of Nebraska.

Devine, D. J., Clayton, L. D., Philips, J. L., Dunford, B. B., & Melner, S. B. (1999). Teams in organizations: Prevalence, characteristics, and effectiveness, *Small Group Research, 30*, 678-711.

Earley, P. C., & Mosakowski, E. (2000). Creating hybrid team cultures: An empirical test of transnational team functioning. *Academy of Management Journal*, *43*, 26-49.

Festinger, L., Schachter, S., & Back, K. (1950). *Social pressures in informal groups: A study of human factors in housing*. Palo Alto, CA: Stanford University.

Graetz, K. A., Boyle, E. S., Kimble, C. E., Thompson, P., & Garloch, J. L. (1998). Information sharing in face-to-face, teleconferencing, and electronic chat groups. *Small Group Research, 29*, 714-743.

Griffith, T. L., Mannix, E. A., & Neale, M. A. (2003). Conflict in virtual teams. In C. B. Gibson & S. G. Cohen (Eds.), *Virtual teams that work* (pp. 335-352). San Francisco: Jossey-Bass.

Griffith, T. L., & Neale, M. A. (2001). Information Processing in Traditional, Hybrid, and Virtual Teams: From Nascent Knowledge to Transactive Memory. In B. M. Staw & R. I. Sutton (Eds.), *Research in organizational behavior* (Vol. 23, pp. 379-421). Stamford, CT: JAI.

Griffith, T. L., Sawyer, J. E., & Neale, M. A. (2003). Virtualness and knowledge in teams: Managing the love triangle of organizations, individuals, and information technology. *MIS Quarterly*, *27*, 265-287.

Hambrick, D. C. (1994). Top management groups: A conceptual integration and reconsideration of the "team" label. In B. M. Staw & L. L. Cummings (Eds.), *Research in organizational behavior* (pp. 171-214). Greenwich, CT: JAI.

Hewitt, J., & Scardamalia, M. (1998). Design principles for distributed knowledge building processes. *Educational Psychology Review, 10,* 75-96.

Hinds, P., & Bailey, D. (2003). Out of sight, out of sync: Understanding conflict in distributed teams. *Organization Science*, *14*, 615-632.

Hoag, A. M., Jayakar, K. P., & Erickson, K. (2003, Winter). The role of trust in virtual and interpersonal environments: Implications for team learning and case method pedagogies. *Journalism and Mass Communication Educator*, 370-383.

Hogg, M. A., & Turner, J. C. (1984). Social identify and conformity: A theory of referent information influence. In W. Doise & S. Moscovici (Eds.), *Current Issues in European Social Psychology* (Vol. 2, pp.139-182). Cambridge, UK: Cambridge University.

Hollingshead, A. B. (1996). Information suppression and status persistence in group decision making: The effects of communication media. *Human Communication Research*, *23,* 193-219.

Huws, U. (1993). *Teleworking in Britain* (Report #18), London: The Employment Department Research Series.

Jarvenpaa, S. L., Knoll, K., & Leidner, D. E. (1998). Is anybody out there? Antecedents of trust in global virtual teams. *Journal of Management Information Systems*, *14,* 29-64.

Johnson, D. W., & Johnson, R. T. (1989). *Cooperation and competition: Theory and research.* Edina, MN: Interaction Book.

Johnson, D. W., & Johnson, R. T. (1994). *Leading the cooperative school* (2nd ed.). Edina, MN: Interaction Book.

Johnson, S. D., Suriya, C., Yoon, S. W., Berrett, J. V., & LaFleur, J. (2002). Team development and group processes of virtual learning teams. *Computers and Education*, *29*, 379-393.

Kinsman, F. (1987). *The telecommuters*. Chichester, UK: John Wiley.

Kramer, R., & Brewer, M. (1984). Effects of group identity on resource use in a simulated commons dilemma. *Journal of Personality and Social Psychology, 46*, 1944-1057.

Lau, D. C., & Murnighan, J. K. (1998). Demographic diversity and fault lines: The compositional dynamics of organizational groups. *Academy of Management Review, 23,* 325-340.

Lawler, E. E. (1999). Employee involvement makes a difference. *The Journal for Quality and Participation*, *22*, 18-20.

Lee, Y., & Ottati, V. (1993). Determinants of in-group and out-group perceptions of heterogeneity: An investigation of Sino-American stereotypes. *Journal of Cross-Cultural Psychology*, *24,* 298-318.

Lipnack, J., & Stamps, J. (1997). *Virtual teams* (2nd ed.). New York: John Wiley.

Lengnick-Hall, C. A., & Sanders, M. M. (1997). Designing effective learning systems for management education: Student roles, requisite variety, and practicing what we teach. *Academy of Management Journal*, *40,* 1334-1368.

Majchrzak, A., Rice, R. E., King, N., & Ba, S. (2000). Technology adaptation: The case of a computer-supported inter-organizational virtual team. *MIS Quarterly, 24,* 569-600.

McGrath, J. E., & Hollingshead, A. E. (1994). *Group interacting with technologies: Ideas, evidence, issues, and agenda.* Thousand Oaks, CA: Sage.

Michaelson, L. K., Jones, C. F., & Watson, W. E. (1993). Beyond groups and cooperation: Building high performance learning teams. In D. L. Wright & J. P. Lunde (Eds.), *To improve the academy: Resources for faculty, instructional, and organizational development* (pp. 127-145). Stillwater, OK: New Forums.

Moreland, R. L. (2000). *Transactive Memory: Learning who knows what in work groups and organizations*. In L. Thompson, D. Messick, & J. Levine (Eds.), *Shared cognition in organizations: the management of knowledge* (pp. 3-31). Hillsdale, NJ: Lawrence Erlbaum.

Mugny, G., Sanchez-Mazas, M., Roux, P.,& Perez, J.A. (1991) Independence and interdependence of group judgments: Xenophobia and minority influence. *European Journal of Social Psychology, 21*, 213-223.

O'Neil, H. F., Allerd, K., & Baker, E. L. (1997). Review of workforce readiness theoretical frameworks. In H. F. O'Neil (Ed.) *Workforce readiness: Competencies and assessment* (pp. 3-25). Mahwah, NJ: Lawrence Erlbaum.

Ramsower, R. M. (1985). *Telecommuting: The organizational and behavioral effects of working at home.* Ann Arbor, MI: UMI Research.

Richter, J., & Meshulam, I. (1993). Telework at home: The home and the organization perspective. *Human Systems Management, 12,* 193-204.

Rock, K. W., & Pratt, M. G. (2002). Where do we go from here? On the relationship between identification and employee dispersion patterns. In G. Soenen & B. Moingeon (Eds.), *Organizational identities: An integrative perspective* (pp. 51-71). London: Routledge.

Rockmann, K. W., & Northcraft, G. B. (2005). The ethical implications of virtual interaction. In A. Tenbrunsel, E. Mannix, & M. Neale (Eds.), *Research on managing groups and teams, 7* (in press).

Rockmann, K., Pratt, M. G., & Northcraft, G. B. (2004). *Overcoming multiple subgroups in distributed teams: The impact of subgroup alignment and communication media on team identification and expertise recognition.* Working paper. University of Illinois.

Schmuck, R. A., & Schmuck, P. A. (1997). *Group processes in the classroom* (7th ed.). Chicago: Brown & Benchmark.

Schneider, S. K., & Northcraft, G. B. (1999). Three social dilemmas in managing the diverse organization: A social identity perspective. *Human Relations, 52*, 1445-1467.

Smith, K. G., Smith, K. A., Olian, J. D., Sims, H. P., O'Bannon, D. P., & Scully, J. A. (1994). Top management team demography and process: The role of social integration and communication. *Administrative Science Quarterly, 39*, 412-438.

Solomon, N. A., & Templer, A. J. (1993). Development of non-traditional work sites: The challenge of telecommuting. *The Journal of Management Development, 12,* 21-33.

Stasser, G., & Stewart, D. (1992). Discovery of hidden profiles by decision-making groups: Solving a problem versus making a judgment. *Journal of Personality and Social Psychology, 63*, 426-434.

Starbuck, W. H., & Milliken, F. J. (1988). Executives' perceptual filters: What they notice and how they make sense. In D.C. Hambrick (Ed.), *The executive effect: Concepts and methods for studying top managers.* Greenwich, CT: JAI.

Stevens, M. A., & Campion, M. J. (1994). The knowledge, skills, and ability requirements for teamwork: Implications for human resource management. *Journal of Management, 20*, 503-530.

Stunkel, K. R. (1998). Point of view. *Chronicle of Higher Education, 44,* A52.

Turner, J. C. (1985). Social categorization and the self-concept: A social cognitive theory of group behavior. In E. Lawler (Ed.), *Advances in Group Processes* (Vol. 2, pp. 77-122). Greenwich, CT: JAI.

Warkentin, M. F., Sayeed, L., & Hightower, R. (1997). Virtual teams versus face-to-face teams: An exploratory study of a Web-based conference system. *Decision Science, 28*, 975-996.

Wegner, D. M. (1987). Transactive memory: A contemporary analysis of the group mind. In B. Mullen & G. R. Goethals (Eds.), *Theories of group behavior* (pp. 185-208). New York: Springer-Verlag.

Zajonc, R. B. (1968). Attitudinal effects of mere exposure. *Journal of Personality and Social Psychology, 9*, 1-27.

Chapter VII

Computer-Supported Collaborative Learning:

The Role of the Instructor

Kara L. Orvis*
The Consortium of Universities of the D. C. Metro Area,
U. S. Army Research Institute, USA

Andrea L. R. Lassiter*
Minnesota State University - Mankato, USA

Abstract

In collaborative learning, interaction among learners is essential for effective knowledge acquisition and increased understanding. Computer Supported Collaborative Learning (CSCL) environments often inhibit or cause problems with learner-learner interactions. This chapter takes an applied perspective of what the instructor can do to identify and manage learner-learner relationships in a CSCL environment. Using a model of virtual team effectiveness, we identify potential motivational, cognitive, and affective problems between learners that are often exacerbated by computer-mediated technologies. Recommendations for instructor interventions designed to promote effective learner interactions are offered. This information will provide insight to both corporate trainers and K-12 educators on how instructors can promote appropriate and positive learner-learner interaction in CSCL environments.

Introduction

Computer-supported collaborative learning (CSCL) allows group learning to take place in computer-mediated environments. To receive the full benefit of social learning, collaborative learners must interact with each other, share information, and coordinate actions. Unfortunately, research has indicated that computer mediation contributes to potential barriers to learner-learner interaction. Specifically, members of computer-mediated teams tend to experience slower development of trust, cohesion, efficacy, and shared cognition, all of which impact whether learners interact effectively. A concern for instructional developers and designers is how to foster effective learner-learner interactions in CSCL environments.

This chapter proposes that instructors have the ability to influence and promote effective learner-learner interactions by identifying problems and stepping in to facilitate their processes. However, most CSCL course developers and instructors have not focused on the instructor's role of promoting learner-learner interaction. Rather, attention has been paid to the choice of technologies used to support this interaction, even though research on virtual teams has found that a leader is able to influence the processes (e.g., coordination and information sharing) and relationships (e.g., cohesion, efficacy, and trust) between team members (Zaccaro, Ardison, & Orvis, 2004; Orvis, 2004). This chapter will incorporate virtual team and CSCL research to focus on the role of the CSCL instructor as a promoter, facilitator, and manager of positive learner-learner relationships and interactions.

The specific objectives of this chapter will be to:

- Describe the importance of learner-learner interactions in collaborative learning environments

- Describe the influence of dispersion and computer-mediation on learner-learner processes
- Focus on the instructor's role in facilitating learner-learner processes
- Suggest practical guidelines for what an instructor can do to overcome problems with learner processes at the group level

Collaborative Learning

Learning is undoubtedly influenced by interactions. Whether in a traditional classroom setting or through computer-mediated learning technologies, we acquire knowledge through our interactions with others. The basis of collaborative learning is grounded in the belief that learning is a social, rather than an individual, phenomenon (Bonk & Cunningham, 1998). It is an interactive process where students work together to construct knowledge and solve problems, first through an expression of their ideas and then by way of an augmentation of those ideas as influenced by others. Through collaborative tasks such as discussing, summarizing, clarifying, and integrating course content into an overall framework, learners acquire knowledge and gain a deeper understanding of course material (Deatz & Campbell, 2001).

With the introduction of collaborative technologies, there are opportunities for collaborative learning to take place across barriers of time and space. CSCL allows for team learning through electronic means. In addition, many educators believe that CSCL environments are the most promising next generation of distance learning tools (Kreijns, Kirschner, & Jochems, 2002). However, the move to a computer-mediated environment raises some concerns. Collaborative learning is built on the premise that individual learning is promoted through group processing (Enerson, Johnson, Milner, & Plank, 1997). Therefore intra-group interaction is the key element (Kreijns, Kirschner, & Jochems, 2003), regardless of the technology used to support that interaction. Unfortunately much of the literature on dispersed collaborations has shown technology and dispersion makes traditional team processing more difficult (e.g., Avolio, Kahai, Surinder, Dumdum, & Sivasubramaniam, 2001; Webber, 2002), which is problematic, considering quality of the interactions determines the extent and depth of individual learning (e.g., Kreijns et al., 2003).

Kreijns et al. (2003) identified two major pitfalls to meaningful interaction in collaborative learning. The first is the common assumption that merely providing opportunity for collaboration will result in collaborative actions. However, classroom studies have found that the simple act of placing people in a team does not automatically promote cooperation and interaction (Johnson & Johnson, 1999). As an example, CSCL typically results in low participation rates and short discussion threads (Hewitt & Teplovs, 1999; Lipponen, 2001). The second pitfall is the tendency for instructors to restrict social interaction to cognitive processes while ignoring socio-emotional processes. This is a mistake; conditions such as cohesion and trust between team members must exist if students are to offer ideas, critique each other, and interpret critiques as valuable rather than personal insults (Rourke, 2000). Regrettably, these conditions often are absent or take longer to develop in computer-mediated environments (Webber, 2002). However, the CSCL instructor can play a part in making sure these two pitfalls do not interrupt or inhibit learner-learner interactions.

Key Points

- The extent to which students in a collaborative learning environment acquire knowledge and achieve a deeper understanding of content is dependent on the level and quality of interaction between learners.
- CSCL environments create difficulties in necessary learner-learner relationships and interactions.
- Instructors and course developers make the mistake of assuming interaction will take place if the technology supports it, and of ignoring socio-emotional processes between learners.

Instructor Role

There is little doubt that technology changes the role of the instructor (Palloff & Pratt, 1999). Not only do CSCL instructors need to be informed of the difference technology makes in their role as course designer, but instructors now need to take the role of interaction facilitator, rather than that of knowledge dispenser. Unfortunately, with the introduction of CSCL technology, attention is focused on the changes an instructor has to make as a course designer, rather than as an interaction facilitator. The majority of instructors are captivated by new technologies and increased choices for technology and pedagogy. The role of a CSCL instructor in promoting these interactions, outside of the technology or pedagogy, has been largely ignored. Once the course is designed and the technology chosen, instructors often sit back and wait for students to participate (Lane & Shelton, 2001), rather than actively engaging in leadership processes to promote and encourage effective interactions among learners.

As mentioned earlier, technology plays an important role in supporting collaborative learning, yet it does not ensure that interaction will take place. Relationships and conditions between students, such as social cohesion, shared cognition, and collective efficacy, dictate how and how well learners are able to work together to collaborate and share information. These processes in turn influence whether individual learners are able to benefit from the collaborative learning experience (Deatz & Campbell, 2001; Kreijns et al., 2003). A major concern for CSCL instructors should be how to promote essential learner-learner interactions by attending to the conditions and processes at the group level. Such attendance should ultimately influence the effectiveness of collaborative learning as it promotes the acquisition and understanding of content for the individual learner.

Given the unavailability of theoretical models which describe the relationship between instructors and student processes at the group level, we look to the virtual leadership and team literature for a framework of leadership and group process relevant to collaborative learning environments. Zaccaro, Rittman, and Marks (2001) proposed a framework which outlines the leader's contribution to team effectiveness by influencing team member processes. This model, which has been applied to virtual teams (Zaccaro et al., 2004), is based on functional leadership theory which proposes that the leader's main preoccupation should be to do, or get done, whatever functions are impeding group effectiveness. According to the Zaccaro et al. (2001) team leadership model, if problems with critical functions between group member interactions are identified, then leaders should facilitate or promote the appropriate quality of interactions. For example, if a team was performing poorly because team members were not sharing information, it would be the leader's responsibility to identify the cause. If the leader recognizes a lack of trust between team members, they should adjust trust levels within the team to improve team effectiveness. This adjustment of trust could take place through a number of leadership processes, whereby the efficacy of each is dependent on contextual influences. Rather than prescribing specific behaviors, one of the benefits of Functional Leadership Theory is that it leaves room for a number of ways in which a leader can accomplish a critical function.

In this chapter we propose an augmented version of the Zaccaro et al. (2001, 2004) model that is more relevant to instructors of computer supported collaborative learning teams. Whereas the Zaccaro et al. (2001, 2004) framework explains team effectiveness via group processes, when considering collaborative learning environments the outcome of interest is the knowledge gained by an individual learner. However, as team performance is dependent on the processes that take place between team members, the basic premise of collaborative learning suggests (and is further supported by research) that individual performance, as measured by knowledge acquisition and level of understanding, is also dependent on the processes that take place at the group level (Deatz & Campbell, 2001; Kreijns et al., 2003). Zaccaro et al. (2001) propose that leaders contribute to team effectiveness by influencing three team processes which ultimately drive coordination between team members: cognitive, motivational, and affective. As supported in the literature, collaborative learning teams must engage in similar sets of processes to achieve success at the level of the individual learner. If the requisite processes between students are not taking place, then individual performance, as it relates to individual knowledge, will suffer. Therefore, as a leader influences the processes that take place among team members to ensure team effectiveness, an instructor influences processes that take place among collaborative students to ensure the quality and depth of individual learning. The model in Figure 1 specifies these relationships.

Although CSCL instructors and team leaders are different in many respects, they are similar in their potential influence on group level processes and states. Just as a leader must attend to group processes to ensure team performance, instructors must facilitate individual learner effectiveness by shaping, directing, encouraging, and managing these same processes in CSCL environments. This is especially important in environments where people are dispersed and rely on technologies for interaction. Such environments influence the interactions taking place among learners. Therefore instructors can play an important role by attending to learner-learner interactions throughout the course. If they intervene where there are problems between learners, instructors have a chance to reverse the potentially negative effects of computer-supported environments and can better manage barriers to learner-learner interactions.

Figure 1. CSCL group characteristics and instructor-group relations as they influence individual learning (adapted from Zaccaro, Ardison, & Orvis, 2004).

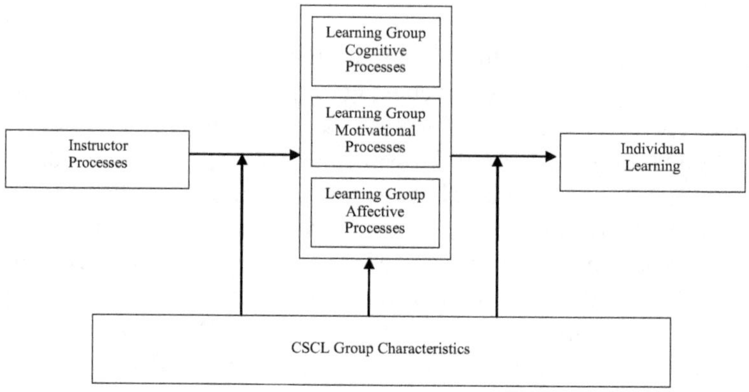

Key Points

- Technology has changed the role of the instructor
- More attention has been paid to the instructor as a course designer rather than as an interaction facilitator
- Instructors can play a significant part in influencing learner-learner interactions

Process of CSCL Student Interaction and Recommendations for Instructor Support

To determine appropriate instructor actions, first we must identify potential problems in learner-learner cognitive, motivational, and affective processing resulting from the nature of a CSCL environment. This section will detail the importance of learner-learner cognitive, motivational, and affective processes in promoting learner-learner interaction. A "key recommendations" section will provide general suggestions for instructor interventions to tackle these problems. The goal is to provide CSCL instructors with a guide for monitoring learner-learner relationships and interactions along with suggestions for interventions when problems occur. It is important to note that the suggestions made are not inclusive of all possible actions an instructor can take if there are problems at the group level (e.g., with cohesion). Given the complexities in situations, rather than prescribing one type of leadership or style, the virtual leader-team model suggests there are a number of ways in which an instructor can promote effective interactions.

Cognitive Processes

Cognitive processes involve collective information processing and the generation of shared knowledge. Although cognition has traditionally been examined as an individual mental process, recent attention has been paid to the socially distributed (or shared) nature of cognition among group members (Salomon, 1993). Some of the commonly discussed concepts of cognition among team members are shared mental models (e.g., Cannon-Bowers, Salas, & Converse, 1993) and transactive memory (e.g., Wegner, 1995). In CSCL environments, cognitive structures can include knowledge about the purpose of the group, characteristics of the task, linkages among group members, collective actions, and roles of team members (Klimoski & Mohammad, 1994). Similarity in these structures represents "sharedness" or common understanding of the group, their purpose, and how they should coordinate. When knowledge is shared, it contributes to effective group member coordination (Cannon-Bowers et al., 1993), because members are able to anticipate the behavior of other group members (Rentsch, Heffner, & Duffy, 1994). Shared knowledge also improves communication and processing required for successful collective performance and coordination (Klimoski & Mohammed, 1994), allowing many people to accomplish something that one person could not do alone.

Members of computer-mediated groups often take longer to develop shared cognition, leading to difficulties in early learner-learner interaction. This is especially true when groups are working on an unfamiliar task with unfamiliar members (Webber, 2002). When there is ambiguity in roles, group members may not act as others anticipated, because they did not know it was their job to get something done. This creates frustration for learning partners. Also, because they have not worked together before, assumptions may be made that group members all share the same information when they do not. Cascio (1999) and Hackman (1990) also note the importance of clear roles and leadership structures to minimize ambiguity about who decides what, especially in those teams that are physically separated (Oakley, 1998; Townsend, DeMarie, & Hendrickson, 1998). In such dispersed situations, a decreased awareness of others' actions is associated with a lack of rich cues, which are normally experienced in co-located team member interaction.

Structuring explicit rules of coordination and clarifying learner roles early on are crucial for dispersed learning groups who do not have time to identify roles and form norms about how to interact (Avolio et al., 2001). Given their status and power, instructors are an avenue through which structure can take place immediately (Feldman, 1984). Such early intervention can influence information sharing (Cramton & Orvis, 2003), build shared expectations (Avolio et al., 2001), influence team potency and performance (Sivasubramaniam, Murray, Avolio, & Jung, 2002), and support well being (Townsend et al., 1998). When an instructor provides group learners with role clarification, structure, and guidelines for how to work together early in the team's tenure, they are helping the group members develop shared cognitive structures of how they should interact with one another. Learners who do not receive this information will be less likely to have a shared understanding of interaction and will take longer to determine how to work together.

Key Recommendations for Instructors:

- Specify both academic objectives and teamwork skills objectives
- Explain and provide structure for academic tasks
- Structure well-defined patterns of communication
- Train learners how to work together as a collective
- Clarify roles of learners within the group, including role distinctions and role expectations
- Specify expected behaviors (e.g., within what timeframe learners must respond to an e-mail)
- Maintain frequent task-oriented communications, so that learners can monitor group and team member progress

- Provide a learner with a clear mission and specify the purpose and/or importance of interdependent interaction

Motivational Processes

Motivational processes involve the choice that team members make to engage in tasks and whether they will allocate resources toward task accomplishment (Kanfer & Ackerman, 1989). Although it is important that the learners know *how* interact effectively and have the technological resources to do so, they must also have the *desire* and *willingness* to coordinate their efforts to work collaboratively. Group learning effectiveness is grounded in the learners' collective effort to work hard on behalf of the group. Collective motivation originates from particular group states such as cohesion, trust, and collective efficacy. If such social needs are not met, learners are likely to be unwilling to take risks in collaborative learning, such as sharing information and depending on others (Wegerif, 1998).

Cohesion

One way to foster motivation is to facilitate the formation of team cohesion. Cohesion is most commonly defined as members liking for one another (Evans & Jarvis, 1980) and the extent to which group members are attracted to the group (Hogg, 1992). Cohesion has been found to be directly related to group functioning (e.g., Evans & Dion, 1991) as those with high levels of social cohesion tend to have more motivation to work together as a collective. In CSCL, students who are cohesive should be more willing to work hard on behalf of the group. They will be motivated to spend more time providing thoughtful contributions and engaging in meaningful dialogue, instead of giving half-hearted efforts toward their part of the task.

Computer-mediated environments often lead to lower levels of cohesion and members tend to like each other less than face-to-face groups (McGrath & Hollingshead, 1994). Computer-mediation decreases the opportunities for interaction, often inhibiting friendship formation. In addition, there is a decreased awareness of team members' actions and a reduction in an individual's self-awareness, promoting feelings of anonymity (McKenna & Green, 2002). Computer-mediated communications also tend to be more formal and task focused, with less time spent on socio-emotional processes. As a result, little social information is shared among group members and social relationships often develop more slowly over time (Lebie, Rhoades, & McGrath, 1996). Therefore, dispersed learners may experience increased ambiguity and artificiality (team opacity) associated with interaction in a computer-mediated environment (Fiore, Salas, Cuevas, & Bowers, 2003), and may be dissatisfied with the impersonal experience (Lebie et al., 1996).

A common suggestion for practitioners is that dispersed group members be allowed time early in their development to interact socially and to build interpersonal relationships (e.g., Jarvenpaa & Leidner, 1998; Walther & Burgoon, 1992). Sharing personal information at the beginning of team formation influences the liking of group members (Weisband & Atwater, 1999), boosts member satisfaction and communication (Kahai & Cooper, 1999), and increases feelings of social cohesion (Zaccaro & McCoy, 1998). Instructors, who facilitate a social environment in a CSCL team, can help learners feel that they are working with real individuals on the other end of the computer (Kimball & Eunice, 1999). This can be done by implementing routines of interaction and promoting a common identity (Axtell, Fleck, & Turner, 2004).

Trust

Trust is another important ingredient for motivation and effective interactions (Meyerson, Weick, & Kramer, 1996). It involves putting oneself in a position of risk and relying on others to honor commitments (Mayer, Davis, & Schoorman, 1995). Trust can be in the form of cognitive trust (based on expectation that others will be reliable and dependable) or affective trust (that others will reciprocate care and concern) (McAllister, 1995). Within computer-mediated environments, it is difficult for group members to monitor individual member actions, so group members must rely on trust more than control (Handy, 1995; Lipnack & Stamps, 1997). Unfortunately, low trust leads to excessive monitoring of others and duplication of effort (Ashforth & Lee, 1990). In addition, learners may be less willing to share information, which is critical for the construction of knowledge. Higher levels of trust also contribute to better interaction processes (e.g., less conflict and better group climate) and more effective progression toward task accomplishment (Jarvenpaa, Knoll, & Leidner, 1998).

However, evidence of the impact of computer mediation on trust is inconclusive (Wilson, Straus, & McEvily, 2002). Many have concerns that trust is difficult to develop in dispersed collaborations; however others have found that it does develop just as strongly as in face-to-face groups (Zheng, Bos, Olson, & Olson, 2001; Wilson et al., 2002). In addition, some researchers have found that trust is low early in a group's life span, developing slowly over time (Wilson et al., 2002), while others have found trust to be very strong at the beginning of a group's life span (McKnight, Cummings, & Chervany, 1998), even when there is no shared interaction history or shared personal knowledge. This notion of "swift trust" has been shown to be relatively fragile, and can unravel fairly easily (McKnight et al., 1998).

While there is no definitive understanding of trust mechanisms in dispersed environments, one thing is for sure: trust is important for learner-learner interaction. Instructors can facilitate the development of trust by encouraging the exchange of social information and by helping learners stay focused on the task (Jarvenpaa & Leidner, 1999). Development of cognitive-based trust can be fostered by demonstrating one's reliability and competence. On the other hand, development of affective-based trust can be fostered through a series of non-task contact and conversations. To do this, instructors should help learners engage in social dialog apart from the task and help encourage an understanding and appreciation of the unique perspectives each learner brings to the situation.

Efficacy

Collective efficacy, whether or not learners believe that together they can accomplish their tasks for successful outcomes (Bandura, 1986), influences to whether group members are willing to put effort toward the group. It is important that collaborative learning students believe they can form relationships with team members and work together to develop deeper levels of learning. Research on teams has shown a cyclical relationship between collective efficacy, performance, and coordination processes (e.g., Marks, 1999). When individuals are first brought together and experience ambiguity as to who should be doing what and at what time, they are likely to fail and feel as though their efforts are in vain. If individuals are not able to successfully work together, they will experience reduced feelings of efficacy, which will negatively influence later interactions and the spiral will continue downward. On the other hand, if students experience success in collaborating with one another, they are more likely to be efficacious about their ability to interact and be successful.

Computer-mediated environments may serve as a barrier to collective efficacy in several ways. First, when learners are dispersed and interacting through technology, the amount of unique information to be shared increases (Cramton & Orvis, 2003). There is also evidence that dispersed individuals are not able to share as much information as face-to-face teams early-on (Lebie et al., 1996; Webber, 2002), taking them longer to develop role and task norms. As a result, there is increased ambiguity regarding the task and the roles that each team member is responsible for (Avolio et al., 2001). Finally, by decreasing awareness of other learners' actions, there are limited opportunities for monitoring and evaluating other's performance, therefore hindering the development of positive collective efficacy (Fiore et al., 2003).

Clear definition of roles and knowledge of how to interact is imperative for developing collective efficacy. Instructors can help overcome barriers to collective efficacy by reducing ambiguity and establishing rules of interaction, such as encouraging the sharing of unique information. In this way, structuring group member interaction is particularly important for dispersed collaborative learning teams (e.g., Avolio et al., 2001). When an instructor provides structure for how interaction should occur, more effective interactions are likely to occur. Additionally, when interaction is successful near the beginning and performance is high, higher efficacy will be experienced and learning will continue to improve.

Key Recommendations for Instructors:

- Focus on learner-learner interaction as early as possible
- Emphasize the importance of learner-learner interactions in promoting individual learning
- Allow students some time in "getting to know you" activities
- Focus on the development and maintenance of swift trust
- Frame feedback in a way that helps students believe they can accomplish the tasks
- Identify learners who are not interacting and help them feel as though they are a part of the group
- Plan learning materials to emphasize a collective identity instead of an individual identity among learners
- Monitor and encourage full and complete information exchange and minimize biased discussions

- Encourage communication that confirms information receipts as well as provides information about local contextual constraints on other learners
- Routinize the use of e-mail, computer bulletin boards, chat rooms, and video and audio conferencing to monitor and record learner action and progress

Affective Processes

Affective processes refer to the expression and modulation of emotion and affect (Zaccaro et al., 2001). The emotional or affective climate within the team can greatly influence team effectiveness, information processing, and creativity (Rhoades & O'Conner, 1995). For example, a collective negative mood can be harmful by introducing personal conflict and a reduction in willingness to work together. In this way, negative affect leads to negative motivational and coordination processes, resulting in lower performance (George, 1990). Instructors can encourage healthy affective processes in learner interactions by promoting a collective positive mood. At the same time, instructors should promote a learning environment that prevents negative affect.

Group member interaction can be influenced by whether or not a positive mood exists. Specifically, a positive mood among CSCL learners should encourage more cooperation, more participation, less conflict, and stronger social cohesion (Carnevale & Isen, 1986; Rafaeli, & Sutton, 1989; Rhoades and O'Conner, 1995). In this situation, learners will be more willing to cooperate and participate in group level tasks and will likely experience less affective conflict and stronger social cohesion. Relational links between learners will lead to positive outcomes such as creativity and motivation, increased morale, better decisions, and less process loss (Walther & Burgoon, 1992).

Negative affect often results from working in a dispersed environment. Dispersed teams who are more temporary in nature tend to be task-oriented and exchange little social-emotional information, negatively effecting the development of relations among group members (Chidambaram, 1996). As mentioned previously, dispersed team members tend to be generally less satisfied than face-to-face teams (Wartiken, Sayeed, & Hightower, 1997) and tend to like each other less (Weisband & Atwater, 1999). In a dispersed environment they may also have inaccurate perceptions of other members and of the task (Reinig, Briggs, Shepherd, Yen, J., & Nunamaker, 1995), fostering weak relational links among learners (Warkentin, Sayeed, & Hightower, 1997).

Key Recommendations for Instructors:

- Develop electronic communication norms that emphasize mutual interaction and minimize affective conflict
- Foster strong relational links among learners to promote positive outcomes
- Confront negative emotion or affective conflict among learners quickly in order to maintain effective processes
- Convey enthusiastic messages encouraging collective effort
- Act as gatekeepers for all team members and avoid misinterpretations of silence and member non-responsiveness

Interdependency of Learner-Learner Processes

It is insufficient for an instructor to focus solely on one or two processes between learners. For example, members must be motivated to interact *and* must have the resources to interact. Often, there is a delicate balance of processes necessary to achieve the appropriate amount and types of interaction. In addition, attention to certain processes might be more important early in group formation rather than later. Ideally, in the ambiguous early stages of team development, leaders should be concerned both with how to work together, and with the team members' desire and motivation to work together. Groups with higher levels of social cohesion are more likely to be motivated to work together as a team, be willing to make mistakes, and be willing to ask for help. Groups who understand the structure of their interaction and the roles of each learner will know how to interact together. Therefore, groups who have instructors providing structure for interaction and facilitating a socially cohesive environment are likely to have learners who collaborate more so than in learning groups whose instructors do not attend to those functions.

It is important to point out that computer-mediated environments do not always lead to problems in group member relationships and willingness to interact. When groups are provided with enough time, are familiar with other members, and working on simple non-interdependent tasks, they are likely to function just as well as face-to-face groups (Webber, 2002). Therefore, the leader may not need to provide intervention at all or possibly only during the beginning stages of group formation. However, because of the increases in unique information, learner communication modes, and the likelihood that CSCL students will be working with students they do not know, the instructor needs to be aware of the areas in which problems may occur between learners.

Summary and Future Directions

Not only has the emergence of new technologies challenged the interactive processes of collaborative learners, but it has challenged and changed the instructor's role. Instructors must be more concerned with facilitating the interactions taking place between learners. Such concern includes identifying the potential pitfalls of computer-mediation on learner-learner interactions. Existing research suggests that problems with team processing and learner-learner interactions in CSCL can be overcome with appropriate leader behaviors.

Future research should continue to examine the role and duties of CSCL instructors and what can be done to better support learning in these environments. Without a doubt, learners need guidance on how to work together in computer-mediated environments, and instructors need to know how to provide such guidance. The goal of this chapter was to suggest ways that appropriate instructor behaviors can overcome problems associated with learner interaction processes in CSCL. By drawing on existing virtual team leadership and CSCL literatures we have provided a wide range of recommendations that instructors should consider to promote and manage effective learner-learner interactions.

References

Ashforth, B. E., & Lee, R. T. (1990). Defensive behavior in organizations—A preliminary model. *Human Relations, 43*(7), 621-648.

Avolio, B. J., Kahai, S., Surinder, K., Dumdum, R., & Sivasubramaniam, N. (2001). Virtual teams: Implications for e-leadership and team development. In M. London (Ed.), *How people evaluate others in organizations* (pp. 337-358). Mahwah, NJ: Lawrence Erlbaum.

Axtell, C. M., Fleck, S. J., & Turner, N. (2004). Virtual teams: Collaborating across distance. In C. L. Cooper & L. T. Robertson (Eds.), *International review of organizational psychology* (Vol. 19, pp. 205-248). Chichester, UK: John Wiley.

Bandura, A. (1986). *Social foundations of thought and action: A cognitive theory.* Englewood Cliffs, NJ: Prentice-Hall.

Bonk, C. J., & Cunningham, D. J. (1998). Searching for learner-centered, constructivist, and sociocultural components of collaborative educational learning tools. In C. J. Bonk & K. S. King (Eds.), *Electronic collaborators: Learner-centered technologies for literacy, apprenticeship, and discourse* (pp. 25-50). Mahwah, NJ: Lawrence Erlbaum.

Cannon-Bowers, J. A., Salas, E., & Converse, S. (1993). Shared mental models in expert team decision making. In N.J. Castellan, Jr. (Ed.), *Current issues in individual and group decision making* (pp. 221-246). Hillsdale, NJ: Lawrence Erlbaum.

Carnevale, P. J. D., & Isen, A. M. (1986). The influence of positive effect and visual access on the discovery of integrative solutions in bilateral negotiations. *Organizational Behavior and Human Decision Processes, 37*, 1-13.

Cascio, W. F. (1999). Virtual workplaces: Implications for organizational behavior. In C. L. Cooper & D. M. Rousseau (Eds.), *Trends in organizational behavior* (Vol. 6, pp. 1-14). Chichester, UK: John Wiley.

Chidambaram, L. (1996). Relational development in computer-supported groups. *MIS Quarterly, 20*(2), 143-163.

Cramton, C. D., & Orvis, K. L. (2003). Overcoming barriers to information sharing in virtual teams. In C. Gibson & S. Cohen (Eds.), *Creating conditions for effective virtual teams.* San Francisco: Jossey-Bass.

Deatz, R. C., & Campbell, C. H. (2001). *Application of cognitive principles in distributed computer-based training* (Research Product 2001-03). Alexandria, VA: U. S. Army Research Institute for the Social and Behavioral Sciences.

Enerson, D., Johnson, R.N., Milner, S., & Plank, K. (1997). *The Penn State Teacher II: Learning to Teach; Teaching to Learn.* University Park, PA: Center for Excellence in Learning and Teaching, Pennsylvania State University.

Evans, C. R., & Dion, K. L. (1991). Group cohesion and performance: A meta-analysis. *Small Group Research, 22,* 175-186.

Evans, C. R., & Jarvis, P. A. (1980). Group cohesion: A review and re-evaluation. *Small Group Behavior, 11,* 359-370.

Feldman, D. C. (1984). The development and enforcement of group norms. *Academy of Management Review, 9*(1), 47-53.

Fiore, S. M., Salas, E., Cuevas, H. M., & Bowers, C. A. (2003). Distributed coordination space: Toward a theory of distributed team process and performance. *Theoretical Issues in Ergonomic Science, 4*, 340-363.

George J. M. (1990). Personality, affect, and behavior in groups. *Journal of Applied Psychology, 75*, 107-116.

Hackman, J. R. (1990). Work teams in organizations: An orienting framework. In J. R. Hackman (Ed.), *Groups that work (and those that don't)* (pp. 1-14). San Francisco: Jossey-Bass.

Handy C. (1995). Trust and the virtual organization. *Harvard Business Review, 73*, 40-49.

Hewitt, J., & Tevlops, C. (1999). An analysis of growth patterns in computer conferencing threads (pp. 232–241). *Proceedings of Computer Support for Collaborative Learning: Designing New Media for a New Millennium: Collaborative Technology for Learning, Education, and Training*. Palo Alto, CA.

Hogg, M. A. (1992). *The social psychology of group cohesiveness: For attraction to social identify.* London: Harvester Wheatsheaf.

Jarvenpaa, S. L., & Leidner, D. E. (1999). Communication and trust in global virtual teams. *Organization Science, 10,* 791-815.

Jarvenpaa S. L., Knoll K., & Leidner D. E. (1998). Is anyone out there? Antecedents of trust in global virtual teams. *Journal of Management Information Systems, 14*, 29-64.

Johnson, D. W., & Johnson, R. T. (1999). *Learning together and alone: Cooperative, competitive, and individualistic learning* (5th ed.). Boston: Allyn & Bacon.

Kahai, S., & Cooper, R. A. (1999). The effect of computer mediated communication on agreement and acceptance. *Journal of Management Information Systems, 16,* 165-188.

Kanfer, R., & Ackerman, P. L. (1989). Motivational and cognitive abilities: An integrative/aptitude treatment interaction approach to skill acquisition. *Journal of Applied Psychology, 74*, 657-690.

Kimball, L., & Eunice, A. (1999). The virtual team: Strategies to optimize performance. *Health Forum Journal, 42*(3), 58-62.

Klimoski, R., & Mohammad , S. (1994). Team mental model: Construct or metaphor? *Journal of Management, 20,* 403-437.

Kreijns, K., Kirschner, P. A., & Jochems, W. (2002). The sociability of computer-supported collaborative learning environments. *Journal of Education Technology & Society, 5*, 8-22.

Kreijns, K., Kirschner, P. A., & Jochems, W. (2003). Identifying the pitfalls for social interaction in computer-supported collaborative learning environments: A review of the research. *Computers in Human Behavior, 19*, 335-353.

Lane, D. R., & Shelton, M. W. (2001). The centrality of communication education in classroom computer-mediated-communication: Toward a practical and evaluative pedagogy. *Communication Education, 50*, 241-255.

Lebie L., Rhoades, J. A., & McGrath, J. E. (1996). Interaction Process in Computer-Mediated and Face-to-Face groups. *Computer Supported Cooperative Work, 4*, 127-152.

Lipnack, J., & Stamps, J. (1997). *Virtual teams: Reaching across space, time, and organizations with technology.* New York: Wiley.

Lipponen, L. (2001). *Computer-Supported Collaborative Learning: From Promises to Reality*. Turku: Department of Education, Report 245.

Marks, M. A. (1999). A test of the impact of collective efficacy in routine and novel performance environments. *Human Performance, 12*(3-4), 295-309.

Mayer, R. C., Davis, J. H., & Schoorman, F. D. (1995). An integrated model of organizational trust. *Academy of Management Review, 20*, 709-734.

McAllister, D. J. (1995). Affect and cognition based trust as foundations for interpersonal cooperation in organizations. *Academy of Management Journal, 38*(1), 24-59.

McGrath, J. E., & Hollingshead, A. B. (1994). *Groups interacting with technology ideas, evidence, issues, and an agenda.* Thousand Oaks, CA: Sage.

McKenna, K. Y. A., & Green, A. S. (2002). Virtual group dynamics. *Group Dynamics: Theory, Research and Practice*, 6, 116-127

McKnight, D. H., Cummings, L. L., & Chervany, N. L. (1998). Initial trust formation in new organizational relationships. *Academy of Management Review, 23*(3), 473-490.

Meyerson, D., Weick, K. W., & Kramer, R. (1996). Swift trust and temporary groups. In R. M. Kramer & T. R. Tyler (Eds.), *Trust in organizations: Frontiers of theory and research* (pp. 166-195). Thousand Oaks, CA: Sage.

Oakley, J. G. (1998). Leadership processes in virtual teams and organizations. *Journal of Leadership Studies, 5*(3), 3-17.

Orvis, K. L. (2004). Leadership and team performance in collocated and distributed teams. Doctoral dissertation, George Mason University. *Dissertations Abstracts International.*

Palloff, R. M., & Pratt, K. P. (1999). *Building learning communities in cyberspace: Effective strategies for the online classroom.* San Francisco: Jossey-Bass.

Rafaeli A. & Sutton R. I. (1989). The expression of emotional expression in organizational life. In B. M. Staw & L. L. Cummings (Eds.), *Research in organizational behavior* (Vol. 11, pp. 1-42). Greenwich, CT: JAI.

Reinig, B. A., Briggs, R. O., Shepherd, M. M., Yen, J., & Nunamaker, J. F. (1995). Developing and validating an instrument to measure the impact of group support technology on affective reward. *HICSS 4*, 798-807.

Rentsch, J. R., Heffner, T. S., & Duffy, L. T. (1994). What you know is what you get from experience. *Group and Organization Management, 19*(4), 450-474.

Rhoades, J. A., & O'Connor, K. M. (1995). Affect in computer-mediated and face to face work groups: The construction and testing of a general model. *Computer Supported Cooperative Work, 4*, 203-228.

Rourke, L. (2000). *Operationalizing social interaction in computer conferencing.* Retrieved November 11, 2004, www.ulaval.ca/aced2000cade/english/proceedings.html.

Salomon, G. (1993). No distribution without individual's cognition: A dynamic interaction view. In G. Salomon (Ed.), *Distributed cognitions. Psychological and educational considerations* (pp. 111-138). Cambridge: Cambridge University.

Sivasubramaniam, N., Murray, W. D., Avolio, B. J., & Jung, D. I. (2002). A longitudinal model of the effects of team leadership and group potency on group performance. *Group and Organization Management, 27*(1), 66-96.

Townsend, A., DeMarie, S., & Hendrickson, A. (1998). Virtual teams: Technology and the workplace of the future. *Academy of Management Executive, 12,* 17-29.

Walther, J. B., & Burgoon, J. K. (1992). Relational communication in computer-mediated interaction. *Human Communication Research, 19*(1), 50-88.

Warkentin, M. E., Sayeed, L., & Hightower, R. (1997). Virtual teams versus face-to-face teams: An exploratory study of a web-based conference system. *Decision Sciences, 28*, 975-996.

Webber, S. S. (2002). Virtual Teams: A meta-analysis. In R. J. Klimoski (Chair) & B. Avolio (Discussant) (Eds.), *Virtual teams: The hidden truth.* Symposium conducted at the Academy of Management Conference, Denver, CO.

Wegerif, R. (1998). The social dimension of asynchronous learning networks. *Journal of Asynchronous Learning Networks, 2*(1), 34-49.

Wegner, D. M. (1995). A computer network model of human transactive memory. *Social Cognition, 13*(3), 319-339.

Weisband, S., & Atwater, L. (1999). Evaluating self and others in electronic and face-to-face groups. *Journal of Applied Psychology, 84*, 632-639.

Wilson, J. M., Straus, S. G., & McEvily, B. (2002). *All in due time: The development of trust in electronic and face to face groups.* Academy of Management Conference, Denver, CO.

Zaccaro, S. J., & McCoy, M. C. (1988). The effects of task and interpersonal cohesiveness on performance of a disjunctive group task. *Journal of Applied Social Psychology, 18*, 837-851.

Zaccaro, S. J., Ardison, S. D., & Orvis, K. L. (2004). Leadership in virtual teams. In D. Day, S. Zaccaro, & S. Halpin (Eds.), *Leader development for transforming organizations* (pp. 267-292). Mahway, NJ: Lawrence Erlbaum.

Zaccaro, S. J., Rittman, A. L., & Marks, M. A. (2001). Team leadership. *The Leadership Quarterly, 12*, 451-483.

Zheng, J., Bos, N., Olson, J. S., & Olson, G. M. (2001). *Trust without touch: Jump-start trust with social chat.* CHIOI Conference on Human Factors in Computing Systems, Seattle, WA.

Endnote

* Kara L. Orvis, Research and Advanced Concepts Office, The Consortium of Universities of the Washington D.C. Area and The United States Army Research Institute; Andrea L. R. Lassiter, Department of Psychology, Minnesota State University - Mankato.

Kara L. Orvis is now at Aptima in the Organizational Effectiveness Division.

This document represents the opinions of the authors at the time of publication. It does not necessarily represent the position of the U.S. Army Research Institute for the Behavioral and Social Sciences, Department of the Army or Department of Defense.

Correspondence concerning this chapter should be addressed to Kara L. Orvis, 12 Gill Street, Suite 1400, Woburn, MA (korvis@aptima.com).

Chapter VIII

A Blueprint for Assessing Learning in Virtual Teams

Patricia J. O'Connor
Queens College, City University of New York, USA

Susan H. Godar
William Paterson University, USA

If you don't know where you're going, any road will get you there.
Lewis Carroll

Abstract

Beginning with an explanation of the concepts and strategies of outcomes assessment, this chapter shows how using assessment can assist in maximizing learning gains from virtual teams. Using as an example a course in Global Marketing, we show ways of concretizing the goal of teaching effective teamwork, designing a course to assist rather than to impede learning, and using assessment both to improve student performance while a class is running and to revise the next iteration of the course. Finally, we offer a series of prompts designed to assist faculty in using outcomes assessment techniques to shape their own courses.

Introduction

If asked their pedagogical purpose in using virtual teams, many faculty have only vague responses to make—perhaps because the question seems almost nonsensical. Surely, respondents may think, there are only a couple of things to say here. One is that virtual teams harness the power of collaborative learning: students learn more of the course's content than they would if working alone. The other is that students learn teamwork skills. What other purposes could there be? It is our contention that if faculty make good use of outcomes assessment techniques, beginning with specifying concretely and in detail why they are using virtual teams, they will have a better understanding of what they are trying to accomplish by using them—and have a much better chance of helping their students to achieve those learning objectives.

The first problem addressed by outcomes assessment is this: pedagogical elements such as overall course design, team assignments, and the way the work of the virtual teams is structured can be powerful ways to assist student learning—or they can be massive impediments to student learning. When faculty fail to specify very clear objectives to be accomplished using virtual teams, the fact that any of these components of a course actually helps students to learn what they are intended to learn is, at best, a happy accident. The second problem is that without a clear idea what students should gain from participating in virtual teams, it is unclear how faculty can know to what degree this pedagogical strategy is successful. Since, after all, using virtual teams is more complex (and frequently more worrisome) than many other teaching methods, we want to be certain that it achieve its maximum potential benefit for student learning.

This chapter shows how to use outcomes assessment strategies to maximize student learning in virtual teams. We focus on the second of the two goals cited above—teamwork skills—because it is common to all faculty who use virtual teams. Effective teamwork can be characterized as a "process goal," an attempt to inculcate or to improve the skills students must use while carrying out the process of working together. Often, faculty are not very experienced in assisting students to learn these skills. In contrast, the first response — that virtual teams increase the amount of knowledge students gain (over what they would learn if working alone) — can be thought of as a "product goal." Working in teams produces increased learning of course content. Faculty are experienced at evaluating these knowledge gains. Moreover, along this latter dimension the learning being measured varies with discipline and course. By focusing on teamwork skills, this chapter concentrates on using assessment techniques to improve learning in an area where faculty tend to be less experienced, and where they share a goal.

This is not to say that the approach outlined here cannot be applied to discipline- and course-specific knowledge goals. Not only can it be so applied, but it should be. There is a simple, powerful reason why most regional and discipline-specific accrediting agencies have begun to concentrate on outcomes rather than on "inputs" (e.g., qualifications of faculty, number and type of journals in the library, number of contact hours). There is no necessary correlation between quality of inputs and academic institutions or programs achieving their mission. Accrediting agencies and funding bodies — whether granting or legislative — want to know that the inputs purchased with their dollars are resulting in student learning. Hence, the focus has become outcomes. Faculty who have not yet been confronted with the necessity of using outcomes assessment techniques to show that their students are mastering the content of their courses will soon come under increasing pressure to do just that. They may make use of strategies detailed here, for showing teamwork skills results, to show knowledge goals results.

We begin with a brief account of the concepts and strategies of outcomes assessment, focused on those aspects which are of utility in assessing learning in virtual teams. For some faculty — for example, those whose institutions lie in one of the geographic regions covered by an accrediting body that has long required outcomes assessment — this section will function as a review. For others, it will be an introduction to assessment. Next, we use these assessment strategies on a sample course, Global Marketing, showing how the overall course design, assignments, and structure of the virtual teams' work all cohere to increase the likelihood that students will in fact achieve the specific learning objectives that are the reason why the instructor uses virtual teams in the course. We conclude with a series of prompts designed to assist faculty in using outcomes assessment techniques to shape their own use of virtual teams in a manner that will increase student learning.

Concepts and Strategies of Outcomes Assessment

Outcomes assessment expands the process in which most faculty who seek to enhance student learning already engage. They review how well students are learning, reflect on whether they are satisfied with that level of achievement, and — when they are not — revise their pedagogy or course content to increase learning, either while the course is running or in the next iteration. For many faculty, however, this process is both solitary and more a matter of trial and error experimentation with changes than based upon concrete information.

Assessment makes two changes to the familiar process. First, assessment adds a component: placing courses in the context of the academic programs of which they are a part. Thus, it requires that in designing a course, faculty align its learning objectives with the learning goals of the department or program in which the course has its home. The distinction between "goals" and "objectives" is crucial, for if it is not made faculty will find themselves no closer to a specific and concrete understanding of what they want students to learn in their course than the generalities of "more content" and "teamwork skills" with which this chapter began. A learning goal is non-specific and often abstract. As such, it admits of multiple possible interpretations. This is in fact one of its strengths, for in the context of assessment this feature of learning goals enfranchises faculty: it allows them to decide, and to specify concretely, what contribution they and their courses can make to students' achieving the goal. Those statements of the specific contribution are learning objectives.

To see how this works, consider the learning goal "effective writing." Most academic institutions have this as one of their goals for general education. Students, we agree, should by the time they graduate from our institutions be effective writers. But what exactly does this mean, and how can we tell whether a general education course is in fact helping our students to become effective writers? Faculty in English, teaching the required composition course, may interpret the goal as meaning that students should be able to write an acceptable five-paragraph essay. Faculty in Philosophy, teaching the required ethics course, may interpret the goal as meaning that students should be able to write a single paragraph in which they cogently argue that a given action is either ethical or unethical. Both sets of faculty are correct, even while the learning objectives of the two courses are different.

In the first course, the generality "effective writing" turns into the specificity "students will be able to write a standard five-paragraph essay." In the second, it becomes "students will be able to argue persuasively for or against the ethics of a particular action." Students in both classes are indeed progressing toward the institution's general education goal of effective writing. English's learning objective assists students to achieve an aspect of the goal best suited to the discipline. Philosophy's is an aspect best suited to that discipline. Faculty in the respective disciplines are highly competent to assist student learning in exactly these ways, and well able to recognize both the degree to which it has taken place and how to enhance incomplete learning. When faculty make the pedagogical choice to use virtual teams, outcomes assessment suggests that they should not only know how using them fits within the learning goals of the department or program in which their course is situated, but make that "fit" explicit by a specific and concrete articulation of one or more learning objectives.

The second change assessment makes to the familiar review/reflect/revise process in which faculty already engage begins with the requirement that they collect information on student performance. The use of this information then changes the rest of the process. Review can be based on solid information rather than general impressions or recollections. Reflection is on how to improve the achievement of specific knowledge or skills objectives. Revision consists of targeted changes to bring about a concrete result.

The information of interest in assessment reflects these uses. What is collected is not student course grades, or even student grades on a particular project. In grading, the entirety of the student's response to an assignment is evaluated. All the knowledge, skills, and abilities made manifest in the work are taken into account. In assessment, on the other hand, all that is evaluated is the student's mastery of a single learning objective. At most institutions, there are a minimum of 12 possible grades that can ultimately be assigned (A-F, with pluses and minuses). In assessment, the maximum number of evaluative levels needed is three: not good enough, good enough, and better than good enough.

Assessment provides sufficient information to make an informed judgment about whether students need additional opportunities to achieve mastery of a particular learning objective. Moreover, its focus on that single objective helps faculty to pinpoint the differences between work that is already at least "good enough" and work that is not — and thus helps us to know what feedback to students, or changes in course or assignment design, are most likely to lead to learning that meets or exceeds our intended outcome on a particular learning objective.

Using Assessment Strategies to Structure the Course

With this discussion of how outcomes assessment focuses and concretizes faculty attempts to improve student learning, we can now turn our attention to a specific course that uses virtual teams. The Global Marketing course is a required course within the Marketing concentration, which is one element within the B.S. in Business Administration at William Paterson University. In the B.S. program, one of the goals is "effective teamwork." In Global Marketing, this goal is concretized as learning objectives that appear on the syllabus for the course. Each fragment below is the completion of a sentence that begins "By the end of the course students will be able to:

- Listen respectfully to the ideas of others.
- Comment respectfully on the ideas of others.
- Work together to solve a problem.
- Explain barriers to and facilitators of successful [international] virtual team communication."

The first three objectives clearly aim at fundamental skills necessary for successful teamwork. The final objective, however, is different from these. It requires not that students develop competence in skills, but that they reflect on — and draw conclusions from — their experiences while working in teams. Adopting such an objective represents an attempt to increase the likelihood that students will transfer what they have learned about teamwork in this class not only to other classes, but also to the world outside the classroom. The content-based learning objectives for Global Marketing are not included in the list above because of this chapter's focus on the goal that most courses using virtual teams will have in common.

Students on virtual teams in the Global Marketing course are encouraged to cooperate by the how teamwork is structured. In an article that has become a classic in management literature, Kerr (1995) talks about the folly of rewarding individual effort while hoping for teamwork. He contends that reward systems are frequently set up to promote being a star player rather than a team player. The Global Marketing instructor, mindful of this, has attempted to make certain that all aspects of the course, from how discussion is conducted to the channels by which feedback is given, reward cooperation and respectful listening/commenting while students are working in teams. She has also tried, via gradually increasing the difficulty level of assignments, to make certain that by the time students reach "crisis points" late in the semester they will have established a level of trust within their teams that means they will work together even when not directed to do so.

Global Marketing students are placed in small (five- to six-person) discussion groups in a Blackboard environment. Each week, groups must discuss a question posed by the instructor. In some semesters, students also participate in an international cross-cultural project with students from other countries. (In these cases "international" is included in the fourth objective.) In others, the students instead engage, as individuals, in a simulation exercise on marketing in foreign countries. (In these semesters "international" is omitted from the objective.) Within the context of the discussion question assignment, individuals are not rewarded for behaviors other than respectful listening and comments that seek to deepen or enhance the intra-team conversation.

Students are not, for example, given credit or points for being first to post a response to the question. Nor do any components of the team assignments encourage students to develop other skills that might be useful to them in a business environment, such as the ability to discern how much each of their teammates are contributing to the discussion. Instead, all elements of the assignments, as well as expectations of and rewards for behavior, focus on building trust, respectful communication, and collaboration.

Conducting Assessment During a Class

One of the advantages of virtual teams, from an assessment point of view, is the ability to have an accurate record of the discussions that have occurred within the team. In F2F teams, unless there is a secretary taking excellent notes of all exchanges, much information is lost. In virtual teams, the computer (via a course management system or an e-mail file system) maintains the exchanges.

It is, therefore, relatively easier to gather data for assessment of the first two items in the list of learning outcomes than it might be in a regular classroom setting. The method used is simply reading the exchanges that take place and evaluating whether students have "listened respectfully" and "commented respectfully."

Since the assignment is to discuss possible answers to the question posted by the instructor, respectful listening and commenting is measured by the appropriate use or mention of one student's postings in the posted response of another student. For example, student A might say that she believes something to be true. Students B and C might then take up positions opposing A's. They show respectful listening by accurately depicting A's ideas. They show respectful commenting by offering criticism of the ideas (rather than of A), and by trying to supplement or modify the ideas when possible (rather than by portraying their own ideas as a complete departure from A's — unless, of course, they are).

The rubric for assessing how well students are achieving the learning objective "listen respectfully" is not complex. Inaccurate renditions of the first student's statement show that others are not listening, and that the attainment of the learning objective is "not good enough." An accurate and polite restatement of the idea shows that B and C's work is "good enough." Doing things like asking student A to clarify or expand on her ideas, thereby deepening and enhancing the conversation, shows that B and C are doing "better than good enough." A similar rubric is used for "comment respectfully."

Since the skills of respectful listening and commenting are sine qua non for effective teamwork, it is not possible to wait for the next iteration of Global Marketing to assist students whose achievement of these objectives is not good enough. Waiting would jeopardize both the teamwork and the knowledge learning objectives of the course! This is a case in which the instructor must intervene while class is in progress. Intervention takes the form of a paragraph included either in a general posting to the group or in an e-mail to an individual.

In the public paragraphs, students are praised for positive efforts (e.g., "Your discussion of X showed that you had good grasp of the concepts"). When a majority of team members need to improve their skills in a particular area, this guidance is also given publicly. For example, the instructor might say to the team as a whole: "You need to build upon the ideas of others rather than just making statements of your own position. Remember that this is to be a conversation, a discussion like you might have in any other class." When an individual's performance is not good enough, however, the instructor's critique — for example, "Your comments about Y were harsh and might be misunderstood. Don't attack the messenger; attack the message" — is sent as a private communication.

Assessment of the third objective is conducted later in the semester, after students have developed some expertise in elementary teamwork skills and have worked together on small, contained tasks such as the one described above. At this point, the students are ready to attempt a task closer to the ill-formed, ambiguous problems with multiple possible answers that actually confront marketers working in the global economy. Here the "eavesdropping" technique of gathering assessment information, which takes place while students are engaged in the task, is applied at what the instructor knows — but the students do not — to be points at which the work becomes very difficult.

The object of listening in at these times is to collect information about whether students will now spontaneously seek to work together to solve problems. The instructor's eavesdropping, conducted on the informal exchanges that students post to one another when they reach critical junctures in either the international collaboration project or in the simulation exercise on marketing in foreign countries, does indeed show that students turn to one another, unbidden, for advice on how to solve problems. They post questions to others in their group to solicit this advice, and teammates respond. Thus, assessment makes clear that by this point in the semester, through practice gained on earlier, well-formed tasks, students have gained a modicum of both trust and expertise in teamwork — enough so that they spontaneously use it to solve problems, in preference to struggling with them alone.

The last of the learning objectives is best assessed by means of an individual assignment. It is important to determine the degree to which each student understands the barriers to and facilitators of successful [international] virtual team communication, since each of them as an individual needs to transfer what she or he has learned about teamwork not only to other classes, but also to the world of business. Students submit a paper of approximately five pages in which they briefly enumerate the barriers and facilitators they have identified, then choose one from each of the two categories to explain in greater detail. The detailed discussion must include not only a short narrative explaining how the barrier/facilitator manifested during the team process, but what its effect was, and — in the case of the barrier — how the student himself or herself might have intervened to change the outcome.

A summary of the assessment carried out within Global Marketing, and how it is used to improve student learning, is depicted in Table 1.

Using Assessment After Class Completion

The assessment information collected by the instructor shows that by the end of the semester, most students in the Global Marketing class are able to achieve at the level of "good enough" or "better than good enough" on learning objectives one through three, and hence have made measurable progress toward the "effective teamwork" learning goal of the Business curriculum. In part, the progress is due to being clear about how this goal is to be concretized in the context of this course. It seeks to develop fundamental teamwork skills of respect and cooperation. Progress also results from using assessment information to give formative feedback during the course. Students who are not yet listening and commenting respectfully are encouraged to work harder on those skills, while those who are doing well are publicly praised.

The instructor's assessment work currently shows, however, that most students in the Global Marketing class are not achieving at the level of "good enough" or "better than good enough" on learning objective four. Briefly, the assessment data show the following: many students cannot name more than three facilitators (two of which typically are the skills articulated in first two learning objectives — most commonly, the other is "getting work done on time"). They have even more difficulty identifying barriers—other than the opposites of the three facilitators — and when it comes to imagining how they might have intervened to surmount a barrier students' comments are rarely insightful.

Table 1.

Learning Objective	Tool for Assessment	Feedback and Effect
Listen respectfully	Student discussions in response to instructor's question	Provided to students while class is running, to increase learning
Comment respectfully	Student discussions in response to instructor's question	Provided to students while class is running, to increase learning
Work together	Unprompted student postings/e-mails to one another	Instructor uses to determine whether teamwork structures have produced trust or should be changed in subsequent course iterations.
Communication strategies	Individual student papers	Instructor uses to determine whether students are likely to be able to transfer the teamwork skills learned during the class. If not, changes should be made in subsequent iterations.

Since the instructor believes that enabling students to transfer the skills they have gained by working in their virtual teams is important, she must make changes to the course — and she must do so without disturbing already satisfactory student achievement on the first three objectives. While this may seem difficult, in fact the assessment data, in conjunction with the current assignments in the course, clearly show the direction to be taken. As currently designed, the course contains only one assignment requiring students to reflect on whether team communication is effective, and this is both the last, and an individual, assignment. Chances are that students would be much better equipped to succeed on this assignment if they had more opportunities to do reflective analysis. They might also develop better skills if, at least initially, they practiced within the context of their teams rather than as individuals.

Mindful of not doing anything that might cause intra-team competition, the instructor will avoid one obvious "reflection" assignment: having each team, later in the semester, analyze one of its own early discussions. Instead, she can do one of two things. First, utilizing again the advantage of having an electronic record of discussions within teams, she can take an exchange from a different semester, change the names of the participants, and send it to all the current teams for analysis. Or, she can herself write a "team discussion." Each strategy has advantages and drawbacks. Either will give students practice in reflecting on communication barriers and facilitators. Neither need add to student (or instructor) workload, as this reflective analysis can simply replace one of the existing discussion question assignments.

Applying Assessment to Courses Using Virtual Teams

The instructor of the Global Marketing class has used — and continues to use — the techniques of outcomes assessment to augment the familiar faculty pattern of review/reflect/revise. When designing the course she has concretized the goal of "effective teamwork" and carefully structured team interactions to enhance collaboration rather than to arouse competition. While the class is in progress she has used assessment information to provide formative feedback to students so that they can make progress toward the first three learning objectives. Toward the end of the course she has gathered information that shows her course design and assignments do result in students spontaneously working together to solve problems. Finally, her assessment shows that she must change the course in order to improve students' chances of being able to transfer the skills they have learned while working in virtual teams. Outcomes assessment works for this instructor — and for the students in Global Marketing.

The first step in using outcomes assessment is always concretizing the learning goal: turning it into one or more objectives that state specifically and concretely the knowledge or skills that we want students to develop in a course. "Effective teamwork" is a goal. Each instructor must decide for himself or herself, however, how to translate that into learning objectives. This effort of translation may be made easier by reflecting on two things: first, the assignments used in the course; secondly, how the work of teams is structured.

Since assignments are designed to allow students to develop skills, or show to what degree they have already developed them, existing assignments can provide a number of clues about the specific teamwork skills the course seeks to build. For example, given the discussion question assignments of the current version of Global Marketing, we can see that the course is trying to develop the basic skills necessary for successful teamwork (first and second learning objectives). When the "reflective analysis" discussion is added, that assignment will show that the instructor is trying to develop, rather than simply to test for the presence or absence of, the skill of identifying barriers to and facilitators of communication.

How teamwork is structured may also provide clues to a course's learning objectives. If students are asked to evaluate each other's performance, for example, this may show that an instructor intends that students learn how to manage or facilitate a virtual team, rather than only how to be a productive member of one. Or students may be encouraged by team structure to practice higher-order teamwork skills, such as consensus-testing or norm-setting, rather than (or in addition to) fundamental skills.

Once the learning objectives have been identified, the next step in using assessment techniques is to make certain that the course assignments and structure truly are aligned in an optimum manner, where that is defined as the way in which students are most likely to achieve the objectives at least at the level of "good enough." It is important to recognize that often a wholesale redesign of the course is not necessary at this point. Through their existing review/reflect/revise process, faculty who have repeatedly taught a course may have refined it to such an extent that, without doing actual assessment and looking at the resulting information, it is difficult to determine what should be changed to improve student learning.

What often does need to be done at this juncture, however, is determining what counts as "better than good enough," "good enough," and "not good enough" levels of achievement. This is sometimes surprisingly difficult to do, not because we do not know *where* to look (clearly, at what students do in response to assignments), but because despite — or perhaps due to — all our practice in grading we do not know *how* to look: at achievement in relation to a single learning objective. We are much more accustomed to evaluating assignments as a whole than we are to singling out one aspect of them, more practiced at looking at the compound of knowledge and multiple skills than at a single skill element.

Once the assessment criteria have been established, however, information on student achievement can be collected and used in two ways. During the class, the information allows the instructor to provide targeted feedback that enhances student performance on learning objectives, as the Global Marketing instructor does when she makes public or private comments on whether students are listening/responding respectfully. After the class has finished, assessment information may also provide a basis for redesign of the course at any of many levels, from the learning objectives to the course or teamwork structures to individual assignments. Students are much better able to learn successfully when all the components of a course work together to produce that learning and assessment assists faculty to make certain that virtual teams achieve their maximum potential benefit to students.

REFERENCES

Kerr, S. (1995). The Folly of Rewarding A, while Hoping for B. *Academy of Management Executive, 9*(1), 7-14.

Section III

Teams in Action: International Collaboration

Chapter IX

One School/ Two Campuses: A Socio-Technical Approach for Building the Distributed Classroom

Anne-Laure Fayard
INSEAD, France

Abstract

INSEAD, an international business school with campuses in France and Singapore, discovered first-hand the opportunities and challenges that distance and technology can bring for teams and collaboration among knowledge workers. Using off-the-shelf technologies, I used this situation to experiment with a distributed classroom experience in an MBA course. The course was project-based and students had to work on a consulting project in virtual teams distributed in Asia and Europe. This chapter documents the design and implementation of the course and provides lessons for teaching successful transnational classrooms. Observations conducted during this course suggest that the "class," which is enacted with the feeling of belonging to the same group, is a socio-technical construction. Participants evolved their practices and adapted the technology during the course in order to facilitate communication and smooth out interactions across the sites.

Introduction

"Hi all," a student in Singapore wrote to her teammates, "all the best for the following. It would have been great to meet 'face-to-face' at least once, wouldn't it? Take care."

Two of her teammates in France replied:

We won't see you on this continent in the future, will we? Anyway, it was great to work with you. Good job on the presentation!

You never know what course life can take and where we might end up meeting! Anyway — if not in the near future — we will end up meeting at one of the alumni get-togethers!

This e-mail exchange between team members shows that at the end of the course, students had a sense of being part of a team even though they had never met. One of the major aims of the course — creating a sense of belonging — had been achieved.

INSEAD, an international business school based in France, founded a campus in Singapore as an integral part of its original European campus[1]. Offering a distributed course across the two campuses was in line with INSEAD's strategy to create a two campus–one school concept, as the course aimed to create and nurture the experience of being in one class, of sitting in a shared space, even though students were located in two campuses. This chapter presents a case study that documents the development of a distributed course involving two groups of students based on different campuses — in Asia and Europe — and the methods employed to create the sense of being part of the same class.

Distance education and e-learning have been the subject of many studies since the mid-1990s. The use of the Internet to deliver management education has increased dramatically over the last decade (Alavi & Leidner, 2001). Most of the research is based on the study of Web-based courses (i.e., mostly text-based and asynchronous), and the issues studied are the quality of learning, the satisfaction of the students, and the content and structure of the curriculum (Alavi & Gallupe, 2003; Argaugh, 2000a; Argaugh, 2000b; Hiltz & Wellman, 1997; Leidner & Jarvenpaa, 1995). There have also been several examples of courses with participants based in different locations, the distributed aspect often "built into" a group project with students taking the course working with other students taking a similar course in a different school (Alavi, Yoo, & Vogel, 1997; Yoo, Kanawattanachai, & Citurs, 2002). The distributed course described in this chapter differs on two aspects. First, all the teaching was simultaneous: most of the time via video-conference and a few sessions with a Web-conferencing tool[2]. Second, the course was not offered across different schools, but across two campuses of a single institution, with the course taught simultaneously to two groups of international students as if they were in the same classroom, with the students working together in global virtual teams on a project.

Several studies have compared online and classroom versions of the same course (Alavi, et al., 1995; Alavi & Leidner, 2001; Arbaugh, 2000b; Smith, 2001). This chapter does not aim to do this. Rather the aim is to understand the socio-technical practices developed in order to create an environment where students in two different continents have the feeling of being part of the same class. My observations focused not on the type of learning[3] or its quality, but on the process of designing a learning environment where students could develop a sense of belonging.

Scholars have questioned approaches that consider e-learning an opportunity offered by technology to save costs and add a measure of convenience, using e-learning technologies as another delivery system of the content provided in the bricks-and-mortar classroom (see Weigel, 2002). Media richness (Daft & Lengel, 1986), social presence (Rice, 1984; Sproull & Kiesler, 1991), and distributed learning theories (Walker, 2003) suggest that recreating the classroom learning environment with Web-based courses would be difficult, even impossible. Some researchers have begun to consider the physical and the virtual classroom as distinctively different learning environments (Bowman, 2001; Weigel, 2002). They have suggested that Web-based courses (which are low according to the media richness theory) could be enhanced with other media (with different degrees of richness) to support activities such as case discussions and group projects. Weigel (2002) proposes a blended approach to e-learning that combines co-located education and distance education, and where technology enriches the learning experience. The design of the course described in this chapter was inspired by a similar approach, aiming to go "beyond the virtual classroom" (Weigel, 2002). When I decided to use the opportunity of having two campuses and design this course, my decision was triggered by my interest in distance communication and in the impact of technology on communication and social interactions. I also had a strong belief that technology was only an enabler and was not the only, or even the critical factor in making it a success.

The design of this course was inspired by the socio-technical theory, and the assumption that social systems and technological systems mutually shape one another (Trist et al., 1963). Technology cannot be separated from the people who are interacting with it or with the patterns and practices of that interaction (Blomberg, 1987; Jordan, 1993; Nardi & O'Day, 1999; Suchman, 1987). To understand how to use technology successfully, we need to study socio-technical systems as complete environments where people, while interacting with the technology, modify and adapt the technology to their needs and the context, as well as change their work practices and adapt them to the new constraints and abilities afforded by the technology (e.g., Mackay, 1990; Nardi & Miller, 1990). The course described in this chapter was designed and "evolved" as a socio-technical system, involving the students, the instructor, the different activities going on during the course (case discussions, exercises, group work sessions, presentations, etc.) and technology — seen as only one component of the various components of the system.

Hence, I did not focus on the characteristics of the technology, nor did I compare face-to-face interactions with technology-mediated interactions in terms of better performance and/or a better outcome (Hiltz, Johnson, & Turoff, 1986; McGrath, 1994; Olson, Olson, & Meader, 1995; Short, Williams, & Christie, 1976; Strauss &, Walther, 1995). My interest was in understanding the co-adaptive process (Mackay, 1990) by which people adjust and evolve their practices to adapt to the technology, but also redesign and change the technology to shape it to their communicative practices and needs[4].

Videoconference technology was the main technology used in this course, and since one aim of the course was to create a sense of social presence and belonging, I was influenced by the different attempts to design environments that support informal communication in distributed settings (Abel, 1990; Bly et al., 1993; Dourish & Bly, 1992; Fish, et al., 1993; Heath & Luff, 1991). While I could not recreate a media space[5] (see Mackay, 1999 for a review of the different experiences of media space) in the course, the model of a media space inspired the design of the course. Therefore, I extended the length of the video link (starting earlier and finishing later, including breaks) and I tried to support the development of relatively informal interactions.

This chapter documents the experience of teaching a distributed course, with international graduate students enrolled in the same program but distributed in two different campuses, located in two continents. The chapter focuses on how to build a sense of belonging and social presence across two continents. This case study suggests how we can leverage technology "affordances" (Gibson, 1979) to support teaching and learning. The course as a classroom experience emerged as a socio-technical construction, which was achieved through a co-adaptive process (Mackay, 1990). The chapter proceeds as follows. First, it describes the setting — the structure of the course, the technology used, and the pedagogical approach. Then, major observations relevant to the development and teaching of transnational classes are presented. It concludes with implications for teaching transnational classrooms, the limitations of the study, and possible directions for further research.

The "Managing Global Teams and Projects" Course

INSEAD, an international business school based in France, founded a campus in Singapore in 2000. I used this structure to test a distributed classroom experience with an MBA course on Managing Global Teams and Projects. From a curriculum perspective, I thought this course was important to offer in an institution focusing on the development of international managers. In today's world where globalization is becoming increasingly important, virtual as well as multinational organizations rely heavily on distributed teams and remote collaboration. Many companies are looking for managers who have the skills to work in distributed environment and to manage virtual teams.

The course lasted two months and was taught via a video link to students in both Singapore and France. The participants were full-time MBA students with four- to five-years' work experience and differing cultural and language backgrounds. Prior to participating in the courses by videoconference, some of the students had met each other face-to-face, but most had not. Further, many of the participants had never been to the other geographic location, so they had no prior sense of a common social network other than the fact that they were all part of the INSEAD organization. We used off-the-shelf technologies (video-conferencing, an electronic whiteboard, audio conferencing, a Web-conferencing tool, e-mail, and an Internet forum). Two major aims of the experiment were: (1) to provide students with the experience of remote collaboration and (2) to explore how to create and nurture the experience of being part of the same class.

My teaching philosophy is one of experiential learning, where the learning experience is not a one-way interaction between the instructor and students, with the teacher transferring knowledge for students to memorize. Rather, I believe that is important for students to have an opportunity to experience problems and challenges, to try to solve them and to reflect on the processes they developed. The design of the course was inspired by constructivism (Vigotsky, 1986). According to this approach, learning takes place when students act on content, when they can reflect on it and shape it. This approach has inspired my pedagogy of "learning by doing." Moreover, studies of distance learning (Hiltz & Turoff, 2002) have shown the importance of developing collaborative learning activities in online contexts.

Hence, the course was designed to allow and even encourage students to be active in the learning process. First, it was project-based and much of the learning experience came from the actual experience of working in distributed teams. Students were working for six weeks on a real-world project in dispersed teams (on average eight members, half in Fontainebleau and half in Singapore), in most cases with teammates they did not know before. After the first course (where the project was "internal" — the clients were the MBA office and the Dean of the Singapore campus), I realized that it was important to have a real-word project, i.e., a "client" who would learn something from the students' report. This was therefore the case in the next offerings. Students were given the project brief in the first class and had to form their teams for the second class, beginning work on the project after this second class. The project was defined so that students at both sites had a specific and complementary type of resources. The project brief was different each time,[6] but was similar in nature as it was always presented as a consulting project. This involved data collection at sites (gathering documentation on a company's strategies, interviews, questionnaires, benchmarking the competition), analysis, and brainstorming in order to provide an innovative proposal to the client. The teams' work was partly structured, as they have to deliver specific deliverables (an analysis of the data, the results of a brainstorming session, etc.) at predefined moments in the project. The final project was presented in front of a jury composed of representatives of the client and of faculty members with an expertise related to the topic of the project.

As part of the "learning by doing" approach, students were strongly encouraged to experiment with the technology, the design of the environment and how it worked in practice. The course was also seen as an opportunity for them to reflect on their experience. Students were therefore asked to write (individual and group) papers reflecting on their experience (on team dynamics, project management, and technology-mediated communication). They were also asked to evaluate their peers (part of their evaluation was based on peer evaluation). To support their learning process, I provided teams with detailed feedback on each of their group work sessions.

Arrangements: Schedule, Space, and Technology

The course was composed of eight double sessions (of 3 hours each). As it was very much project-oriented, in six of the eight double sessions 90 minutes were allocated to group-work sessions, half by video-conference and half using teleconferencing. Team members also had access to a Web platform with a dedicated team space and discussion forum. The two facilities were designed to operate as a common media space (e.g., Abel, 1990; Bly, Harrison, & Irwin, 1993) so that when students stepped into the room in their local facility there was the sense of being in a shared facility with the other campus. The video link was therefore set up 20 minutes before the beginning of a class, so that when the students came in the connection was on, enabling them to immediately interact with the other site. During the ten-minute breaks in the middle of a session or between a class and a group-work session, the link was maintained in order to facilitate informal interactions. For the same reason, the video link was disconnected ten minutes after the official end of a class. A similar arrangement was used for group-work sessions. This arrangement (starting the link before the "official" start and ending it after the "official" end) was found to be very important in supporting informal interactions.

In each room, there was an electronic whiteboard and, at the other end of the room facing the whiteboard, a TV monitor with one camera[7]. The tables were positioned so that the ends at each site were connected by video into one long virtual table (see Henderson & Henderson, 2000, for a description of a similar arrangement at SUN Microsystems for a distributed design group).

Table 1. The setting

	Course 1	**Course 2**	**Course 3**	**Course 4**
Technology used	Video-conferencing Electronic whiteboard Teleconferencing Web platform	Video-conferencing Electronic whiteboard Teleconferencing Web platform Dedicated group space Web-conferencing tool	Video-conferencing Electronic whiteboard Teleconferencing Web platform Dedicated group space Web-conferencing tool	Video-conferencing Electronic whiteboard Teleconferencing Web platform Dedicated group space Web-conferencing tool
Numbers of students	7	24	18	13
Numbers of nationalities	6	19	13	11
Numbers of teams	1	2	2	2
Numbers of classes	10	10	10	10
Faculty	One professor (half of the sessions at one site, half of the sessions at the other site) and two teaching assistants	One professor at each site, swapping for 2 sessions	One professor at each site, swapping for 2 sessions	One professor (2/3 of the sessions at one site, 1/3 of the sessions at the other site) and one teaching assistant at the site while she was in attendance
Numbers of group work sessions	6	7	7	7
Numbers of videoconference group work sessions [1]	3	4	4	4
Numbers of teleconference group work sessions	3	3	3	3

**There were six planned group work sessions. Students were also offerend the chance to set up an extra group work session with a video link. They did not use it in the first course, but both teams in the two following courses set up an extra group work session by video-conferencing.*

When the course was first run, one faculty member spent half of the course at each site, helped by a teaching assistant at each location. The fourth run of the course followed a similar model (one faculty member spending time at both sites and helped by a teaching assistant). However, for the second and third runs, there were two faculty members at each site, who swapped for two sessions towards the middle of the course.

Observations

This case study produced several relevant observations for developing and teaching transnational classes and for creating a setting where students develop a sense of belonging to the same "class." My observations are presented around five themes. I first show how the experiential learning approach used in the course was instrumental to its success. I then discuss how the use of technology can be supported to make it transparent to users. I argue that the use of technology requires an evolutionary approach to design. Fourth, I describe the roles — assigned or emergent, new or reinterpreted — that were enacted in the course. Lastly, I show how all these elements were enacted in the building of "the class" as a single location and a social place.

Experiential Learning

The project was central to the course, as it created a rich learning context for the students. The fact that there were "real" clients who would be attending the final presentation created a realistic context. Because of the distributed nature of the teams, each sub-team had access to different resources, which created tensions and power issues, but also led each sub-team to realize that they were complementary to each other and that they needed to engage in collaborative activities. The course involved different kinds of activities using various types of technology. Students could therefore experience the affordances of the different types of technology in several contexts, and compare how efficient these technologies were according to the type of activity (class discussions, lectures, brainstorming, etc.) and the number of people involved (class vs. small group).

As always in such an experiential approach, the reflection phases are key to the learning process. Hence, students had several opportunities to reflect on their experiences—both individually (a questionnaire at the beginning, in the middle, and at the end of the course) and collectively (a presentation on technology-mediated communication — challenges and best practices — based on their experience, a reflective section in their final report, and assessment of their group dynamics). This reflective process was associated with feedback provided by the instructor at each stage of the projects, and more specifically with coaching reports provided after each of the group work sessions. The coaching focused on three major topics: use of technology and its impact on communication, team dynamics, and project management.

Technology

Support the Use and Development

Technology often creates barriers by constraining interactions and leading people to behave very formally. Moreover, some people are fearful of technology, and are uncomfortable in technology-mediated or technology-supported settings. It is therefore important to make technology as transparent as possible. Design can help make it more user-friendly and simple. However, another essential element in this process of making technology transparent is to allow people to play with it, have them change it if possible, and support them as much as possible in this process.

The design of the class triggered the participants to become active users of the technology. They were encouraged to question the arrangement of the room and the technology and to try out different arrangements in order to communicate more smoothly. They were also encouraged to innovate in their use of the different tools. At the end of the class, all of them realized that technology was much more than the set of functionalities, and that what made the difference was the context of use — including the physical arrangement, the practices developed, the personality of the users, and the nature of the task.

First, it is important to realize that technology should work, as students will not try more than twice to use a discussion forum or a Web platform that does not function correctly[8]. Second, a new role was defined. As the instructor was not able to manage the technical details and lead the discussion at the beginning of each class, one student at each site was appointed as "host" to organize the technology and help involve participants (those who were not co-located with the instructor) in the discussion. The host was asked to organize the technology for the session, monitor the picture, ensure that nobody talked off camera, and so on. Appointing a host also forced students to become active users of the technology and to reflect on its use. Third, training can be offered. However, more than training, students needed opportunities to use the technology. Thus, during the first courses, several training sessions for the Web-conferencing tool were offered (to ensure that all participants could attend at least one of the sessions), but only a few students attended. For the last course, I did not offer specific training sessions, but started the first Web-conferencing tool session with a brief overview of the program and a number of exercises to get the students to use the main tools. This approach was effective and students were as comfortable as in the offerings where they had a specific training session before the class. Similarly, during the first run of the course, a person from technical support gave a quick demo of the electronic whiteboard. Students seemed to find it simple to use, but almost never used it. Starting from the second offering of the course, I introduced several exercises to provide hands-on experience of the electronic whiteboard, after which students started using it in their group work sessions.

In the first session, each participant was asked to present himself or herself. To do so, participants had to use the remote control to focus the camera on themselves. This small exercise allowed students to mix a social experience with a technical one. They had at least one experience with the remote control, and some of them continued to use it afterwards. During the first session, other exercises were offered such as a game of Pictionary using the electronic whiteboards and a communication exercise. All these exercises were icebreakers from a technical and social point of view. They offered the participants the opportunity to use the technology, but also allowed them to get to know the people at their site as well as the other site.

Coaching also supported the development of new practices. Part of the coaching focused on the use of technology and patterns of communication. During the meeting, some participants referred explicitly to the coaching reports, or implemented some of the suggestions proposed in the report of their previous meetings. Improvement was rapid, and after the third group-work sessions for most of the teams the coaching reports included very little reference to the use of the technology.

When Technology Becomes Invisible

Technology should become invisible to users. Hence, having a video-conference or using an electronic whiteboard should require as little conscious thought as talking on the phone, using a mouse, or even using a knife and fork or chopsticks. Much of this invisible aspect is related to familiarity. Children require some attention to begin using a knife and fork, or chopsticks, to learn how to talk on the telephone, or to use a mouse, but it does become invisible after a while. The course aimed to offer the students the chance to develop some practices and to learn how to arrange the technology so that it would become invisible.

The course was designed so that participants could "forget" the technology and focus on building relationships. Video-conferences are often seen as formal meetings that require a great deal of technical preparation. If the video link operates during times of informal interaction rather than during designated meetings only, the effect is to create a common "media space" for group interaction (e.g., Abel, 1990; Bly, Harrison, & Irwin, 1993). As sessions started before the "official" time, when students came in, the "classroom space" was "on" and they could interact with the remote site. Similarly, students could continue to exchange information and have informal discussions after the class as the link continued after the "official" time. The link was also maintained during breaks, and drinks and snacks were offered to participants to encourage them to stay and interact.

During one of the project presentations, technology became "invisible" to the participants. The project manager (located in France) of the winning team, which won two bottles of Champagne (one at each site), proposed a toast. All the participants (students and members of the jury) formed a circle across the two sites (with one half of the circle at each site). One of the jury members in Singapore was Chinese and suggested a Chinese toast. Everybody agreed and the 35 people across the two locations raised their glasses and shouted loudly for few seconds before saying the final "Gambei." Several of the jury members later expressed their surprise that this seemed so natural, as if everyone were in the same room. Students seemed to find this situation completely natural, as if after six weeks the technology had become second nature. Some stayed in the classrooms for a while, either talking with classmates at the other site, or talking with co-located teammates and jury members.

Evolutionary Design

I took an evolutionary approach while developing the course. My observations and experience of previous offerings informed the design and practice of the next offering of the course. Hence, the course evolved with the introduction of a real world project (in the second offering), an increasing number of Web-conferencing sessions, and coaching (during the last two offerings).

Moreover, once one stops considering technology as a fixed set of functionalities, rather as an element in a system, which is adapted and changed by the users, one then takes an evolutionary approach to design[9]. While designing the course, I took such an approach and left space for evolution, encouraging participants to change arrangements and evolve practices.

To make interactions smoother, participants continually explored different arrangements, changing the location of the TV and the cameras depending on the size of the group (class session vs. team meeting) and type of activity (brainstorming vs. presentation). For example, the virtual table arrangement described in the research setting and methodology section was the result of several trials by the students. They tried out several locations for the TV monitor, finally deciding to place it at the end of the room facing the electronic whiteboard located at the other end. They then moved the tables closer to the monitors. Chairs were placed around this virtual table, an arrangement that created a feeling of "being part of the same room" supporting interactions. To see those at one's side, one turned one's head left or right, when people were in the remote room, they also turned their heads and looked through the video. The presentations were given using the electronic whiteboards located at each end of the virtual table. Participants turned in their chairs to see the presentation, while those in the remote room saw it via the video.

We also explored various settings with the video-conference — two TV monitors vs. one, two cameras vs. one. In fact, during the first offering, we had two TV monitors and two cameras. The two cameras provided a view of the instructor (standing by the electronic white board) and a view of the students. However, we finally decided to have only one camera, as it was easier to have only one camera, with someone changing the view depending on who was talking. The rationale for having two monitors was to provide both the instructor and the students with one view of the remote classroom. One of the monitors was located nearby the board so that students could have the instructor, the board with the slides and the other participants in their visual field. The other monitor was located in the back of the room so that the instructor could have a sense of talking to all the participants (co-located and remote). Although in theory, this made sense, in practice, it did not work, and the added value was too low compared to the added complexity, especially, as having the two monitors required having two cameras.

It was difficult to interrupt when participants at the other site were talking, and waving one's arms to gain attention was not effective in gaining the floor. In one class, the participant in charge of the remote control in Singapore, noticing that someone in Singapore wished to comment on what someone in France was saying (he was able to notice the subtle nonverbal behavior because they were co-located), focused the camera on the person who wished to speak. This practice was efficient in signaling to the participants in France that someone in Singapore wanted to take their turn. Over time, this became a convention for assuring that both "sides" were involved in the conversation.

Roles

Hosts

It was found that the appointed hosts soon gave way to emergent facilitators who were much more effective in mediating the group interaction than the appointed hosts. The new or emergent hosts managed the technology as well as the social interactions. They played a similar role and had similar skills to the "translators" or "facilitators" described in various studies of the introduction of technology (Jordan, 1993; Mackay, 1990; Nardi & O'Day, 1999)—i.e., they all possessed or developed technical skills and interests, and were particularly willing to help.

In each course, several hosts emerged both at class and team level. There was generally one host in each team, usually sharing the role in the classroom. The hosts tended to arrive early and stay during the break to arrange things (e.g., relocate the monitor, check the lighting, move the microphones, etc.). They also made adjustments during class discussions and group work. They regularly checked that the other students were on camera or close enough to the microphone, and asked them to modify their behavior when necessary. They pointed to the microphone to tell performers to move closer to it, signaled when a participant was out of the shot, and waved to indicate a problem with the video connection or when slides were not being projected onto the electronic whiteboard. It is important to note that hosts were not necessarily the project manager, or the person chairing the meeting. In fact, in most of our teams (in six cases out of seven), the project manager was not the host.

The Instructor as a Facilitator and Coach

As shown by other researchers studying distance learning (Argauh, 2000a, 2000b; Bowman, 2001; Hiltz & Turoff, 2001; Weigel, 2002), the role of the instructor changes in distance learning situations. The traditional lecture-based format does not seem to be appropriate for this course context (Webster & Hackley, 1997). Instead of delivering content and covering the material, the instructor becomes a learning facilitator who creates a context where students are faced with problems and challenges to solve. The instructor role is to coach the students in their learning experience, by observing them and giving feedback. This course was designed to create a situation where students had to try out different situations, develop new practices, articulate them and reflect upon them. Although I also lectured and moderated discussions, I saw myself increasingly in the role of a facilitator who created a context for learning experiences to take place and as a coach who observed the classroom as well as asked questions and offered feedback on the students' performance. Moreover, as an instructor one needs to invest a great deal of energy and effort to develop a classroom atmosphere, create a learning community, and build relationship and trust—by being active and attentive in class, giving positive feedback, encouraging experimentation and, when not in the classroom, by being frequently online. This also has implications at the organizational level, as noted by Alavi and Gallupe (2003), as it requires training and support that some instructors, and most educational institutions, are not aware of. The importance of getting organizational support for the development of such courses (financial and human resources are one of the many ways organizations can support such courses) should not be undermined and can create a lot of frustrations for the instructors. It is important for the instructors to realize the shift in their role, as well as the extra time and energy required to build and teach such courses. These two issues might explain why faculty members are sometimes reluctant in developing such courses[10].

Building the Class: The Class as a Socio-Technical Construction

Building a Single Distance Place

What happens when there is not one single space in which to interact as in the case of a video-mediated setting, which implies (at least) two rooms? It might be tempting to analyze a video-conference between two sites as a pair of connected local meetings, but such a definition does not take into account the experience described by the participants when they refer to "here" as "one single" meeting place or classroom ("Are you here?" or "OK, let's start as we are all here."). Therefore, it seems that the "space" in which participants interact is less than the shared frame of reference we have when we are co-located, but more than a pair of connected places. Video-conference interactions take place in a single distance place, which is a conceptually constructed place "here," holding all the participants together.

Each site had only limited and constrained access to the other site, through the virtual space. Therefore, there was no true common frame of reference. In order to "build" this single distance place—the "classroom" where they could interact—participants rearranged the room (e.g., by creating a virtual table) or developed new practices (e.g., supporting turn-taking by focusing the camera on the person who wished to speak). Another important practice developed to build a common frame of reference was context sharing. On several occasions, participants made comments in order to share context, which would have been unnecessary in a co-located situation. People make explicit what is usually implicit, letting the "other site" know what is going on "at their site." Often one of the participants acknowledged the presence of new participants. This would not happen in a co-located situation, as everybody would be aware of the presence of this newcomer. In a video-mediated context, the participants at the other site might not have noticed the newcomer's arrival, who might have been out of the shot. This public acknowledgment creates a common frame of reference for participants at both sites. In a similar vein, we heard many similar comments of participants providing the remote participants with information that they could not have access to because of the limited "shared space." This could be either information about what was going on outside or inside the room, or even something relating to an element beyond the range of the camera, such as the weather. Another way of sharing context was enacted during the second course. During the second class of this course, one student in Singapore took a flip chart into the classroom and placed it near to the screen. He drew the tables in France and wrote down the names of students he knew. A second student entered the room and did the same, followed by another.

Building a Social Place

A classroom atmosphere involves a sense of a group, relationships, and some sort of trust. When the instructor and the students are co-located, the classroom atmosphere emerges (partly) "unconsciously." Students are all sitting in the same location, they can see each other and the instructor, they can chat with their classmates as well as with the instructor, and the instructor has a sense of the "atmosphere" and can adjust her or his behavior. As soon as distance is introduced (in distance learning as well as in virtual teams), building a relationship, a sense of group and trust becomes a challenging and non-obvious task (Hiltz & Turoff, 2002; Jarvenpaa & Leidner, 1999; Meyerson, Weick, & Kramer, 1996). Although video is often seen as offering the closest situation to face-to-face interactions (Daft & Lengel, 1986, Rice, 1984; Sproull & Kiesler, 1991), people still do not share the same physical context, e.g., there is limited peripheral awareness, eye gaze, body language, etc. (Heath & Luff, 1991; Henderson & Henderson, 2000), nor do they share the same social context (Heath & Luff, 1991; Mackay, 1999). They have fewer cues to interpret others' behavior. For instance, have the remote participants heard them properly? Have they noticed their quizzical expressions? Are they bored or tired, or is this just an impression due to the quality of the video image?

Using technology to facilitate human interaction required offering activities that would help create a sense of social presence, in the classroom as well as in the project teams. In that sense the first session was key, and I therefore tried to involve participants. The exercises with the technology (presentation of self with the remote control, a game of Pictionary with the electronic whiteboard, and a communication exercise) played the role of team- or class-building exercises. They were perfect icebreakers, as the participants laughed and felt less anxious about the technology. During the third course, I introduced the idea of "taking" a group picture as if it were a regular single location course. We created a "virtual" picture of the whole class with one campus site in front of the camera and the other students on the screen in the background. This was a very powerful visual experience that created a sense of being part of the same class. Additionally, students were asked to post their picture and give some background details on the course Web platform so that they could exchange information that they would have shared in informal encounters — before or after the class, at lunch or while chatting at the bar[11]. During the first group work session, each team had to come up with a name for their team. In most cases, this exercise was an opportunity to create team spirit. Several teams brainstormed seriously and came up with innovative names. During the first group work session, each sub-team had to make a one-minute video to introduce themselves to their teammates at the other sites. Some sub-teams were very creative. This gave their remote teammates a better sense of their personality as well as what they looked like (the quality of the video recording used for this exercise — mini-DV — was much better than the image we had via the video link). As mentioned earlier, starting the video link before the official time, ending it after, and having video coffee breaks played an important role in creating and supporting a sense of social presence. Some participants exchanged their e-mail addresses, or asked their teammates to create a hot-mail account in order to chat. They reported that they could therefore have regular informal discussions with their teammates[12]. Different types of technology were thus used to support the building of a sense of social presence and belonging.

Most of the participants had not met before, although a few knew each other[13] as they had spent some time on the same campus. Those students who had met or knew both locations played a key role in building relationships across the two sites. In one team, two students who had been to Singapore and were currently in the class based in France had many discussions with their teammates in Singapore about diving spots. The swapping process also created opportunities for informal interactions as participants in Singapore asked their classmates in France for help in finding lodging in France, and vice versa. For each course, I spent some time at each site, which was essential in building a relationship with the students. For the two courses that I co-taught with a colleague, we were based for most of the course on one campus, but switched campuses for two sessions in the middle of the course. This switch had an impact on our interactions with the "remote" site, especially when we were back on "our campus." These observations corroborate studies showing the importance of regular face-to-face meetings, rotating members and "traveling managers" in virtual teams (Duarte & Snyder, 2001; Kraut et al., 2002; Lipnack & Stamps, 2000; Nardi & Whittaker, 2002).

A friendly and informal atmosphere developed with teasing between the two locales. Jokes emerged, some relating to students' personalities, many relating to the geographical context. The weather was a frequent topic of conversation. There were often teasing comments about the way people were dressed (leather jackets and scarves vs. flip-flops and shorts). Students occasionally took the camera to the window to show how sunny it was (either in France or in Singapore). In one of the courses, when it snowed in France pictures of the campus under snow were posted on the course platform.

Implications and Conclusions

The course was assessed as successful in meeting its learning goals as the students — although located on two different continents — reported that they felt part of the same class. It can also be described as successful based on the high quality of the projects (evaluated both by the clients and faculty members) and on the formal and informal[14] evaluation of the course by the students.

The shared classroom experience emerged from the development of a set of various socio-technical practices, and can therefore be described as a socio-technical construction. The importance of the practices and roles in the achievement of this classroom experience shows that instead of regarding the technology as a constraint and trying to reproduce a face-to-face setting, one should work to understand the different technologies and play with them in order to create an environment that allows rich interactions supporting learning and a sense of community. Below are some of the practices that were key in teaching this transcontinental classroom:

- Do not view technology as a stand-alone element, but see it as an artifact *used* by the different participants in different situations to achieve different goals;
- Encourage users to *experiment* in order to adapt the technology to their needs and to evolve their practices;
- Recognize the importance of *facilitators* and particularly emergent facilitators;
- Rethink your role as teacher: you have to become a *learning facilitator* and a *coach rather than the focus of the learning;*

- Develop the course as a *learning environment* where students can experience different challenges and problems, explore ways of solving them and reflect on their experience;
- *Create a "place"* where students can interact, develop trust and relationships.

Although technology is only one element, it is an important one and there are several high-level requirements for the technology used in a distributed class:

- **Equality:** Participants must interact on a level playing field. There should be symmetry between the ends, and a reasonable equality (access to information, shared context, etc.) between people "here" and "there."
- **Space:** It is important to see both (all) spaces, and know who is there.
- **Context:** Participants should know who is waiting outside the door, and off-camera.
- **Seeing:** It is important to see all participants, and be seen by them.
- **Hearing:** It is important to be able to hear all participants, and be heard by them.
- **Interacting:** Participants should have high-speed interactions (overlapping, interrupting—which implies full-duplex, echo-cancelled audio).
- **Access:** The management of airtime. In small group settings, the distinction between the presenter and the audience must be questioned, as everyone is a presenter. In larger groups, there is a distinction, but it is not simply that presenters talk and the audience listens. It is important to look at the ease of talking and the management of turn-taking (in larger groups, semi-formal queuing may be used, but even so there may be fast exchanges between audience members).
- **Course Materials:** Participants must be able to see all material including materials handed out before the meeting/class, those carried in, and those created in the meeting (emergent materials).
- **Writing Surfaces:** Shared surfaces should be used to present, annotate, and brainstorm (e.g., electronic whiteboards).

This course demonstrates that technology in distance education and e-learning projects should be viewed as another learning tool to deepen the learning experience of students rather than simply another means to deliver content.

Educators need to see virtual classrooms as complementary to brick-and-mortar classrooms rather than a substitute or replacement. The goal should be to develop classrooms which combine the best features of both worlds. Many of the observations shared in this chapter are also relevant for virtual teams. The high-level requirements listed above should also be concerns of organizations using virtual team meetings or other activities. Our observations of the student teams showed that the most successful teams were those that put some effort in developing social relationships, had a "respected" host, and recognized the importance of developing new socio-technical practices.

As a caveat, I would like to note that such courses require a lot of time and energy, and some sort of devotion for exploring and experimenting with teaching such courses. Moreover, although the experience can be achieved with a lot of effort by one individual, the development of such courses at a bigger scale requires educational institutions to become aware of the amount of work required by these courses (and to develop incentives for faculty to develop such courses) as well as an understanding of the resources (financial, technical and human[15]) required.

The main technology for the course was video-conferencing, although other technologies were introduced to support the sense of belonging and social presence developed in the group. I would like to explore further this idea of "beyond being there" (Hollan & Stornetta, 1992), which challenges us to think of what the technology enables us to do, rather than simply reproducing the face-to-face situation, and explore different ways that communication systems can support interactions and learning.

This chapter provides a rich contextual description of a distributed course across two continents involving international teams of MBA students. Providing qualitative reports of such courses is important as it shows the significance of the context in developing new socio-technical practices and an efficient use of the technology, although it does not allow broad generalizations. However, qualitative studies are valuable for determining how patterns of interaction develop and how learning occurs within these courses (Argaugh, 2000a). I believe that multiplying these types of qualitative studies and comparing them will allow us to find generalizable patterns and to develop richer theories in both learning settings and the larger field of organizational behavior.

Acknowledgment

Thank you to the MBA students who participated in the course and were involved in the study.

Specials thanks to Austin Henderson for his thoughtful suggestions on the course design, to Ariella Aschheim for her help in collecting and analyzing the data during the first course, and to Anca Metiu for co-teaching several offerings of the course.

References

Abel, M. J. (1990). Experiences in an exploratory distributed organization. In R. Galegher, E. Kraut, & C. Egido (Eds.), *Intellectual teamwork: Social and technological foundations of cooperative work.* London: Lawrence Erlbaum.

Alavi, M., & Gallupe, R. B. (2003). Using information technology in learning: Case studies in business and management education programs. *Academy of Management Learning and Education, 2,* 139-153.

Alavi, M., & Leidner, D. E. (2001). Research commentary: Technology-mediated learning — A call for greater depth and breadth of research. *Information Systems Research, 12,* 1-10.

Alavi, M., Wheeler, B. C., & Valacich, J. S. (1995). Using IT to re-engineer business education: An exploratory investigation of collaborative telelearning. *MIS Quarterly, 19,* 293-312.

Alavi, M., Yoo, Y., & Vogel, D. R. (1997). Using information technology to add value to management education. *Academy of Management Journal, 40,* 1310-1333.

Arbaugh, J. B. (2000a). Virtual classroom characteristics and student satisfaction with internet-based MBA courses. *Journal of Management Education, 24,* 32-54.

Arbaugh, J. B. (2000b). Virtual classroom versus physical classroom: An exploratory comparison of class discussion patterns and student learning in an asynchronous internet-based MBA course. *Journal of Management Education, 24,* 207-227.

Arbaugh, J. B. (2001). How instructor immediacy behaviors affect student satisfaction and learning in web-based courses. *Business Communication Quarterly, 64*(4), 42-54.

Blomberg, J. (1987). Social Interaction and office communication: Effects on user's evaluation of new technologies. In R. Kraut (Ed.), *Technology and the Transformation of White Collar Work* (pp. 195-210). Hillsdale, NJ: Lawrence Erlbaum.

Bly, S., Harrison, S., & Irwin, S. (1993). Media spaces: Bringing people together in a video, audio and computing environment. *Communications of the ACM, 36*(1), 29-47.

Bowman, J. P. (2001). The third wave: Swimming against the tide. *Business Communication Quarterly, 64*(2), 87-92.

Cramton, C. (2001). The mutual knowledge problem and its consequences for dispersed collaboration. *Organization Science, 12*, 346-371.

Daft, R.L., & Lengel, R. H. (1986, May 5). Organizational information requirements, media richness and structural design. *Management Science, 32,* 554-571.

Desanctis, G., Fayard, A.L., Roach, M., & Jiang, L. (2003). Learning in online communities. *European Management Journal.*

Dhar, V., & Olson, M.H. (1989). The role of value-based assumptions for the design of collaborative work systems. In M. H. Olson (Ed.), *Technological support for work group collaboration* (pp. 33-50). Hillsdale, NJ: Lawrence Erlbaum.

Dourish, P., & Bly, S. (1992). Portholes: Supporting awareness in a distributed work group. In *Proceedings of Human Factors in Computing Systems, CHI'92,* Monterey, CA (pp. 541-547). New York: ACM Press.

Duarte, D. L., & Snyder, N. T. (2001). *Mastering virtual teams.* San Francisco: Jossey Bass.

Eisenhardt, K.M. (1989). Building theories from case study research. *Academy of Management Review, 14,* 532-540.

Fayard, A. L. (2004). Interacting on a Virtual Stage: An Analysis of Video-Mediated Interactions and their Implications for Goffman's Theatrical Metaphor, *INSEAD Working paper 2004/80/TM/OB*.

Fish, R., Kraut, R., Root, R., & Rice, R.E. (1993). Video as a technology for informal communication. *Communications of the ACM, 36*(1), 48-61.

Gibson, J. J. (1979). *The ecological approach to visual perception.* Boston: Houghton Mifflin.

Heath, C., & Luff, P. (1991). Disembodied conduct: Communication through video in a multi-media office environment. *Proceedings of CSCW'91.*

Henderson, A., & Kyng, M. (1991). There's no place like home: Continuing design in use. In J. Greenbaum & M. Kyng (Eds.), *Design at work: Cooperative design of computer systems.* Hillsdale, NJ: Lawrence Erlbaum.

Henderson, A., & Henderson, L. (2000, Fall). Supporting distance collaboration. *Performance Magazine.*

Hiltz, S. R. (1986). The "virtual classroom": Using computer-mediated communication for university teaching. *Journal of Communication, 36,* 95-104.

Hiltz, S. R., Johnson, K.D., & Turoff, M. (1986). Experiments in group decision making: Communication process and outcome in face-to-face versus computerized conferences. *Human Communication Research, 13,* 225-252.

Hiltz, S. R., & Turoff, M. (2002). What makes learning networks effective? *Communications of the ACM, 45*(4), 56-59.

Hiltz, S. R., & Wellman, B. (1997). Asynchronous learning networks as a virtual classroom. *Communications of the ACM, 40*(9), 44-49.

Hollan, J., & Stornetta, S. (1992). Beyond being there. *Proceedings of CHI'92.*

Jarvenpaa, S. L., & Leidner, D. E. (1999). Communication and trust in global virtual teams. *Organization Science, 10,* 791-815.

Jordan, B. (1993). Ethnographic workplace studies and computer supported cooperative work. In D. Shapiro, M. Tauber, & R. Traunmüller (Eds.), *Proceedings of the Interdisciplinary Workshop on Informatics and Psychol*ogy, Amsterdam: North Holland.

Leidner, D. E., & Jarvenpaa, S. L. (1995). The use of information technology to enhance management school education: A theoretical view. *MIS Quarterly, 19,* 265-291.

Lipnack, J., & Stamps, J. (2000). *Virtual teams.* New York: John Wiley & Sons.

Mackay, W.E. (1990). *Users and customizable software: A co-adaptive phenomenon.* Unpublished Ph.D. dissertation, Massachusetts Institute of Technology.

Mackay, W. E. (1999). Media spaces. In M. Beaudoin-Lafon (Ed.), *Computer-supported co-operative work.* Chichester, UK: John Wiley.

Meyerson, D., Weick, K.E., & Kramer, R.M. (1996). Swift trust and temporary systems. In R.M. Kramer & T.R. Tyler (Eds.), *Trust in organizations* (pp. 166-195). Thousands Oaks, CA: Sage.

Nardi, B., & Miller, J. (1990). An ethnographic study of distributed problem solving in spreadsheet development. *Proceedings of the 1990 ACM conference on Computer-Supported Cooperative Work,* Los Angeles, CA (pp. 197-208).

Nardi, B., & O'Day, V. (1999). *Information ecologies: Using technology with heart.* Cambridge: MIT.

Nardi, B., & Whittaker, S. (2002). Face-to-face communication in distributed work. In P. Hinds & S. Kiesler (Eds.), *Distributed work.* Cambridge: MIT Press.

Olson, J.S., Olson, G.M., & Meader, D.K. (1995). What mix of video and audio is useful for small groups doing remote real-time design work? In *Proceedings of CHI'95.*

Rice, R. E. (1984). *The new media: Communication, research, and technology.* Beverly Hills, CA: Sage.

Short J., Williams, E., & Christie, B. (1976). *The social psychology of telecommunications.* London: John Wiley.

Smith, L. J. (2001). Content and delivery: A comparison and contrast of electronic and traditional MBA marketing planning courses. *Journal of Marketing Education, 23,* 35-44.

Sproull, L., & Kiesler, S. (1991). *Connections: New ways of working in the networked organization.* Cambridge: MIT.

Strauss, S.G., & McGrath, J.E. (1994). Does the medium matter? The interaction of task type and technology on group performance and member reactions. *Journal of Applied Psychology, 79*(1), 87-97.

Suchman, L. (1987). *Plans and situated action: The problem of human-machine communication.* New York: Cambridge University.

Trist, E., Higgin, G. W., Murray, H., & Pollock, A. B. (1963). *Organizational choice: Capabilities of groups at the coal face under changing technologies.* London: Tavistock.

Vygotsky, L. S. (1986). *Thoughts and language.* Cambridge: MIT.

Walker, K. (2003). Applying distributed learning theory in online business communication courses. *Business Communication Quarterly, 66*(2), 55-67.

Webster, J., & Hackley, P. (1997). Teaching effectiveness in technology-mediated distance learning. *Academy of Management Journal, 40,* 1282-1309.

Weigel, V. B. (2002). *Deep learning for a digital age.* San Francisco: Jossey-Bass.

Yoo, Y., Kanawattanachai, P., & Citurs, A. (2002). Forging into the wired wilderness: A case study of a technology-mediated distributed discussion-based class. *Journal of Management Education, 26,* 139-163.

Endnotes

1 The objective was to build a second campus that would not be a simple teaching entity, but a campus in itself.

2 We used a Web-conferencing tool developed for e-learning. It allows all participants to share documents and power point presentations. Participants interact via audio and can also use chat. I taught one session in the second and third courses, and three sessions in the last course.

3 We discussed a number of issues related to learning in the context of this course and two other e-venues in DeSanctis et al. (2003).

4 Some examples of new roles and practices are described in this chapter. However, for more detailed descriptions of the evolution of the communicative practices (see Fayard, 2004).

5 While video-conference systems were designed on the model of a formal meeting (with a clear beginning and end), a media space aims to "create a technology-supported analog to the mailroom or the cafeteria" (Mackay, 1999, p. 57). Hence, it links different rooms, offices, spaces with video-connections that are always "there."

6 They worked on projects for the Singapore Tourism Board, the National Kidney Foundation in Singapore, and the Economic Development Board of Singapore.

7 There was only one camera at each site. For one offering, we tried to have two cameras, but we ended up not switching — mostly because it was adding too much complexity to the interactions, so we decided to use only one camera.

There were no technicians to operate the camera, but we have a remote control that was used by the instructor as well as the students. In fact, there was one student in charge of the remote control for each class and who was supposed to do close-ups when necessary.

8 This is even more the case in organizations.

9 Design is not only the activity of designers designing in a studio (Mackay, 1990; Henderson & Kyng, 1991) — it also involves the continuous adjustments made by users to their everyday practice and the context of use.

10 It is worth noting that at INSEAD, there is only one course building on the existence of the two campuses. Colleagues, both at INSEAD and in other institutions, who either have tried to develop such courses, or just explored the idea, told me that they stopped teaching such courses, and did not even try because of the time and effort it required, and the little support they got.

11 In reality, as one student noted, some of them knew more about each other than a normal single location group.

12 Some even preferred Web chat for one-to-one discussions on the project (rather than a phone call for example).

13 While some students spend their whole program on one campus, others spend part of the program on the other campus.

14 Former students contacted me after they left their programs and told me how the course experience had been useful in their professional experience.

15 At INSEAD, faculty usually do not have teaching assistants for their courses. Hence, it was very hard for me to obtain resources to hire a teaching assistant to host the course at the "remote" site. Moreover, it was hard to convince the management of the school that I did not need a technician from the multi-media services who will come and stay during the first 10 minutes, but someone with social skills that would be able to "represent" me and help me manage the discussions, and that this person had to be there during the whole class.

Chapter X

Students International Collaboration Project (SICP): A Cross-Cultural Project Using Virtual Teams to Learn Communication Styles

Kathryn Hashimoto
University of New Orleans, USA

Jean-marc Lehu
Université Panthéon Sorbonne , France

Abstract

"SICP" stands for Students International Collaboration Project. This chapter describes a project where students create learning with faculty mentors, offering insights into problem solving. Achieving the freedom to learn and broaden students' individual interpersonal skills is the main goal for this new endeavor. This chapter will explain SICP's mission and its procedures, analyze its main concepts, and describe the outcomes. Experiences of past projects in the learning curve will be used to give a

practical framework for teachers who would be interested in initiating such a project, not only for their students but also for themselves. The prototype combined French and American teams who wrote a research paper together. The learned outcomes focused on improved communication skills and team management. In the process, the students also learned about a different culture. This mentoring process constitutes an opportunity for teachers to stimulate learning by involving students in a shared responsibility experience. This project expands traditional classroom learning into an experiential process to learn new concepts.

Introduction

The workplaces of today are changing rapidly as technology races ahead with new hardware and programs. The virtual work environment has grown out of trends in globalization and the development of information technology. Previously, international business people were connected with telephones, faxes, and face-to-face meetings, but essentially operations were self-contained and regional/national. To have a strategic team operate, it was necessary to see people face-to-face in order to create new ideas, organize work, and finalize plans. However, because of mergers, corporate restructuring, and competition, businesses have been forced to operate globally (Furst et al., 2004; Roebuck, Brock, & Moodie, 2004). It is not always possible in terms of time and costs to pull employees together in one place for a meeting. As a result, researchers (Roebuck, Brock, & Moodie, 2004) have defined virtual teams as teams who conduct their work mostly through electronic technology. These cyberspace teams allow an organization to pool the talent and expertise of their employees by eliminating space and time barriers. Virtual encounters have "been characterized by high productivity, participation, satisfaction, and synergy among group members" (Nemiro, 2002, p. 70).

Background

Like the business environment, universities are also following the technological trends to provide for customer needs, to cut costs, and to compete effectively.

Creating virtual classrooms meets the growing need of people who cannot come to the university once a week. For example, students in virtual classes can travel to work without missing classes, and people who are not located near universities can still obtain a degree. Virtual classes do not need as much physical space, so universities can reduce the number of classrooms and technology labs, which cuts down on physical plant and maintenance costs. Therefore, virtual classes generate revenue without increasing budgets. Finally, classes can be offered anywhere in the world, which increases revenue. In this time of shrinking budgets, a project that decreases costs and increases revenues sounds like the perfect solution for education.

However, Kirschner and VanBruggen (2004) questioned whether the technologies designed for functional collaboration actually support learning. They theorized that for valued learning to take place, three factors must be working together: functional pedagogy, relevant content, and a sense of community. If any of the variables approached ratings of zero, then the valued learning experience would also approach zero. In the Students International Collaboration Project (SICP), all three factors are present to induce valued learning: the functional pedagogy is mentored self-learning; students are given objectives and relevant content; and professors mentor teams through the problem of creating a sense of community and trust. Therefore, theoretically, the SICP project includes all of the ingredients for success.

However, in another study, Berry (2002) asked whether virtual teams were more efficient and satisfying than traditional face-to-face teamwork. He studied the efficacy of electronic communication by using marketing students' perceptions of virtual teams. His research focused on the process rather than the design. Dr. Berry explored three success variables: perception of group cohesiveness, perception of satisfactory group interaction process, and perception of satisfactory group outcomes. His findings suggest that virtual teams can be just as efficient and satisfying as teams in face-to-face encounters. Therefore, the use of virtual teams allows universities to be more competitive, while at the same time accommodating student needs, and training them for the new work environment.

SICP — Students International Collaboration Project

Project Background

Near the end of the 1990s, Professor Stefaan Van Ryssen at the Hogeschool Gent University in Belgium developed an original project, *Marctica*, which used the Internet and the freedom of discovery as a new way to teach. Keeping the original philosophy of student collaboration, the SICP has been designed to focus on the behavioral lessons that can be brought to the students. SICP stands for Students International Collaboration Project. There are several goals to this project. The first goal is to create a virtual team crossing international borders and cultures. The second is to organize the relevant content by assigning a team-building project. The third is to learn about another culture by designing the project such that the students must integrate their efforts to accomplish their objective. The fourth goal is to learn team strategies by creating an environment where teams must work together without any interference. The fifth is to create the role of mentor where advice is given when asked, but is not mandated for action. Finally, the last objective is to give the students the opportunity to learn effective national/international communication skills on their own.

Project Organization

In the last few iterations of SICP, the French teams have been paired with American teams. The project begins by having students pairing up, usually 2-3 students on a team in each country. Then the faculty pair up French and American teams. These teams must get acquainted via e-mail by giving a basic summary of each member's background and interests. Once they have begun a dialogue, they must mutually decide on a topic for research, and the information that is needed. The verbalized objective is to write one paper that compares a French and American industry or business that will be submitted to both professors. Later in the semester, teams give oral presentations of the project, along with their perceptions and experiences. It is in this last stage that the real learning takes place. The true motivation for the assignments are exposed, and discussions commence on what students really learned about their own team-building abilities and communication skills.

The following statements are taken from observations and from more than 100 in-depth debriefings with the students, conducted each year after a project is completed. They are the result of longitudinal exploratory qualitative research on the SICP case. The external validity is limited, of course, but those statements can be used to adapt this project to other universities for the profit of their students.

The Project Process and Rationale

1. *Faculty pair up French and American teams.* The SICP relies on e-mail exchanges between the American and French students, so pairing is essential to the project. In a previous version, pairing was left to the students. Some may think that the exchanging of detailed group profiles among students could reflect Winch's (1958) theory that suggests students will be attracted to other students who would be able to satisfy their needs, thus creating compatible teams. But as Berscheid and Walster (1978) observed, the need-for complementarity rarely occurs, and experience from past SICP iterations backs up this theory. In fact, debriefings indicated that when students are left to their own devices, the pairing tends to follow Seyfried's (1977) hypothesis that complementarity and similarity of needs could exist together, but students have other priorities which are more important.

   So the coordinators handle the international pairing. In fact, post-debriefings have suggested that students are more amenable with the final choices and work better toward a positive solution when they are assigned partners. Also, it appears to be more efficient if the professors are involved in the beginning. Sometimes the pairing matches two groups with exactly the same interests. But in most cases, the profiles are too vague or too precise to allow for a perfect matching. As a result, the introductions between the two groups can last longer than the suggested time.

2. *Teams mutually decide on a topic for research.* To begin, the students must start their collaboration by collectively choosing a subject. The first step of the social exchange theory suggests that the individuals tend to behave in ways that produce benefits for themselves (Homans, 1961). This project is no different. Since the project is just beginning, the possibility of a fruitful compromise will not come spontaneously to their

minds. But, the topic decision must start with a compromise game, because each camp has its preferences, usually based upon the relative ease of collecting the necessary data. From their discussions, a common project emerges. Subsequent debriefings have taught us that students are usually not prepared for such talk. Typically, when they have to work in teams, the students are assigned a project and then form their team. The SICP sequence reverses the process. The teams are formed first and then they decide on the project. Since the two parties have equal status, they have to find a way to present the strongest arguments if they want their choice to be the one selected.

3. *Students must agree on information needed to learn about the subject.* Time is of the essence in this project. The teams only have five to six weeks to get acquainted and write a common marketing report about a service they choose to study and analyze. This service has to be provided both in the United States and in France to allow direct comparison. Students have to gather the most recent strategic and marketing data to make an interesting comparative analysis. The set of necessary topics and information has to be collectively determined by the teams. This is an important step, because if not accurately done, the comparison will be very difficult. Strategic analysis is not necessarily taught the same way in the United States and in France, which makes the exercise even more interesting.

   The chosen companies do not necessarily have to be the same in the United States and in France, but they do, of course, have to run the same type of business. Because students have to determine a common check-list, arguments arise about using a specific item. At this stage, it is typical for students to run to their respective professors and ask for them to step in and handle the argument. However, it is essential for faculty to offer suggestions, but not mediate. Therefore, the end result means that the students will have to talk and commonly settle the way that they wish to work.

4. *The final project is to write one paper for both professors on the findings and comparisons between the French and American industries, to be delivered on the same date.* A typical common problem at this step is procrastination. Many American students like to write their papers at the last minute, usually the night before. However, with the time difference and the delay in obtaining consensus with e-mail, last minute writing is not possible, if they want to turn the paper in on time. In addition, the French students must work hard at translating their thoughts into

English, which takes more time for them to edit and discuss. Finally, American students find that they have to correct grammar and sentence structure after the paper subjects have been addressed. So there are more steps to writing a paper than both sets of students realize.

On the final project, because academic systems are different in the United States and in France, it is not a good idea to decide a common grade. It would never be possible to have a weight and a balance that would be exactly the same for both teams. However, the level of importance that is assigned to the project on both sides should be meaningful. Experience has shown that when students do not have the similar classroom driven motivations and time constraints, it can become a major obstacle to success. Another issue with the common paper is to assure students that their own coordinator will be an autonomous evaluator. Even if the two coordinators are working as one, they have to give advice and complementary recommendations to their own students, so they are in the best position to analyze the achieved result. However, since both professors are grading the same paper, equal amounts of information from both sides are necessary to receive an excellent grade. Debriefings have taught us that it is reassuring for the students to know that their work — even if conducted with a foreign partner — will be evaluated by their own teacher, especially since it is common for the local group to request permission to add appendices to their own copy of the report. They have no authority to change the report, of course, but they can add to it.

Issues, Controversies, and Problems

Background

Any collaborative efforts are always subject to controversies and problems. Several of these are: the "free-rider effect," which refers to one team member not working and letting everyone else do the task; the "sucker effect," which is just the opposite — one member doing all the work; and the "ganging up on the task" which refers to everyone agreeing to do as little work as possible to make it easy while still getting the job done (Hakkinen, 2004). Any time a group of people comes together to do a task, these problems always come up, and computers and e-mail do not make these problems vanish. People still need to mutually develop goals, to negotiate their own conditions of collaboration, and to build common ground, especially given the different cultural norms (Hakkinen, 2004).

However, according to researchers (Archer, 2004; Roebuck, Brock, & Moodie, 2004; Chinowsky & Rojas, 2003), there are special challenges for teams operating in virtual space. First, there is the lack of face-to-face communication. People understand words, but they also rely on nonverbal gestures and body positioning to comprehend subtle innuendoes like humor. A quizzical look or a rolling of the eyes can speak volumes about how well the message is being communicated. "People who are corresponding online often seem to be or are brusquer, and sometimes even rude, than they would be in face-to-face conversation" (Bock, 2003, p. 43). Therefore, care in wording is more critical in cyberspace communications than in face-to-face meetings.

Second, teams need to develop a rapport so that they can trust one another. This trust allows people to express their opinions without fear, or to suggest new ideas without feeling intimidated. Trust is believing that teammates are there to work together in completing a common task. Especially in a virtual space, it is important not to judge each other (Archer, 2004), but to recognize individual differences in order to work more effectively. These differences are not only personal, but also variations in organizational cultures, and different accountabilities. Trust is much harder to develop without physical human interaction.

A third challenge is to agree on a method of governance that develops a way for each team member to share information so that nothing important is left out. In some ways, e-mail is easier to be heard because everyone automatically has a space for their opinion. However, cultural differences, styles of conflict management, and trust issues may change the way people communicate. Therefore, there should be extra time to allow for people to get to know each other (Bock, 2004).

Goals

The verbalized official goal of SICP is to conduct a strategic marketing analysis with a foreign partner but, of course, the real objective is to learn lessons in communication. Nevertheless, it is important not to fully reveal this objective at the beginning. This allows the students to freely discover these objectives while working with their partners. The most important component of the

SICP's philosophy is that collectively the teams will share the *same* project until the end, when they release their common report. So for several weeks the students have to create, install, develop, manage and protect a virtual relationship. Most of them are comfortable using the Internet, but they have not developed the skills to meet a new person and efficiently collaborate and adapt plans with that other person in order to finish a project.

The purpose of SICP was not to create a new pedagogical exercise to produce a grade, a new report to force students to learn, or a new exam to make them memorize data and regurgitate on command. The core purpose was to initiate a new kind of learning experience where the students could have a maximum amount of intellectual freedom and autonomy. From the debriefing results, it really works: "This is the first time teachers think we can do something completely on our own, and that's really great" or "I didn't like it when you left us alone at the beginning, telling us we were free to manage our project, but in fact we are not [alone], there are four of us that think we are alone on the same project, so finally we realized that we are not at all alone" or "The central principle of virtual exchange emphasizes the feeling of great autonomy, but therefore and thankfully it has to be shared with the foreign team." The new generation of students usually don't want to learn for the sake of learning. Instead of squandering time trying to generate student interest, this project hints, suggests, and explains that the mission is not just for the lesson or for the University. It is for the participants themselves to discover what working with somebody one does not know and does not see could mean. Some might say that this is just adding a few pinches of mystery. So what?! If it will bring natural interest and involvement, why couldn't this natural curiosity be an invisible part of the project?

Problems/Possibilities of International Teams

This project could be handled inside the same class. But the international side of the SICP is one of its core assets. Because of the differences in language, culture, and geographical distance, the exercise is similar in team-building strategies, and yet totally different in implementation. Even when working groups are formed in a classroom for an exercise, adaptation problems could happen. It's only human. But with the SICP, those "problems" are multiplied. And as the working time is limited, the involved students have no other choice but to adapt. Participants have to quickly learn to improve their communication capacities. They have to be permanently sensitive to potential inconsistencies in messages that vary in origin and credibility (Brody, 1991), as they will always be involved in a "virtual contact."

Team Strategies

At the master's level, students have already conducted many exercises and/or reports with a partner. So they think they know what teamwork is and how to develop a consistent strategy. But the new variable brought by the SICP is that they will be teamed with a foreign partner who is an unknown quantity, and who remains abroad. In the United States, as in France, schools and universities already include many different cultures. However this time, students are not only from different cultures, but also have different lifestyles, working techniques, and university training. School and public holidays interfere with plans, especially when each culture assumes that the other knows about their holidays. In addition, the students are separated by several time zones, which creates problems with organizing deadlines. And to add a little bit more complexity to the game, the clock is ticking away.

The project is scheduled to last a maximum of two months, so adaptation strategies should be known, mastered and most importantly, applied. As in the real world, strategy for virtual teams requires constant change management for maximum efficiency. During the debriefings, some students explained that adaptation is a "key element" or a "necessity," because there is no time to block the project if they do not agree with their foreign partners. Therefore, students have to deepen their understanding and open their minds to try to understand why they and their foreign counterparts are reacting to a situation in a certain manner.

Trust

Trust also has a great part to play in the "*game*." Each team will remain on its own territory during the entire project. This means that American students have to trust their French partners about the data collected in France, and vice versa. Strain, grievance and contention could then occur about delays, and the quality and/or sources of the data. If major problems occur, students will be encouraged to think back about the quality of their exchange while preparing their papers and writing their common lists. If discrepancy and criticism occur, then the students are invited to root out the reason for such behavior. It then becomes quickly obvious to the students, the reason is that the bases for trust were not created and the resulting distrust prevented planning from being fulfilled. So even if the situation was sometimes unfruitful because of adversarial conflicts, those students learn what started the complete lack of trust. As one of them admitted during the debriefing: "I just realize now some opportunities we didn't seize, just because we were a little bit too shy to communicate further with them." As a result, learning still takes place even in unproductive encounters.

Information Exchange

The students are strongly encouraged to continuously exchange information with their foreign partners. Nevertheless, the temptation remains high for groups to work on their side of the ocean and to combine their work at the end. Only a few groups define regular checkpoints to verify whether they are on the right track or not. Final results usually reflect the nature of the infrequently used process. But once again, results are not the main goal. Debriefings allow the coordinator to help the students understand why it was so difficult to adjust the data at the end, and that it would have been easier if they had constantly been in touch with their partners. The main reasons to explain unconstructive behavior are usually the same. Systematically, students perceived that it is much easier to just agree at the beginning about what has to be done than to maintain a continuous flow of information. However, this lesson can be learned by discussing and comparing the perceptions of teams who worked with a constant link and the others who did not.

International/National Communication Skills

At the master's level, French students are supposed to practice enough English to understand and be understood. But offering the teams a common language appears to be insufficient. Knowing another language's words and definitions is not the same thing as creating a comprehensible thought. The style of the phraseology and the colloquialisms from each country are very different. Learning to express oneself so that other people can understand the idea is difficult when speaking to fellow countrypersons, but the thought is infinitely more problematic when adapting to different thought patterns and different linguistic experiences.

Distance

Because this is a common comparison report, both groups must be involved in the writing. However, distance is a variable that most students don't understand right away. They believe that it will be just like e-mailing their friends. However, this distance is both geographical and temporal. It is geographical, because one part of the team is in the United States and the other one is in France. When teams are formed among students in the same classroom, they usually have the same timetable. However, virtual groups mix people not only with different cultures and habits, but also with very different academic calendars. For example, New Orleans has a Mardi Gras break, which means that the American students may be unavailable for three days. On the other hand, the French students had two weeks where they were in class from 8 a.m. to 8 p.m. Monday through Friday. Because of these different schedules, students had a hard time communicating in a timely fashion and questions were raised on both sides about the commitment of the other team. This was especially difficult when the project began at the same time as the two weeks of intensive French classes. Each group had to learn, as soon as possible, to consider their partner's timetable. This means not assuming that work is done at their own pace, but teams need to talk together to find a commonly profitable rhythm. It means mutual times to meet on the Internet, commonly accepted deadlines, and agreed-upon ways to format the data.

The distance between the teams is also temporal, because most of the time the exchanges are not handled *via* instant messaging but *via* traditional e-mailing. This delay offers opportunities for more thinking and better arguments from each team, but it also creates frustration at not being able to get a response immediately. Interaction effectiveness in this situation is of course lower than during a face-to-face discussion. For example, when asking students about electronic mail interviews (Schaefer & Dillman, 1998), students believed it offered "richer content," "more structure" and was "more adapted for an immediate use." On the other hand, e-mail does require knowledge about the other person's style of humor and personality, because the nonverbal part of the message is left out. Therefore, one needs to adapt the verbal message to incorporate the nonverbal inferences in order to communicate effectively. Another problem with temporal distance relates to the deadlines for writing the paper. Obtaining agreement from both teams takes time and usually the students forget that e-mail responses do not necessarily happen rapidly.

Problems in Communication

A *priori*, we could think that problems in communication could be more important on the French side of the SICP, as the officially used language is English. Obviously, French students have to make an effort to use a foreign language. But the potential communication problem is also on the American side. For example, American students can believe that their international counterparts are being difficult, or they can learn that words are not interpreted the same in all cultures. For example, a coffee shop in America is quite often a place to pick up coffee on the way to somewhere, and occasionally one sits at the location to drink it. On the other hand, a coffee shop in Paris is primarily a place to sit and watch people go by, and is rarely a quick stop. Therefore, questioning and defining words and terms to assure common understanding is always an ongoing process, rather than initially assuming everyone understands the topic and words.

Solutions and Recommendations

Student Learning Perspective

Bushman et al. (2001) suggest that complaining is a way to just feel a little bit better. In this case, those complaints constitute a wonderful lever for the learning process for the teacher. Because, as we naturally could expect, every complaint is targeted towards the foreign group. It's the most simple and usual illustration of Heider's (1958) observation about attributing causes to events. If a problem happens, the cause must be found in the foreign partner's behavior! Would this mean that the foreign partner is seen as having a systematic out-role, as defined by Jones and Davis (1965)? Probably not. Our debriefings do not allow us to go that far. But some students are not at all convinced that the foreign group has exactly the same goal and the same motivation to succeed in the SICP.

The main recurrent complaints are: "Oh, the foreigners didn't play the game" or "They never answered the e-mails" or "They didn't do their part in a timely fashion" or "How could we efficiently work together, as we do not share similar values?" As in the "real" world, value conflicts are often quite difficult to resolve simply because it hurts our system of beliefs (Susskind & Field, 1996). In the most serious cases, it can move toward intractability (Northrup, 1989), just because one part of the team feels threatened. Maintaining the conflict then appears necessary to the concerned students, because they are "defending" their values. Fortunately, in most of the cases, it leads to compromise. However, it is not easy for many students who do not succeed quickly, to step back to see the big picture. Then the intervention of the tutor might be necessary to ensure that teams do not waste too much time.

It is necessary to always keep in mind that as the exchange remains virtual, reactions can be very harsh towards the foreign team. Debriefings about identified problems (delays in answering, repeated criticism of the foreign team, complaints about the way they work, etc.) indicate that while the global team might be fragile in its relationships, the national aspects appear to be very strong. As a result, some students analyze afterwards that they wouldn't have acted as "badly" as they think they acted, if they would have been alone. This behavior illustrates Homes' (1990) analysis of the "easier" bad behavior against others, in the name of others, instead of for your own sake. Because the exchange is not face-to-face, people cannot look at one another and laugh at their stupidities. What is written is the only expression that each side has in evaluating behaviors.

Obviously, students are not aware of their personal progress while working on the SICP, because usually they are too busy focusing on the other side's misdemeanors rather than on their own behavioral evolution. But the limited time of the project forces them to work quite quickly, and therefore does not offer them the possibility to pause and reflect on "so what did I learn about myself today?" Even if this is the heart of the project, personal learning must be discovered by themselves and cannot be lectured. Nevertheless, when debriefed a few weeks later and questioned about personal communication problems, it is very interesting and reassuring to see how much less embittered students became about their foreign "partners" when they began to understand and reflect on their own behavior. It appears then that they begin to perceive what this project is about: adapting, if not correcting, their own communication problems.

This is a time for individual assessment and growth. Students learn to exchange information by drawing on all members of the team to share experiences. This creates confidence, raises challenges, develops adaptation skills, and identifies shared responsibilities. As a result, the main goals are for students to develop communication and team skills. Looking deeper into the project, some might say that it is too ambitious to produce efficient results when its success relies on giving the students the reins most of the time. However, in fact, the attempt is not so difficult if the framework is clearly given to the participants at the beginning. They need to understand the possibilities of the freedom to choose. Typically, teachers are always telling their students what the correct answer is. In this project, students have the right to choose what the "correct" decisions are. This should be the main part of the teacher's intervention, to transform this perceived freedom into a strongly bolstered personal challenge for each student.

Faculty Perspectives

Every teacher should keep in mind Galileo's well-known maxim: "You cannot teach a person anything; you can only help him find it within himself." If Galileo's thoughts are still true, then SICP represents a practical application of it. Every problem, even those with a precise framework, sets in motion a team perception of the problem, which has to be solved *by* the team. Even if the teacher took care to give preliminary advice about the fact that the project was not as easy as it might seem, eventually, every team learns this whenever there is a different point of view, different styles of communication, and of course, organizational problems. The natural classic reflex of the students is to put the blame on the foreign team partners. They run to the professor and demand solutions. The teacher's authoritarian solutions are usually obvious and could be implemented very quickly. But solving the problem for the students is much less interesting than inviting the students to find their own *ad hoc* solution. Learning by doing has always been the best teaching device. Pushing the students to make their own choices forces them to learn to identify the precise problem, to understand its roots, and to develop the role for the processor. The teacher's role is to make sure that teams are making problem-solving a top priority before other corollary problems occur. Here, the role of an efficient mentor is essential. If students are aware from the beginning that the coordinators keep in touch during the entire project, they are more likely to stay on top of their situations. Also, as faculty collaborate with each other and voice the foreign partner's complaints, students are forced to examine their own role in the effort.

However, it is always important to remember that coordinators are separated by the same geographical and temporal distances and, therefore, subject to the same issues as the students. A study among employees revealed that feedback tends to be considered unfair by employees when the boss did not succeed in collecting all the data (Leung et al., 2001). The same unsuccessful result could happen with the SICP, so the permanent connection between the coordinators is very important to help fill gaps in information so that students can gain a more complete picture of the situation. When a teacher observes that the students are sending regular e-mails to their counterparts, it is easy to assume that the foreigners are not doing their part. However, one needs to step back as a mentor to ask, "What is going on that I do not know about?" In one instance, some of the American teams were frustrated with slow responses, until they found out that the French students were preparing their graduation celebrations and had temporarily been overwhelmed with work. If those exchanges happen quickly and efficiently, the students perceive that there are two sides to every story, and that they need to think about their own actions before they complain about others. After all, they are technically on the same side because they, as a team, must be productive and create a product within a specified period of time.

If this bulwark is not commonly and permanently defended by the coordinators, then interest in the SICP can rapidly die. It's a double-trigger process. First, complaints must always be put into context. Each of them should be heard, of course, just because each student has to be supported during the project to keep their motivation high. But the limit of this support has to be the limit of the effort done by the student himself. So the student must be questioned about his own group's behavior concerning a complaint to allow him to appreciate a wider perspective. If the core purpose of the complaint remains, then the student is informed that the mentor will quickly contact the foreign coordinator. The most important rule is that things have to be understood and treated very quickly. In the past, teachers didn't have the opportunity to meet their students every day. In most of the cases, it was once a week. However, the Internet now represents a permanent convenient link. In less than 24 hours, coordinators can have a clear view of the situation that gives them the opportunity to give both sides a similar adequate response.

Of course, the students make many mistakes and errors during the SICP. As might be expected, from a learning point of view, teams that are making mistakes are much more interesting than the ones for which SICP seems to be a very simple and convenient game. It is useful to follow Funder's (1987) distinction between error and mistake, to be able to explain the different situations to the students. Explaining to students who complain that it is an *error* to do so without trying to talk with their partners beforehand and trying to solve the problem on their own, this often reveals the *mistake* that triggered the whole thing (a forgotten message, data collected the wrong way, a missed deadline, a non-shared decision about the chosen enterprises, etc.).

Naturally, such a project can also be very productive for the teacher as well. With just two students, on average, teams remain small and easy to manage. So the teacher will be able to develop a different academic relationship with his or her students. Of course, as mentioned above, complaints do occur, but keep in mind that the purpose of the faculty is not to solve problems, but to aid the students in finding ways to solve problems within their own virtual relationship. Therefore, the faculty represent potential support, more a guide than corrector, more a coach than just a lecturer. And even more importantly, it allows faculty to learn more about the individual students and their capacities (or lack of) to manage this kind of project.

Satisfaction with the Process

Whatever the quality of the coordinator's original speech to the SICP to motivate his or her own troops, the interest, and so the motivation, will of course differ from one student to another. Beyond the natural motivation of each student, SICP represents a real challenge from more than just the academic point of view. The final obtained grade or mark is not the main goal, so satisfaction should not be linked to formal evaluation.

Using e-mail and only e-mail for their exchange appeared to be an important constraint to many at the beginning of the process. As debriefing quotes mention: "It's not fully reliable in fact, I was really scared about what to do if they didn't answer?" "Many messages are lost on the Web and we didn't know if they would really play the game" or "As the rule was to manage by ourselves, I think that we didn't use the e-mail as usual, but much more carefully." Two populations can be observed here: the students with, and those without, concrete professional experience. The students without any business experience were generally more afraid about using the e-mail as the communication tool. The others were far less concerned because when questioned about it, it appeared that e-mail is considered to be just a cost-effective communication tool for professionals (Stevens, 2004).

Outcomes

Just like some employees do not appreciate facing challenges in the enterprise (Wanous, 1974), some students do not appreciate challenges during their studies. Debriefings sadly confirm that for some of them studying "has to be done whatever the exercise, the lesson, the teacher, the university." All the students who did not consider the SICP as a challenge appeared to be unsatisfied at the end, or without any opinion about their satisfaction. But in a very reassuring point of view, a majority of students understand from the beginning that SICP represents a real challenge. However, most of them admit that they did not understand that the challenge was about themselves, and not just about writing a common report.

The American students only had class discussion as they turned in their papers. At the time, it was an oral team presentation. It would be more productive if an individual reaction paper were written discussing the informal lessons students learned during the project. On the French side, debriefings are conducted one week after the end of the SICP and a second wave of debriefings with the same students at the end of their term four months later. During those four months, they are trainees in different enterprises. As a result, student consciousness is truly different between those two waves. If a satisfaction rate could be measured, the increase would be obvious four months later. The reason is that soon after the project, most students are just beginning to realize that they have learned something about the way they work and the way they could improve. Many of them who considered the SICP as a challenge admit during the second debriefing that it really helped them to communicate differently with people inside the enterprise.

Some would think that the debriefing results might be different between the American and the French groups. Not at all. All of them found the SICP more original than a standard exercise. All of them are conscious that in a way, SICP put them under stress. All of them could list complaints (usually the same) against the foreign part of their team. All of them realized they probably did not organize their work in the most efficient way possible. And all of them believed that they learned more than just the content of their report. Chris Argyris' (1982) works could easily apply here, as under those "difficult" conditions, a large majority of the students admitted that they only reacted in a certain way to keep the situation under their control without really trying to make the team progress as a whole. This arrangement is similar to the kind of projects that the students will have to manage when on the job. They will have to work with people they don't choose and/or even know. A virtual team project offers a small-scale test of the real world. And, using cross-cultural teams like SICP offers students the possibility to learn about cultural and individual differences in ways of thinking, ways of working and ways of managing people.

What seems interesting is that many participants admitted that SICP changed the way they were using e-mail, forcing them to: "better read the content before pushing the send button"; "check all the points mentioned in the partners' request before replying"; "slow the pace of the exchange"; "always check that all the partners are put in the copy"; "never send a message without a receipt request because it lets you know it arrived even if the reply could be delayed because of your question." The student rethinking of e-mail was never a planned objective of the SICP, but obviously we considered that it could help the participants to really make a more efficient use of e-mail communication in their professional life.

Reflections and Future Trends

Learning projects like SICP are fertile training grounds to improve virtual team communication. Warkentin and Beranek (1999) found that teams that were given appropriate training over time exhibited improved perceptions of the interaction process, specifically with regard to trust, commitment, and frank expression between members. It appears that to get the most out of virtual teams, people need to learn new communication skills that are adapted to the new methods. Crossing boundaries and cultures requires rethinking communication patterns and ways of using words. When Pauleen and Yoong (2001) analyzed many different studies on relationship building and the use of information and communication technologies (ICT), they concluded that the ultimate challenge is to work at merging the individual cultures of the teams into a team culture. This "cultural melding" is a key to success that takes a high level of relationship building in order to succeed.

The media revolution strongly contributed to opening students' minds about life in general and their social environment in particular. Past generations of students could be described as studious, disciplined and easily manageable, if not simply compliant. On the other hand, many teachers today would probably be hesitant to use those same adjectives to describe their students. The current generation is less compliant, more questioning, and may just be more aware in general because of their easy access to information. In the past, teachers were the sole masters of knowledge in the classroom. If a student wanted to learn more, it was the teacher who was the natural, legitimate authority and guardian of the gateways to knowledge. French author Charles de Secondat, Baron de la Brède et de Montesquieu, wrote that the man who teaches could easily become stubborn, because he is doing the job of a man who is never wrong. Today, the media, and more recently the Internet has opened a wide door to an endless, easily accessible, and usually free knowledge base to any person who seeks information. Some might think that teachers could become useless in such a new world. However, students need someone to stimulate and motivate them about the excitement of learning. If teachers are still potentially useful, they have to be defined differently in order to operate effectively. The main reason may rely on a single word: "freedom." Once students learn about the Internet, they want to feel the same freedom to access knowledge in the classroom that they have at home.

Student Learning in Virtual Groups

So, does the SICP create a good application for virtual team collaboration? Like some kind of sleeper effect that will reveal itself to the protagonists after the exercise, the learning process in virtual groups that are involved in SICP differs deeply from what could happen in face-to-face groups. Students have to learn to handle conflict in a different way than they would have normally used. Gathering debriefing results about conflicts helped the coordinators to understand, as Robbins (1974) noted, that most of the conflicts do not arise from a lack of communication. Sometimes, the number of exchanges between two groups of a team increases without any improvement in communication. The problem usually lies on the original foundation of the teams' relationship. In the problem teams, the two groups usually did not take time to understand each other at the beginning of the exercise, so doubt and suspicion permeated the relationship. Therefore, when even a little problem occurs, blame is placed on the other party. On the other hand, with trust comes respect.

For a large majority of the students, the SICP was their first experience working with foreign partners. Debriefings with the students told us that it was very rare that relationships lasted after the project. Deeper analysis has been done during the last two years to identify the reasons. Could the fact that their relationships remained virtual simply explain it? But none of the students agree with this reason, always giving other examples of relationships they strongly nourish *via* the Internet. The two main reasons systematically given are the pairing system and the duration of the project. For reasons of academic planning and compatibility, the SICP lasts roughly two months and, as explained above, the coordinators now organize the pairing. Therefore, the team often does not really have time to develop their partnership long enough to develop a real relationship.

The research project is an opportunity for students to create their own learning. It is not the usual procedure of learning a lesson organized by the teacher, keeping it in mind until the exam, and regurgitating the right and wrong answers on a test to show that they understood the basics. With SICP, most students see just the fun and frustration of communicating with another student thousands of miles away. However, if the students are not made aware of their objective, the project could easily fail. This is not conditioning, but letting participants fully understand their responsibilities toward their partners and, of course, toward themselves. Once the task is over and the paper turned in, they can look back and evaluate the implications of their behaviors and decisions.

Therefore, the purpose of this chapter is not to offer a perfect instrument to every interested teacher, but to share the SICP experiences. The overall philosophy of the project was to allow students to adapt to this feeling of freedom, and for faculty to let go of control. This, of course, does not mean that teachers are only involved at the beginning and at the end, and not for the remainder of the project. It means that the professor is there to support this freedom by aiding in the learning process.

While there are many issues to explore, the virtual teams of the SICP are exciting and creative. Students enjoy meeting people from outside their cultures and getting to know them. As the problems begin to arise with communications, students learn that there are two sides to every story, and that productivity is a matter of understanding everyone's role in the process. And then at last, they start to really think about their own behavior and what they really learned from this exercise. It's amazing to then hear that it was fruitful, even funny sometimes, or that they didn't figure it could require some special skills to just talk with a foreign project partner and build something in common with him. And that is it! That is the lesson.

We believe that the learning process has just started. American and French students will have other opportunities to remember some working situation or exchange of the SICP project in the future. At that time, they will consider that it was much more interesting than the sole marketing project itself. And then we will have our full reward.

References

Archer, D. (2004, October/November). The myths of teamworking. *IEE Engineering Management*, 16-18.

Argyris, C. (1982). *Reasoning, learning and action: Individual and organizational.* San Francisco: Jossey-Bass.

Argyris, C. (1991, May-June). Teaching smart people how to learn. *Harvard Business Review,* 99-110.

Berry, R. W. (2002). The efficacy of electronic communication in the business school: Marketing students' perceptions of virtual teams. *Marketing Education Review, 12*(2), 73-78.

Berscheid, E., & Walster, E. (1978). *Interpersonal attraction* (2nd edition). Reading, MA: Addison-Wesley.

Bock, W. (2003, Fall). Profundity. *The Journal For Quality And Participation, 43.*

Brody, E. W. (1991). *Managing communication processes — From planning to crisis response.* New York: Praeger.

Bushman, B. J., Baumeister, R. F., & Phillips, C. M. (2001). Do people aggress to improve their mood? Catharsis beliefs, affect regulation opportunity, and aggressive responding. *Journal of Personality and Social Psychology, 81,* 17-32.

Chinowsky, P. S., & Rojas, E. M. (2003, July). Virtual teams: Guide to successful implementation. *Journal of Management in Engineering,* 98-106.

Funder, D. C. (1987). Errors and mistakes: Evaluating the accuracy of social judgment. *Psychological Review, 101,* 75-90.

Furst, S. A., Reeves, M., Rosen, B., & Blackburn, R. S. (2004). Managing the life cycle of virtual teams. *Academy of Management Executive, 18*(2), 6-20.

Hakkinen, P. (2004). What makes learning and understanding in virtual teams so difficult? *Cyberpsychology & Behavior, 7*(2), 201-206.

Heider, F. (1958). *The psychology of interpersonal relations.* New York: John Wiley.

Homans, G. C. (1961). *Social behavior: Its elementary forms.* New York: Harcourt, Brace & World.

Homes, S. (1990). The secret history of self-interest. In J. J. Mansbridge (Ed.), *Beyond self-interest* (pp. 267-286). Chicago: University of Chicago.

Jones, E. E., & Davis, K. E. (1965). From acts to dispositions: The attribution process in person perception. In L. Berkowitz (Ed.), *Advances in experimental social psychology, Vol. 2* (pp. 219-266). New York: Academic.

Kirschner, P. A., & Bruggen, J. V. (2004). Learning and understanding in virtual teams. *Cyberpsychology & Behavior, 7*(2), 135-139.

Leung, K., Su, S., & Morris, M. W. (2001). When is criticism *not* constructive? The roles of fairness perceptions and dispositional attribution in employee acceptance of critical supervisory feedback. *Human Relations, 54,* 1155-1187.

Nemiro, J. E. (2002). The creative process in virtual teams. *Creativity Research Journal, 14*(1), 69-83.

Northrup, T. A. (1989). The dynamic of identity in personal and social conflict. In T. Kriesbergy, T. A. Northrup, & S. J. Thornson (Eds.), *Intractable conflicts and their transformations* (pp. 55-82). Syracuse, NY: Syracuse University.

Pauleen, D. J., & Yoong, P. (2001). Relationship building and the use of ICT in boundary-crossing virtual teams: A facilitator's perspective. *Journal of Information Technology, 16,* 205-220.

Robbins, S. (1974). *Organizational conflict: A nontraditional approach.* Upper Saddle River, NJ: Prentice Hall.

Robbins, S. (2002). *The truth about managing people... and nothing but the truth.* Upper Saddle River, NJ: Prentice Hall PTR.

Roebuck, D. B., Brock, S. J., & Moodie, D. R. (2004). Using a simulation to explore the challenges of communicating in a virtual team. *Business Communication Quarterly, 67*(3), 359-367.

Schaefer, D., & Dillman, D. (1998, Fall). Development of standard e-mail methodology: Results of an experiment. *Public Opinion Quarterly, 62*(3), 378-397.

Seyfried, B. A. (1977). Complementarity in interpersonal attraction. In S. Duck (Ed.), *Theory and practice in interpersonal attraction*, London: Academic.

Stevens, G. (2004). New technology briefing. Best practices technology options for optimal e-mail marketing. *Interactive Marketing, 6*(1), 62-70.

Susskind, L., & Field, P. (1996). *Dealing with an angry public: The mutual gain approach*. New York: Free.

Wanous, J. P. (1974, October). Individual differences and reactions to job characteristics. *Journal of Applied Psychology, 59,* 616-622.

Warkentin, M., & Beranek, P.M. (1999). Training to improve virtual team communication. *Information Systems Journal, 9,* 271-289.

Winch, R. F. (1958). *Mate selection: A study in complementary needs.* New York: Harper & Row.

Section IV

Teams and Technology

Chapter XI

Computer Mediated Technology as Tools for Social Interaction and Educational Processes: The Implications for Developing Virtual Teams

Karen Rohrbauck Stout
Western Washington University, USA

Abstract

Computer mediated technologies (or CMTs) enhance educational processes and are tools that have particular implications for learning and interacting in virtual teams. To better understand how educational tools may be implemented to enhance student learning in virtual teams, the author addresses Wartofsky's (1979) explication of tools as cultural artifacts. Distinctions about primary, secondary, and tertiary tools provide a framework to analyze implementations of educational CMT research. Implications of these tools on virtual team's cognitive skills and collaborative learning are explored. Tertiary tools are explored in particular, as they may provide virtual teams with shared interaction space and alternative representations of the social world. The author provides examples of CMT implementation and suggestions for technological and pedagogical advancements.

Introduction

Among faculty, students, academic leaders, and the general public, there is a growing recognition of the power of information technology to help improve the quality of teaching and learning, improve the motivation and attention of students, and improve students' career preparation. (Gilbert, 1996, p. 12)

Technology has the potential to transform learning. It has already transformed organizational environments, as computer mediated and satellite technologies make collaboration possible among geographically dispersed individuals without face-to-face interaction. In organizational environments, virtual team members collaborate via computer mediated technologies (called CMTs) to accomplish goals or outcomes. These computer mediated interactions and relationships hold potential value for organizations, as time (i.e., across time zones) and space (i.e., across geographic distance) hold particular challenges for accomplishing and coordinating goals. Increasingly, educators create virtual teams (i.e., in graduate and undergraduate programs, for business training) to provide geographically dispersed individuals access to educational experiences. Advancements in the development of educational CMTs have led to popular perceptions of technology as capable of widespread, qualitative change. Implementations of educational CMTs have been limited, however, particularly in training students for virtual teamwork.

Educational CMTs are tools to enhance teaching and learning. To demonstrate how these tools may be implemented, the author addresses Wartofsky's (1979) explication of tools as cultural artifacts. Wartofsky's distinctions about primary, secondary, and tertiary tools provide a framework to analyze, design, and implement educational CMTs and hold particular implications for virtual teams. The author reviews current implementations of technology in light of

Wartofsky's framework, exploring how technology mediates cognition and interaction. This review highlights tool use with implications for virtual teams' learning and interacting. Virtual teams may think and talk about material in an alternative, motivating learning environment when Wartofsky's framework guides CMT applications. Wartofksy's theory offers direction for technological development, and this study provides examples for higher education in general and organizational communication courses specifically.

CMT as a Cultural Tool and Artifact

Tools preserve and transmit skills, which allows the continuation of social and cultural organizations. Our perception of the world occurs through the context of tool creation and use (Wartofsky, 1979). Because tools alter human perception, they constrain the possibilities of action and thought (Resnick, 1991). Our perception is filtered through representations of cultural values:

> *The human intention is embodied both in the tools used in production, in the skills acquired and adapted to this use, and in the forms of symbolic communication which develop in language, in art, in dance and poetry, in their origins . . . the dominant forms of representation are the filters . . . and more than this, actually transform the function (and speculatively, also the structure) of these mechanisms.*(Wartofsky, 1979, p. 205)

Humans cycle tools back into the culture, altering modes of action and perpetuating the cycle. This feedback loop results in human perception and praxis that are mediated by action and tools (Wartofsky, 1979). Like those who create and use them, CMTs are embedded in a larger culture that socializes learners into a particular social and cultural milieu (Lambrecht, 1993). As representations of a culture, CMTs contain the culture's intellectual history and particular theories. This may have significant implications for mental work, as tools assist in cognitive processing needs (Resnick, 1991). Therefore, tools warrant great scrutiny and reflection.

The continued examination of the design and implementation of educational CMTs is an important part of this feedback loop. Educators can play proactive roles by carefully selecting CMTs for students and learning goals. Information derived from virtual teams' classroom learning directly parallels organizations' virtual team efforts. As technology is an artifact and tool of our culture, we need to reflect on embedded cultural representations and how technology mediates the learning process. In time, educators can cycle appropriate tools back into culture as representations and modes of action, thereby unleashing the power of technology (Gilbert, 1996) to improve learning in educational and organizational teams.

Levels of Tool Development and Potentiality

Wartofsky (1979) identifies three levels of cultural tools (i.e., primary, secondary, and tertiary) that differentially contribute to modes of action and, therefore, perception. *Primary artifacts* accomplish tasks directly related to the production and reproduction of the species. These may be physical objects (e.g., clubs, axes, and bowls) necessary for existence. They can also include the development of survival skills (e.g., hunting and foraging) and practices (e.g., division of labor), conveyed in a social group across generations (Wartofsky, 1979). Primary tools allow people to master their bodies and to develop perceptions related to signs and patterns. In short, primary tools encourage the mind's mastery over the body to actively produce and reproduce existence. The use of language as a tool for communicating is an example of a primary artifact (Wartofsky, 1979). Primary tools such as overhead projectors, presentation software, e-mail, and bulletin board systems (or BBSs[1]) assist with the act of communication. These tools make communication more effective and efficient in educational, social, and organizational contexts. Virtual teams rely heavily on primary tools like e-mail and BBSs to communicate.

Secondary artifacts use symbols to communicate, perceive, and *represent* primary modes of activity. They are mimetic in nature and become modes of activity unto themselves. They imitate and represent objects and activity associated with primary tools. They are not internal perceptions but external embodiments, or products, of direct outward action. They are used in the fundamental human activity of teaching. Teachers use symbols to communicate and represent knowledge and activity for students' perception. Secondary artifacts perpetuate culture through the teaching/learning process. They preserve and transmit the status quo and current modes of action back into the culture through students' activity and communication (Wartofsky, 1979).

Examples of secondary artifacts include the software, hardware, and teaching practices that construct online, distance, or "virtual" teams and classes. Blackboard© and other similar Web-based team and learning platforms are also secondary tools, as they are multi-modal electronic representations (via multiple primary tools like e-mail, BBS) of traditional face-to-face environments. These tools attempt to replace and represent existing teaching or small group work practices. They are preserved (i.e., saved electronically) and transmitted (whether synchronous or asynchronous) via primary tools to accomplish goals (i.e., the absorption of disciplinary specific knowledge or practices). The Internet and World Wide Web are also examples of secondary artifacts. They are cultural models of actual worlds represented through action and physical objects, as well as abstract worlds constructed through social interaction and discourse. They are symbolic representations of extant modes of action (e.g., commerce, community building, and entertainment), and as such, represent and feed current cultural representations back into discourse and view. Organizational and educational virtual teams use secondary tools to accomplish goals and tasks in an Internet-based instructional environment.

Wartofsky (1979) identifies a third level of tool or artifact called *tertiary*. These artifacts provide imaginative worlds (i.e., "off-line" worlds) where individuals can prepare for future genuine interactions and experiences by engaging in spontaneous play-activity without negative consequences. Wartofsky (1979) argues humans need this free activity to give us practice for future "online" worlds (p. 207). He ties human play activity to animal play activity to demonstrate the importance of these artifacts. Young animals, for example, do not imitate adult animal hunting behavior when they playfully fight amongst themselves. Instead, they imaginatively construct possible future hunting actions through play-instinct. By doing so, they learn future modes of action (Wartofsky, 1979). Artifacts used in free-play often contain imagery similar to dreams, as these tools are derived and abstracted from (but not bound to) perceptions, history, and actual world praxis. Potentially, tertiary artifacts feed creative imagery back into actual praxis and represent possibilities beyond present actualities (p. 209). This feedback loop feeds cultural evolution as alternative representations influence perception, action, communication, and production (Wartofsky, 1979). Virtual teams may use imaginative "play" games as tertiary tools. This chapter will expand upon those possibilities in the recommendations section.

Analyzing CMT Literature with Wartofsky's Model

Primary Tool Use: Producing and Reproducing Knowledge through CMT

At the primary level, educational CMTs consist of computer software and hardware that assist in the communication process. They convey information more efficiently and effectively, which assists in the higher order processing of disciplinary content, problem-solving, and critical thinking. In addition, these tools change the nature of interaction between teachers and students, making the classroom more student-centered. These primary tools enhance the *cognitive* and *interactive* nature of educational process and have important implications for virtual teams.

Primary tools that serve as *cognitive enhancers* alter student behavior and comprehension of material, resulting in higher order processing and cognitive skill development. Often these software programs allow students to progress at their own rate, which encourages learning through mastery. A number of scholars have reported the value of software programs designed to model and represent information, particularly information difficult to convey through face-to-face communication (e.g., Lambrecht, 1993; Mioduser & Marin, 1995; Shih & Alessi, 1993-4; Swan & Mitrani, 1993; Wizer, 1995).

Research indicates that software programs enhance student cognition. They perform tedious mathematical functions and provide visual representations of material, which frees students to more deeply process and understand course material (Lambrecht, 1993). Students who use such software organize declarative knowledge better than those who do not (Shih & Alessi, 1993-4). Schemas develop because of such representations, allowing abstract information processing and reasoning about dynamic processes. This is important as schemas do not naturally develop as a by-product of schooling. They develop through participation in and control of the learning process (Mioduser & Marin, 1995).

Enhanced cognition can lead to enhanced student-led interaction that indicates higher-order thinking usually performed by teachers. Students ask for help, ask and answer questions, and in general, direct their own learning more when using such software (Swan & Mitrani, 1993; Wizer, 1995). When compared to traditional classrooms, students in CMT classrooms engaged the teacher in *any type* of conversation and provided explanations to each other (Swan & Mitrani, 1993).

Some primary CMTs (e.g., e-mail, synchronous chat, BBS, and programs like Group Support Systems[2]) replace aspects of face-to-face communication by design. These communication technologies are *interactive enhancers* and have several advantages: flexibility of time (as communication can be synchronous or asynchronous and occur when convenient), access to others (through multiple interactional modes), speed of feedback (helpful for facilitating group projects), and student-directed problem-solving. Virtual teams need e-mail because of its speed and ease of use, which helps team members to remain in almost constant contact. But e-mail has the additional benefit of communicating and managing multiple identities (Sunderland, 2002). In a study of a primarily distance-learning doctoral program, many enrolled students worked as professionals in other organizations. Students used e-mail to obtain social support, but also marked their multiple identities within their e-mail messages (Sunderland, 2002). E-mail needs to be recognized by educators and team members as a tool worth more than a quick response across distances. E-mail is also a primary tool in communicating who we are and what we need from others across time and space.

Bulletin board systems are used in educational environments to continue class discussions or introduce new topics. The expectation is that CMT provides a free, egalitarian forum for student participation, although that may not always be the case when people with their histories, prejudices, and flaws put these technologies into use. Althaus (1997) found that BBSs successfully facilitated small-group discussions about course topics, allowing more views to be heard. Such enhancements to interaction encourage students to be more engaged in learning, as well as process information at higher levels. Thus virtual teams should use these primary tools to facilitate interaction, as well as enhance learning.

Researchers have compared and coordinated technology and discussions to explore the impact on classroom interaction. Face-to-face discussions were qualitatively improved when sequenced after computer-mediated interactions (i.e., BBS for some, chat for others). Students provided a greater diversity of perspectives in class and enjoyed the computer-mediated discussions more (Dietz-Uhler & Bishop-Clark, 2001). Pena-Shaff, Martin, and Gay (2001) compared BBS-based discussions with synchronous chats and found chats to be more collaborative and social, but often off-task and conflicting. However,

BBS postings were well developed and structured, but "genuine" interactions did not occur (p. 41). The potentialities and characteristics of technology and implications for educational and organizational virtual teams require educators to carefully select and enhance technologies for use.

Primary tools also enhance students' decision-making and small-group capabilities. For virtual teams, these functions are critical. Collaborative, synchronous computer-mediated systems, such as GSS, enhance the productivity and quality of discussions by coordinating idea generation and evaluation, building consensus, managing information, and collaborative writing. In short, they facilitate discussion and decision making: an advantage for virtual teams. In one study, students using GSS brainstormed a larger quantity of quality, innovative solutions than those without GSS (Jessup, Egbert, & Connolly, 1995-6). A similar program called Idea Web© provided students an opportunity outside the classroom to discuss course topics, which resulted in better test scores and course grades (Ahern & Durrington, 1995, 1996; Ahern & Repman, 1994; Everett & Ahern, 1994). Marjanovic (1999) details a number of pedagogical uses for GSS, including interactive lecturing and students' collaborative development of a course dictionary. These computer-mediated practices engage students in interaction with each other and encourage higher-order processing of material. Marjanovic (1999) argues these methods encourage students' interactive learning, but increase teachers' preparation time and alter their pedagogical assumptions. Primary tools facilitate interaction and cognition in virtual teams, as well as improve instructors' abilities to gauge student learning and activity.

Primary tools enhance students' cognition about course concepts by providing basic calculations and mental models. More attention must be paid to modeling and representations of content for students and virtual teams. Certain concepts or theories may be particularly suited to computer modeling, as models represent processes and free students to creatively internalize information. If these models are made available via textbooks, teachers' manuals, research publications, and educational DVDs and CD-Roms, scholars will contribute to the evolution of instruction.

Secondary Tool Use: Reproduction of Processes through Technology

Secondary tools reproduce classroom and workplace environments (i.e., synchronous and local) into virtual environments (i.e., asynchronous/synchronous and distant) through the collections of ideas, skills, and *primary tools*. Combinations of primary tools (e.g., e-mail, BBS, Web pages, etc.) and teaching practices provide multiple modes for interacting among team members, teacher, and course material. Secondary tools retain the benefits of primary tools, but hold their own challenges as they represent and perpetuate the status quo (Wartofsky, 1979). Secondary tools *reproduce* aspects of educational interaction like classroom environments, workspace, tutoring, and social presence. This is important for virtual teams, as secondary tools replace aspects of face-to-face, real-time educational interaction. This implicates the supervision of virtual teams and the construction of educational workspace (i.e., the "classroom").

Secondary tools attempt to replace and represent existing teaching practices. Primary level CMTs are used in conjunction to discuss, complete, and share course assignments, replacing face-to-face interaction, which offers a variety of implications for virtual teams. In an educational psychology course, e-mail and BBS replaced and represented the administration, organization, creation, and evaluation of student group projects (Anderson, 1996). These technologies provided students with increased access to each other, the instructor, and course information. Students were not bound by space or time to read each other's questions and responses, which often included answers to questions they had not yet thought of. Further, the instructor could better assess individual participation and contribution to group projects by reading BBS posts, and, in essence, attend group meetings (Anderson, 1996). Students and faculty both benefit from secondary tools' capability for representing communicative activity and information preserved and transformed through primary tools.

Web sites are secondary tools used by educators to construct and share course assignments, which have important implications for virtual teams. In a study of high-school and graduate-school students' use of the World Wide Web for assignment completion, students researched, developed, and posted group projects. The Web pages helped students structure participation in project groups, provided them personal work space, supplied them access to others' work, and demarcated individual members' contributions (Pychyl, Clarke, & Abarbanel, 1999). In a study exploring the use of GroupShare software, students collaborated in anonymous groups to complete multiple class assignments. They used this Web-based software, which allowed asynchronous communication and text sharing, but kept participants anonymous (Flanagin, 1999). Even in these anonymous groups, students formed bonds with each other and enjoyed collaboration. Their satisfaction was influenced, however, by the complexity of the task (Flanagin, 1999). Secondary tools provide virtual teams essentially with educational workspaces that replicate and, in some ways, improve the face-to-face classroom environment. Further, even if anonymous, virtual teams can be satisfied with collaboration via secondary tools, task complexity should be kept in mind.

Secondary tools' ability to present and communicate student work and activity is important to the education of our students, as students learn from each other's work. At Texas Tech University, communication has been enhanced between virtual team members, distance education students, and clients. They have all responded positively to significant curriculum design changes where students create and present their work via Web sites (Bagert & Mengel, 2005). HTML document templates facilitate students' creation of projects and a class Web page presents these projects for others to view. This work has been so successful that the undergraduate and graduate software design curriculum (a total of 12 courses) has been designed around this technology. The challenge, however, is to develop such curriculum and learning opportunities for students outside the disciplinary area of software design (i.e., in business, communication, and psychology).

Conventional tutorial programs are secondary teaching tools that CMT has the potential to transform. Tutorial programs can be inconvenient for many students (Weller, 2000) and often costly for universities. Geographical isolation, time commitments, disabilities, and lacking motivation keep students from seeking out traditional tutorial assistance (Weller, 2000). Universities must find accessible office and work space, develop a convenient schedule, and a knowledgeable staff. Group tutoring sessions associated with particular classes can be difficult to schedule and under-attended. Secondary CMTs alleviate many of these issues, however, as demonstrated in existing literature. In one tutorial program, students interacted with tutors and each other via synchronous "chats," e-mail, and BBS. They posed questions to the tutor via chat sessions, as well as to the BBS for the tutor or others to answer. Students appreciated the program's flexibility and access, as most of them had not sought out tutors previously. They also appreciated learning vicariously from other students' questions or interactions with the tutor. Interestingly, however, interactions were reported to be more student-led than tutor-led, as students solved problems together (Weller, 2000). This holds important implications for virtual teams, as group conferencing and mentoring can be conveniently and successfully accomplished without face-to-face meetings and at any time or day. Virtual teams may be more group-led than instructor- or supervisor-led. Virtual tutorial programs are a promising development for secondary level tools with important implications for virtual team interaction and supervision.

In another study of a tutorial program, researchers explored the importance of social presence on tutor-student interaction (Schweizer, Paechter, & Weidenmann, 2001). Students received photos of the tutor, audio recordings of the written feedback, or both to manipulate the variable of "tutor social presence." Researchers found that student communication was more task-oriented, formal, and highly emotional when the tutor's social presence was lacking, although the effect lessened over time. The researchers also found that students added social presence in their own e-mails by the use of sideways typographic symbols called "emoticons" (i.e., :-)); (Schweizer et al., 2001). While this study is limited in its generalizability because of its small sample size, it indicates the need to develop technological means of increasing audio, video, and textual modes of social presence for virtual teams.

Social presence is an important issue for secondary level tools, as they represent and replace face-to-face, synchronous, local interaction. Low social presence was a problem in an asynchronous online graduate course, as students missed interacting with other students (Russo, Campbell, Henry, & Kosinar, 1999). The instructor's social presence was effectively conveyed in the course through a combination of audio-lectures, text slides, illustrations, lecture notes, readings, BBS discussions, and photographs. Students complained, however, at the loss of social presence among students themselves, a benefit of traditional classrooms lost in the virtual learning environment. This indicates a significant challenge for virtual teams, as the loss of face-to-face interaction also means a loss of social co-presence. Technologies need to improve and virtual team members need to be aware of perceptions of social presence.

Educational secondary CMTs represent working in professional virtual teams, which benefits students' learning about course material and enhances their understanding about professional and organizational life. One study directly addresses the parallels between educational tools and professional virtual teams. Students used Blackboard© in a graduate-level knowledge management class to perform a creative group task. They then individually reflected upon their learning via BBS postings, assignments posted to the site, and other activities (Pauleen, Marshall, & Egort, 2004). Students applied course concepts and theories from traditional lecture to their Blackboard© creations and reflections, which indicated higher-order thinking. Students recognized this benefit and found this activity useful. In another study, high-school students used the Learning through Collaborative Visualization Project (i.e., CoVis) to create final projects and reflect on their learning. This CMT platform (i.e., e-mail, Usenet news, and a multimedia "notebook") was funded by the National Science Foundation to transform traditional science education classes. The technology mirrored scientists' daily practices, as they work collaboratively with others via technology. Some teachers completely altered their curriculum to incorporate CoVis, while others added it as an option to existing curriculum. Students mirrored their teachers' adoption of the technology, evidenced in the quantity of their CoVis submissions (Fishman, 2000). Thus, the ability of educational teams to transform and resemble professional science virtual teams depended upon teachers' rigorous implementation of CMT as secondary tools. This indicates the importance of the teacher acting as guide and role model in the implementation of secondary tools. In addition, we need continued advances in secondary tools, like photo, video, and visual/graphical technologies, as technology replaces or replicates aspects of face-to-face interaction evident in traditional classroom environments. Social presence and immediacy may encourage student motivation to improve study habits and learning.

Tertiary Tool Use: Learning through Play

Tertiary tools represent aspects of our social world (e.g., cultural rules, symbols, communication, and behavior) in the creation of imaginary "off-line" worlds. These representational worlds allow learners, individually or in groups, to engage in "free-play" activity to practice communication and behaviors associated with particular course content. Such experiential application of concepts encourages higher-order reasoning. Through multiple technologies and types of interactions, learners practice particular skills and reasoning, recognize course concepts demonstrated via computer generated interactions and models, and engage in representational interaction. Since this takes place in an educational context, it is practice and therefore does not contain "real-world" consequences. Internet-based games with interactive interfaces such as Multiple-User Dimensions (MUDs), Multiple-user Object-Oriented environments (MOOs), and Massive Multiple Player Online Role-Playing Games (MMPORPGs) function as tertiary tools. They transport interactants to imaginary worlds that are comprised of cultural rules, expectations, and appropriate behaviors. Interactants compete and collaborate to accomplish tasks on successive levels. Several educational programs across the country have focused on developing video-gaming technology that teaches. For example, the mission of the program at Massachusetts Institute of Technology (MIT) is to "demonstrate the social, cultural and educational potentials of games by initiating new game development projects, and by informing public conversations about the broader and sometimes unexpected uses of this emerging art form in education" (Dr. Henry Jenkins III, as quoted in Roach, 2003, p. 42).

The "Fifth Dimension" was a MUD that altered children's learning and behavior (Cole, 1995), as students moved through rooms to complete tasks, problems, and games. Through their accomplishments, students obtained declarative knowledge, practiced reasoning skills, and interacted with others. The interactive and imaginative games provided students with shared experiences that enabled them to assist and understand others. Interactions outside the MUD increased, as students communicated to overcome challenges and develop strategies inside the MUD. In order to move up levels, students had to accomplish all tasks. This required students to reflect on successes and failures, which encouraged learning to transfer across contexts (Cole, 1995). The Sims© video game was used by an instructor to engage students in ethical education activities and improve students' knowledge acquisition (Ruggeroni, 2001). Students played the game in two experimental conditions for a few hours in each condition. Students interacted in orderly and chaotic environments, while video data were collected of them playing the game. Students developed and transferred knowledge from one condition in the game to another. In addition, students had increased concentration on the game with decreased acknowledgment of external distractions (Ruggeroni, 2001). Faculty members in Sociology, Economics, and other disciplines use the video game *Civilization*, created by Sid Meier (also known for the popular Sims© series), to demonstrate economic and cultural development (Foreman, 2004). Students simulate a variety of cultural, political, and social developments across the globe, as they act as warring invaders or collaborating neighbors. Such simulations model complex cultural, political, and social processes over an abbreviated time period.

Gaming software can model theories and allow students to engage in simulations of course concepts. Computer animation provides examples of social interaction for analysis. Virtual teams may "play" with various organizational roles and career choices affecting their socialization and professional development. As a part of a broader curricula, tertiary artifacts make learning more interesting for students, encouraging them to spend more time engaging other course material (i.e., research, theories). Finally, tertiary artifacts improve virtual team-building and distance learning by providing a visual and auditory virtual, local "space" for interaction with others and to engage course content.

Recommendations and Implications for Tertiary Learning

Video-gaming software can portray relatively realistic visual representations of the physical world (i.e., physical structures, animals, and humans). But they often do not accurately represent the social world, as portrayals of gender roles convey traditionally stereotypic female identities or neglect them altogether (Dietz, 1998). Educators and computer programmers can modify social representations in gaming technology to reflect other worlds, experiences, and roles. These representations can push conventional constraints and encourage tool users to think imaginatively and interact in alternative worlds (Wartofsky, 1979). As all tools have particular histories and theories embedded within them that enable and constrain thought (Resnick, 1991), alternative representations can provide avenues for creative reflection and adaptation. Scholars could actively develop tertiary artifacts that promote positive cultural evolution with representations that demonstrate disciplinary and academic knowledge. Educators who work closely with software programmers can help develop tertiary artifacts that allow students to engage in diverse representations of social and cultural milieus. Computer graphics can represent alternative worlds, encouraging students' awareness and understanding of global and multicultural interaction. However, educators must make informed, careful decisions because CMT could reinforce stereotypes and the status quo.

Players in tertiary games, represented by computer-generated characters, can develop, alter, and sustain interaction with each other. Virtual teams can play in groups or alone, either synchronously or asynchronously. Game producers have created virtual community development tools, requiring as much effort as the game's creation itself (Min, 1999). Players can further build virtual community by viewing each other's personal Web sites and interacting via chat rooms and BBS. Such tools foster student interaction and sense of social presence.

While CMTs are enticing and offer great promise for educational processes, problems will arise from our implementations, including lack of economic resources or access, technological failures, and the pace of technology. In addition, instructors must be aware of how technology communicates complementary or contradictory messages about social processes under study. We must resist the perpetuation of stereotypes via CMT, and instead use technology to challenge assumptions. It is through careful selection of these tertiary tools that cultural evolution may occur (Wartofsky, 1979).

The implementation of tertiary learning tools requires educators to rethink pedagogical assumptions regarding traditional learning and teaching methods. Foreman (2003) argues that the "leading candidate for . . . change is the large lecture. The costs for students is a lost opportunity for more meaningful and enduring learning" (p. 12). Educators will be leery of such collaboration, however, if large lectures (which are introductions to disciplines and their curricula) are to be "replaced by the video game industry," as Foreman (2003, p. 12) suggests. Instead, "[academia] needs to drive the 'why,' government needs to drive the 'how,' and industry needs to drive the 'what,' so that they can produce the market and the technologies to make this easy" (Randy Hinrichs, quoted in Foreman, 2004, p. 64). Creating relationships and collaborating across the education and computer programming industries may be difficult. Collaboration needs to occur, but industry attitudes will determine how much trust is built. Faculty will resist this venture if IT needs and profits, rather than pedagogical needs and quality, drive educational tool development.

Tertiary Tools in Organizational Communication Classrooms

Tertiary tools will be effective in a variety of disciplines, including Communication, to convey and explore social interaction. Organizational Communication courses, for example, could have some of the following innovations. Virtual teams, via tertiary tools like gaming software, can accomplish a variety of tasks to make a "virtual" organization function. Individually, students could mediate a conflict generated in the game, write memos regarding policy changes, plan/schedule organizational tasks and work, and develop leadership skills. Collaboratively, teams could solve simulated problems related to improving employee morale, managing organizational and workgroup identities, and controlling external organizational messages and images. While some educators have developed in-class activities to replicate working organizations, tertiary artifacts allow on-going replication of organizational interaction that increases in complexity throughout the term and varies based on the topic or text. In teams, individuals could rotate organizational roles to experience changes in leadership, work groups, and tasks to understand the dynamic nature of work groups. Students and teams could also experience working in a variety of virtual organizations (e.g., non-profits, small businesses, and large corporations) to experience the range and multitude of challenges faced daily in organizations. These simulations could be particularly useful for exploring a broad array of course issues. Students could understand differences in human relation theories and the impact on a supervisor's communicative behavior with a subordinate. They could try a number of different messages representing different theories and witness the varying consequences of their choices, even with results elapsed over time. Social interaction space could be built into these virtual organizations, so students could enter a "break room," or synchronous chat room, to engage in social talk or plan work.

In future Organizational Communication classrooms, tertiary tools will contain multiple representations of interaction, including audio/visual clips of employee communication behaviors, conflict styles, or miscommunication for students to analyze. Using gaming tools, students can select multiple possible responses in order to witness multiple outcomes that would be difficult or time-consuming to replicate in a classroom environment. Such activities hone students' ability to apply course content, evaluate and judge behavior, and develop higher-order processing skills. Students may eventually create simulations or challenges in the organizational environment based on course material as a final course project. Such assignments put students in the role of teacher, thereby enhancing their own learning and higher order cognitive skills (Swan & Mitrani, 1993).

Future Implications for Virtual Teams

Tertiary educational tools may be used in conjunction with other CMTs to enhance the learning and interaction process for virtual teams. Virtual teams may use synchronous chat, BBS, e-mail, and the transfer of audio/visual files (e.g., of lecture content, pictures of individuals) to replicate interaction among participants. However, extra efforts are needed to facilitate interaction and immediacy between team members. Personal Web pages can introduce students or work teams to each other and serve as repositories for information. Chat rooms and BBSs facilitate social interaction among team members differentially (Pena-Shaff et al., 2001). These steps may not be enough for virtual teams, however, to develop a sense of social presence and immediacy among themselves.

Tertiary tools (e.g., MUDs, MMPORPGs) used in conjunction with primary and secondary artifacts provide opportunities for richer interaction and a sense of social presence. Tertiary artifacts provide virtual teams with shared experiences, and this learning may transfer to other social contexts. Tertiary worlds can be complicated ones in which activities and assignments can provide challenges related to logic and reasoning, discovery, and problem-solving. These challenges can be designed for individuals or groups. Virtual teams can be "transported" to imaginary situations to develop communication skills and team interaction. In essence, tertiary tools provide imaginary "virtual field trips" to visual, symbolic, interactive worlds based on real issues or problems. Team members draw on these shared experiences when engaging in discussion, thereby placing alternative representations of action into discourse and view. These experiences may also have important implications for the development of trust between virtual team members.

Further, tertiary tools can influence cultural change through career and life modeling. Students can simulate the work necessary in particular career paths to "play" biologist, nurse, psychiatrist, etc., to determine if a particular career is suitable for them. This may increase students' affective learning and appreciation for careers, even if they do not personally select the careers. Further, this could have important pedagogical and practical implications for some disciplines like engineering, as engineers could become better designers for others by role playing those for whom they design. Simulations can be valuable for natural, physical, and social sciences as they are capable of modeling processes, systems, or equations that are difficult for students to understand: "things like multivariable calculus . . . people wouldn't struggle with it. Being able to ask 'what if?' is tremendously enlightening in a way that looking at equations on a page of a textbook is not" (J. C. Herz, in Foreman, 2004, p. 54).

Tertiary technologies such as educational video games provide the potential for cultural change, as they provide the tools for simulating multiple identities, as students witness and make decisions across socio-political history, space, and time. The great potential of video games for education is that they are "worlds in a box." Video games allow new identities:

People learn most deeply when they take on a new identity . . . Let's say I really want to know what it's like to be a biologist of a certain sort. I really want to know what it's like to feel that way, to value that way, to talk that way . . . That's going to be a deeper form of learning. (James Gee, as quoted in Foreman, 2004, p. 54)

Gaming simulations provide team members with the opportunity to engage in behaviors, learn content knowledge and language, and experience daily life in a variety of circumstances, roles, or worlds. Simulations may encourage empathy and understanding to develop, as students experience others' identities or witness the consequences of their decisions on groups or even entire civilizations. Learning empathy through technology is important and necessary. Empathy takes a long time to develop anywhere, but especially in virtual teams where group members may never meet face-to-face.

Summary

This chapter has examined literature detailing CMT implementations that can transform educational contexts. CMT implementations can be difficult (Gilbert, 1996), but CMT can qualitatively enhance learning when students process information at higher levels (Lambrecht, 1993). Wartofsky (1979) identifies primary, secondary, and tertiary artifacts as tools that represent modes of action and worlds that mediate individuals into the culture. In educational forums, primary tools enhance cognition and interaction. They accomplish mental work and facilitate interaction to improve teaching and learning in a number of ways. Secondary artifacts represent modes of activity like teaching and learning. Thus these tools make it possible to replicate educational interaction when face-to-face meetings are not possible. While these tools make it possible to create alternative teaching and learning strategies, they are limited in their ability to convey social presence and construct helpful interactions. Tertiary artifacts, however, allow learners to engage in activities that develop their play-instinct (Wartofsky, 1979) and explore alternative representations. As tools have particular histories and theories embedded within them (Wartofsky, 1979), they are representational artifacts of culture that enable and constrain thought (Resnick, 1991). Educational tertiary artifacts should be co-created by scholars and computer programmers so that particular theories and concepts are embedded that allow students to "play" with course content, explore many possible outcomes of behavior, and reflect on experiences with other students. Possibilities for the development of CMT in Organizational Communication classrooms were explored.

References

Ahern, T. C., & Durrington, V. (1995-6). Effects of anonymity and group saliency on participation and interaction in a computer-medicated small-group discussion. *Journal of Research on Computing in Education, 28,* 133-147.

Ahern, T. C., & Repman, J. (1994). The effects of technology on online education. *Journal of Research on Computing in Education, 26,* 537-546.

Althaus, S. L. (1997). Computer-mediated communication in the university classroom: An experiment with on-line discussions. *Communication Education, 46,* 158-174.

Anderson, M. D. (1996). Using computer mediated conferencing to facilitate group projects in an educational psychology course. *Behavior Research Methods, Instruments & Computers, 28*, 351-353.

Bagert, D. J., & Mengel, S. A. (2005). Developing and using a Web-based project process throughout the software engineering curriculum. *The Journal of Systems and Software, 74*(2), 113-120.

Cole, M. (1995). Socio-cultural-historical psychology: Some general remarks and a proposal for a new kind of cultural-genetic methodology. In J. V. Wertsch, P. del Rio, & A. Alverez (Eds.), *Sociocultural studies of mind* (pp. 187-214). New York: Cambridge University.

Dietz, T. (1998). An examination of violence and gender role portrayals in video games: Implications for gender socialization and aggressive behavior. *Sex Roles, 38,* 425-443.

Dietz-Uhler, B., & Bishop-Clark, C. (2001). The use of computer-mediated communication to enhance subsequent face-to-face discussions. *Computers in Human Behavior, 17*, 269-283.

Everett, D. R., & Ahern, T. C. (1994). Computer-mediated communication as a teaching tool: A case study. *Journal of Research on Computing in Education, 26,* 336-357.

Fishman, B. J. (2000). How activity fosters CMC tool use in classrooms: Reinventing innovations in local contexts. *Journal of Interactive Learning Research, 11*, 3-27.

Flanagin, A. J. (1999). Theoretical and pedagogical issues in computer-mediated interaction and instruction: Lessons from the use of a collaborative instructional technology. *The Electronic Journal of Communication, 9*(1). Retrieved October 1, 2004, from http://www.cios.org/getfile.Flanagin_v9n199

Foreman, J. (2003). Next-generation: Educational technology versus the lecture. *EDUCAUSE Review, 38*(4), 12-22.

Foreman, J. (2004). Game-based learning: How to delight and instruct in the 21st century. *EDUCAUSE Review, 39*(3), 51-66.

Gilbert, S. W. (1996, March/April). Making the most of a slow revolution. *Change,* 10-23.

Jessup, L. M., Egbert J. L., & Connolly, T. (1995-6). Understanding computer-supported group work: The effects of interaction frequency on group process and outcome. *Journal of Research on Computing in Education, 28,* 190-208.

Lambrecht, J. J. (1993). Applications software as cognitive enhancers. *Journal of Research on Computing in Education, 25,* 506-520.

Marjanovic, O. (1999). Learning and teaching in a synchronous collaborative environment. *Journal of Computer Assisted Learning, 15*, 129-138.

Min, A. (1999). Multitude's fireteam. *Game Developer, 6*(4), 50-58.

Mioduser, D., & Marin, M. S. (1995). Students' construction of structured knowledge representations. *Journal of Research on Computing in Education, 28,* 63-84.

Pauleen, D. J., Marshall, S., & Egort, I. (2004). ICT-supported team-based experiential learning: Classroom perspectives. *Education & Training, 46*(2/3), 90-99.

Pena-Shaff, J., Martin, W., & Gay, G. (2001). An epistemological framework for analyzing student interactions in computer-mediated communication environments. *Journal of Interactive Learning Research, 12*, 41-68.

Pychyl, T. A., Clarke, D., & Abarbanel, T. (1999). Computer-mediated group projects: Facilitating collaborative learning with the World Wide Web. *Teaching of Psychology, 26*, 138-141.

Resnick, L. B. (1991). Shared cognition: Thinking as social practice. In L. B. Resnick, J. M. Levine, & S. D. Teasley (Eds.), *Perspectives on socially shared cognition* (pp. 1-23). Washington, DC: American Psychological Association.

Roach, R. (2003). Research schools work to improve classroom use of computer games. *Black Issues in Higher Education, 20*(21), 42.

Ruggeroni, C. (2001). Ethical education with virtual reality: Immersiveness and the knowledge transfer process. In G. Riva & F. Davide (Eds.), *Communications through virtual technology: Identity community and technology in the Internet age* (pp. 119-133). Amsterdam: IOS.

Russo, T. C., Campbell, S., Henry, M., & Kosinar, P. (1999). An online graduate class in communication technology: Outcomes and lessons learned. *The Electronic Journal of Communication, 9*(1). Retrieved October 1, 2004, from http://www.cios.org/getfile/Russo_v9n199

Schweizer, K., Paechter, M., & Weidenmann, B. (2001). A field study on distance education and communication: Experiences of a virtual tutor. *Journal of Computer Mediated Communication, 6*(2). Retrieved October 1, 2004, from http://jcmc.indiana.edu/vol16/issue2/schweizer.html

Shih, Y., & Alessi, S. M. (1993-4). Mental models and transfer of learning in computer programming. *Journal of Research on Computing in Education, 26,* 154-175.

Sunderland, J. (2002). New communication practices, identity and the psychological gap: The affective function of e-mail on a distance doctoral programme. *Studies in Higher Education, 27*, 233-246.

Swan, K., & Mitrani, M. (1993). The changing nature of teaching and learning in computer-based classrooms. *Journal of Research on Computing in Education, 26,* 40-54.

Wartofsky, M. W. (1979). Perception, representation, and the forms of action: Towards an historical epistemology. In R. S. Cohen & M. W. Wartofsky (Eds.), *Models* (pp. 188-210). Boston: D. Reidel.

Weller, M. (2000). Implementing a CMC tutor group for an existing distance education course. *Journal of Computer Assisted Learning, 16*, 178-183.

Wizer, D. R. (1995). Small group instruction using microcomputers: Focus on group behaviors. *Journal of Research on Computing in Education, 28,* 121-132.

Endnotes

1 Bulletin board systems, hereafter referred to as BBS, are asynchronous Web- or HTML-based networked e-mail systems that allow students to access text-based messages among class participants. The term BBS is used to refer to such systems also called "list-servs."

2 Group support systems, hereafter referred to as GSS, are synchronous hardware and software systems that mediate students' interactions. The systems moderate students' brainstorming and evaluative discussions, poll interactants on issues, and, in theory, guide discussion and decision-making in an unbiased way.

Chapter XII

Virtual Teams in the Traditional Classroom:

Lessons on New Communication Technologies and Training

Stephen A. Rains
University of Arizona, USA

Craig R. Scott
University of Texas at Austin, USA

Abstract

This chapter examines the technologies available to virtual teams and issues associated with training virtual teams. We first evaluate the benefits and limitations of technologies to aid communication and collaboration. We consider the merits and limitations of asynchronous and synchronous discussion tools, groupware and collaboration tools, and electronic meeting systems. We then offer three different levels of training possible for virtual teams and discuss some key issues associated with training. Each level of training varies in intensity and is dependent upon the nature of the assignment and team objectives. The chapter concludes with some predictions and recommendations about the future of new technologies and virtual teams in the educational setting. Throughout the chapter, special considerations are made for those virtual teams operating in the traditional classroom.

Introduction

During the past 20 years, team-based movements have enjoyed considerable popularity in educational settings and organizations throughout the country. LaFasto and Larson (2001) suggest that most of us are "...well past the point of needing convincing that collaborative teamwork is an effective tool for managing complex tasks in a rapidly changing environment" (p. xvii). In the past few years, however, the nature of teams and teamwork has begun to change. Pauleen (2004) explains that "growing concern with globalization, the rise of the knowledge worker, the need for innovation, and the increasing use of information and communication technology" have resulted in a new form of "virtual" teams (p. viii). As organizations move increasingly toward such teams, it becomes essential to provide students with experiences working in a virtual environment.

The purpose of this chapter is to examine the role of new communication technologies in virtual teams in the educational setting. In particular, we examine the breadth of technologies available to students in virtual teams, consider the importance of technology-based and general training for team members, and speculate about the future of virtual teams and technologies to support them in an educational setting. Throughout the chapter we draw heavily on our own experience as instructors actively using different types of virtual teams in three college courses we teach—paying special attention to practical implications/lessons for the use of virtual teams in the traditional classroom. To begin, we first briefly address the importance of virtual teams in educational settings and provide some background about our use of virtual teams.

Background: Virtual Teams in the Traditional Classroom

Scholarly writing related to virtual teams in the classroom tends to come in two broad forms. First, there is the research literature — on both teams of students assembled purely for research study purposes (e.g., see Chidambaram, 1996; Ocker & Morand, 2002) as well as teams that appear more integrated into actual classrooms (e.g., see Aubert & Kelsey, 2003; Jarvenpaa, Knoll, & Leidner, 1998; Jarvenpaa & Leidner, 1999; Kayworth & Leidner, 2002; Warkentin & Beranek, 1999) — where the use of virtual student teams for learning purposes is secondary to broader goals of studying virtual teams more generally. Second, the role of virtual teams can also be seen in work on education and learning. As one group of scholars explain, "In the expanding market of virtual universities and online degree programs, virtual learning teams are being used to increase collaboration, communication, and ultimately student learning" (Johnson, Chanidprapa, Yoon, Berrett, & La Fleur, 2002, p. 381). As we will show in this chapter, virtual teams also have a place in more traditional university classrooms to help facilitate learning. This interest in virtual student teams is captured in part by the work on computer-supported collaborative learning, or CSCL. Brandon and Hollingshead (1999) suggest CSCL "seeks to combine classroom-based collaborative learning theory with theory and research on CMC in order to provide a foundation for understanding how CMC-based group projects can enhance learning" (p. 110).

Our focus builds on work related to both research about virtual teams in organizations and CSCL that utilizes teams to facilitate learning. However, we also wish to emphasize a more pragmatic and experiential purpose for using virtual teams: many students will likely find themselves working in and being members of virtual teams in the future, so it is important to provide them with educational experiences related to this in the classroom. We believe virtual teams should be used in traditional and virtual classrooms to teach students to be effective and responsible organizational members and to help meet the increasing demand for communicatively competent virtual workers.

For educators, the increased use of virtual teams creates a new set of responsibilities and issues that must be considered. Thus, in this chapter we focus on the types of communication technologies and training useful for virtual student teams so that they will be better prepared to work and interact on such teams beyond the classroom as well. Considering this goal, we make several basic assumptions about the role of technology and training to support virtual teams in traditional classrooms.

First, it is important that technologies for students are inexpensive or already integrated into existing courseware systems. Given the limited funds of many students and institutions of higher learning, instructors must often find low-cost tools that are accessible by all (or risk nonuse on this basis). Second, it is important to let students discover benefits and limitations of these technologies as a learning experience. In other instances, such as in contemporary organizations, it is often important to find the most effective/efficient tools or even focus on a single technology. Part of the student's experience, however, should be learning how to identify and evaluate the strengths and weaknesses of various tools. Finally, because many virtual teams operate in the scope of a traditional classroom, it is important to address issues of combining tools with face-to-face meetings. Indeed, virtual teams in any context vary in their degree of virtuality and opportunities for face-to-face interaction should be considered as a possible communication option for team members. Given these assumptions, we next offer a description of the courses in which we have integrated virtual teams.

Our Courses

Throughout our tenure at the University of Texas (UT) at Austin we have had the opportunity to each instruct and/or team up as instructor and teaching assistant with three courses that incorporate virtual teams. In each of the courses, virtual teams play a substantial part of student learning. Although the courses themselves are primarily taught in a traditional classroom setting and include only UT-Austin students, we create virtual student teams from within the enrollment of each class. Students have the opportunity to participate in a virtual team in the process of completing class projects and are encouraged to formally evaluate their experience in this unique working/learning environment. In the following paragraphs, we briefly describe the three courses in which we have been involved to provide a foundation for our discussion of the new technologies and procedures for training students.

In our course on Team-Based Communication, students participate in semester-long virtual teams. This lower-division course typically has 24 students per each of four sections, though logistics have forced us to keep the virtual teams within each section. For every section, we create four teams of approximately six individuals each. Students are assigned to their group during the first two weeks of the semester. Throughout the remaining weeks they complete two substantial group assignments (totaling 40% of each student's final grade). The two assignments ask students to train the rest of the class on some aspect of small group communication and to complete a service learning project that results in a case study of their team. In completing these projects, student teams have a variety of tools for communication. In addition to meeting face-to-face, teams rely heavily on the groupware that is part of the course Web site (we have used both *Blackboard* and *WebCT*[1]). Each team has an area to post and share documents, a discussion board, and access to a common chat tool. Teams are strongly encouraged to complete at least two meetings using the chat tool, and the use of this tool is incorporated into one of the assignments for the course. Each student has the opportunity to complete a brief essay developing and analyzing strategies to make chat-based or virtual meetings effective. The semester long experience gives students the opportunity to participate on a virtual team and to develop a better understanding of how new communication technologies can be used to facilitate, or in some cases hinder, collaboration.

In our course on New Communication Technologies in the Workplace students participate in virtual teams over the course of six weeks to complete a training project. This upper division course is taught once or twice per year with approximately 40 students. Typically, there are five to six teams of seven to eight students each. Student teams in this course are each assigned to a different commercial courseware tool (e.g., *HotOffice*, *SmartGroups*, *YahooGroups*, etc.). As students work together they are encouraged to use and incorporate the groupware tool. Students also complete a complementary assignment that asks them to formally evaluate the merits and limitations of their respective groupware site. Students post to the course discussion board about their tool and their experience as a member of a virtual team. As a whole, these assignments provide students with the opportunity to participate in a virtual team and think critically about the components (including the technologies) that make them successful/unsuccessful. Like teams in the team-based course, students in this class also have access to a variety of tools found on their course Web site.

Finally, we conduct a course on Organizational Communication, which is offered in both traditional and predominantly online formats. The class — historically upper division but recently revamped as an introductory lower-division course — ranges in size anywhere from 40-90 students. Students are assigned to small groups of four to six members to complete two online case study projects (as well as an online practice case). The graded case study periods typically last for 11-12 days in a long semester, and are done immediately following the first and second exam (out of three) in the course. For each project, students rely primarily on the bulletin board to conduct the case study work. However, they also make use of a chat tool, e-mail, and even occasional face-to-face meetings to help coordinate their work.

Communication Technologies for Virtual Teams

Although the technologies available to virtual teams have been assessed in previous scholarship (e.g., Ferris & Minielli, 2004; Scott, 2003), the focus of our chapter is on those technologies most useful to virtual student teams in the educational setting. In particular we examine technologies dedicated to facilitating discussion, groupware tools for coordination/ collaboration, and electronic meeting systems. Throughout this section of the chapter, we consider the benefits and limitations of each tool for virtual student teams. We pay special attention to those technologies that will be useful for students to experience as future organizational members.[2] A review of the key benefits and limitations of each class of technologies is available in Table 1.

Discussion Tools

Asynchronous

Among tools that facilitate asynchronous discussion, listservs and discussion boards are useful means for teams to communicate. Listservs are a special case of e-mail. Listservs involve a group e-mail list that is subscribed to by team members. Messages sent to the listserv are broadcast to all members. Similarly, a discussion board, or electronic bulletin board, is typically a Web-based tool accessible to all members in which ideas and questions can be posted and addressed. Discussion boards allow group members to engage in an asynchronous, threaded dialogue. Both of these tools are often available free of charge as a feature of a university/college e-mail service and/or as part of Web-based course management systems (e.g., *Blackboard* or *WebCT*).

Table 1. Key advantages and disadvantages of new communication technologies available to virtual student teams

Technology	Key Advantages	Key Disadvantages
Asynchronous discussion tools: list-servs, discussion boards, e-mail	• Members do not have to be online at the same time • Tools can complement face-to-face interactions • May provide a record of the interaction	• Do not work well for intensive discussions • Takes time -- may not be useful when nearing a deadline • Some uneven participation
Synchronous discussion tools: audio-conferencing, chat, video-conferencing, instant messaging	• Useful tool for brainstorming • Can engage in an in-depth discussion • Provides a record of the interaction	• Requires everyone meet online at the same time • All members must have access • Cost for video-conferencing tools
Coordination / collaboration groupware tools: *Blackboard, SmartGroups, HotOffice*	• Can aid coordination with calendar • Can aid collaboration via file sharing, shared documents, and tracked changes • May serve a symbolic / identity function for team	• Must be maintained and kept up to date • Price of commercial tools • Privacy may be lost or diminished
Electronic meeting systems	• Adds structure to discussions, brainstorming, and decision making • Creates opportunities for all members to contribute to discussions and decisions	• Access and financial cost • Requires a trained facilitator / technographer • Uneven acceptance of decisions

The asynchronous nature of listservs and discussion boards makes them an effective method for students to exchange information. Because students need not be online at the same time, information is exchanged when convenient for each member of the team. For virtual teams in traditional classrooms, this feature is particularly helpful to complement face-to-face meetings. Additionally, students have time to think through their responses or contribution. Another beneficial feature of listservs and discussion boards is that both supply a record of the interaction occurring between team members. The team has a record of the agreements made, deadlines set, and objectives achieved. As such, these tools are useful for keeping each member current on the team's progress and for documenting who is responsible for certain tasks.

There are, however, key limitations of each tool that are important to consider. In general, we have found that the listserv was the most utilized tool for virtual teams interacting regularly for extended time periods — most likely because messages were delivered to the students' in-box where they checked their e-mail. However, the listserv did not work well for more intensive discussion of project specifics where threaded conversation was beneficial. Discussion boards were most appropriate for teams working on a specific project that spanned several days (e.g., online case study, discussion and reactions to new software programs). However, students were generally less likely to regularly check the discussion board forums — sometimes producing uneven participation across the team.[3] In large part, these tools are similar enough that our virtual student teams with access to both utilized only one or the other (rarely, if ever, both at the same time). Furthermore, neither provided especially rapid options for addressing problems or meeting short deadlines.

Synchronous

In addition to discussion boards and e-mail listservs, there are a number of synchronous communication options available to virtual student teams for discussion. These include conference calls, instant messaging and even some text messaging between team members, and (of course) face-to-face meetings. Two additional synchronous technologies we have utilized in our virtual students teams are chat and video-conferencing. Chat tools are available commercially through companies such as Microsoft and Yahoo as well as a part of many course management programs. Each member of the group can join the chat using some type of online name (which can be an actual name or some other screen identity) and these text-based interactions typically take place in a specified room often designated strictly for the virtual team. Video-conferencing tools, which can include meeting rooms but are now increasingly common on desktop systems, are also real-time — but include vocal and visual cues. Many videoconferencing tools also integrate with other tools (e.g., a chat feature, a whiteboard for displaying ideas, document camera, display of information on a personal computer). Microsoft's *NetMeeting*, which we have used with some of our virtual student teams, is free software that allows for desktop videoconferencing (with many of the additions noted above).

We have noticed several benefits of these synchronous tools, especially chat, for students. Chat, in particular, provides a useful means for students to brainstorm and to work out problems that can be more difficult (and less efficient) using asynchronous channels. Students can engage in an in-depth discussion using a chat tool. Chat also provides an online meeting environment where students can ask, and receive answers to, questions from other team members. Chat, like the asynchronous tools, usually provides a log/record of the conversation that is useful to the team. In our experience, chat has been particularly valuable for teams in instances where the team could not all meet face-to-face.

Despite such benefits, there are limitations of chat and video-conferencing that warrant consideration. The most obvious limitation for virtual teams that are dispersed is that all parties must meet at the same time. Additionally, not all virtual team members may subscribe to a common commercial chat provider and the chat feature in some of the courseware programs has not been especially stable in our experience. However, the most notable limitations pertain to video-conferencing. Meeting room sessions were not financially or logistically feasible except for demonstrations, and even desktop video-conferencing requirements (e.g., video camera, microphone, broadband Internet connection, software configuration, etc.) provided enough of a disincentive to discourage use. In short, there was little interest among virtual student teams in exploring video-conferencing as a discussion tool. Although students were provided the opportunity (though there was no formal requirement), this technology was rarely used by student teams beyond the initial demonstration.

Coordination/Collaboration Groupware

Groupware is a collection of Web-based tools designed to aid in coordination, collaboration, and communication. For virtual teams in traditional classrooms, there are a variety of groupware tools available. Some of these tools are found on common courseware sites (e.g., the calendar and file exchange functions in *Blackboard* and *WebCT*). Some are found in tools such as *NetMeeting* (e.g., shared whiteboard and sharing documents) or within the collaboration components of word-processing programs. In other cases, they are provided by more commercial services. For example, *HotOffice* contains a file-exchange, document viewer, calendar, e-mail, and contact manager; *Paltalk* contains a few different features, offering a chat and audio- and video-conferencing tool along with file-sharing; and free groupware, such as *YahooGroups,* typically offer fewer tools, but still include file-sharing, a team calendar, and a discussion tool.

Focusing specifically on the key tools available in most groupware, perhaps the simplest and most useful coordination tool available to virtual teams is a group calendar. An electronic calendar makes assignment deadlines evident to all team members. Setting up and maintaining a team calendar takes relatively little effort, yet is a useful way to keep the team on the same page. The calendar can orient the team, providing an informal map for the semester. If the deadlines are agreed upon by all team members, the calendar can also represent an explicit contract among team members. The calendar makes clear the expectations for group members about the dates for assignment completion and helps foster a sense of structure for the project.

File posting/sharing/exchange is another useful tool available in most groupware programs. This tool allows team members to better collaborate by helping to keep the most recent version of the team's document available in a common online location. It also allows all team members to easily locate and contribute to the team's work from anywhere they have Web access. A different set of collaboration tools is found in *NetMeeting*. Here, one can use shared whiteboards or share other programs. This sort of shared space literally allows virtual team members to work together on digital documents.

Finally, a set of collaboration tools are also available on most word-processing programs. Most notably, "track changes" and other features built into the reviewing function on software such as Microsoft *Word*, allow teams to conduct joint writing and editing. Team members can begin collaborating by inserting suggested changes (additions and deletions; content and formatting) to a document. Then other team members can accept or reject these changes/comments. Multiple versions of the same document can be compared if team members are updating them simultaneously. Finally, a complete history of the virtual team's document can be stored in a single file by using the "versions" function in *Word*. The reviewing tools available in word-processing programs such as *Word* make it possible for each student to actively contribute to the virtual team's project.

In general, our virtual teams have varied markedly in their utilization of these groupware tools — with some groups valuing such technology, some teams finding it of minimal value, and others opting not to use the technology at all. For some students, there are clear benefits of this technology. First, groupware sites provide a common place for team members to store information related to the team's work. If used properly, this keeps current versions of a document accessible to all team members and provides a place to deposit other relevant material for the team (e.g., background readings). A second benefit of groupware is that, beyond aiding collaboration and coordination, groupware sites can also perform a symbolic function for the team. The groupware site may create a sense of a "place" and, as a result, be a source of team identity. What it means to be part of a team is articulated through the team's site.

A third benefit of using groupware is that the students get a sense of what types of technologies exist to support teams. Through experimentation with the tools available, each student develops an understanding of how coordination and collaboration tools aid the virtual team. Finally, concerning the reviewing functionality in wordprocessing programs, we have found that most virtual teams find this a valuable way to conduct some group writing. The tools can be set up so that individual member additions (and deletions) appear in different colors and/or are labeled by team member. This makes it evident what was contributed by each team member. Moreover, simply being able to conduct edits online, involve multiple viewpoints on a single document, and integrate/compare documents seems to be of value to those virtual teams who use this tool.

Despite these benefits, there are drawbacks to groupware that should be considered as well. First, groupware sites must be maintained regularly. The calendar and file sharing tools, in particular, require diligence among team members to update the calendar as well as ensure that a current version of the team's work is available on the groupware site. If team members do not take responsibility for this, these tools will foster confusion, which can undermine trust and create a negative experience for members of the team. A second issue involves cost and privacy concerns. *HotOffice* and *Paltalk* charge a fee for their service. Although there are free trial periods for some groupware sites, the cost may be prohibitive for students. With those groupware sites that do not currently charge a fee, like *YahooGroups* or *MSN Groups*, registration is typically required and team members can be subject to advertisements in exchange for using the service. Given continuing concerns with information privacy, this may well be perceived as a considerable limitation by some students and instructors. Third, despite interest in the collaboration features in *NetMeeting*, our virtual teams rarely used this technology. We suspect this is because students were reluctant to set up an account on the relevant directory and then configure the software on their personal computer before communicating with other team members—each of whom would have to do the same. For some virtual teams, the relative advantage of these tools was not perceived to be great enough to warrant extensive use.

Electronic Meeting Systems

Meetings have historically been performed with people gathered in a common location. Although face-to-face meetings are a possibility for virtual teams (and were clearly used in the teams in our more traditional classrooms), electronic meetings have also emerged. Electronic meeting systems are a broad class of computer-based software designed to aid group discussion and decision-making processes. Electronic meeting systems, such as group support systems (GSSs) and group decision support systems (GDSSs), contain tools to facilitate group activities like brainstorming, decision-making, voting, discussion, and planning. A number of electronic meeting systems are available at a fee, including: *The Meeting Room*, *MeetingWorks*, *Facilitate*, and *GroupSystems*. These tools can be used to support teams who are co-located or dispersed, and they typically require a technographer to operate the equipment. GDSS/GSSs provide a structured agenda and utilize both parallel participation and the opportunity for anonymous contributions to avoid common meeting problems in teams.

This specialized technology was used only once by the virtual teams in one of our classes—but that meeting was a crucial one for the entire project. Despite this infrequent use, electronic meeting systems offer a number of opportunities for virtual teams (for reviews of the impact of GSS/GDSS use on decision-making processes and outcomes, see Benbasat & Lim, 1993; McLeod, 1992; Rains, 2005; Scott, 1999). One benefit of electronic meeting systems is that they add structure to discussion and decision-making processes. Groups using an electronic meeting system typically follow a systematic procedure that consists, generally, of brainstorming, discussion, and voting. Another benefit of these meeting systems is that they help foster opportunities for participation and influence that is not possible without the system. Unlike a face-to-face brainstorming session where only one individual speaks at a time and participants are aware of status differences between group members, all team members have the opportunity to contribute and offer input. The ability to be anonymous and contribute simultaneously to the discussion should ensure that all team members are able and feel comfortable participating in discussion and decision making. In our course, students used a GDSS to select the topic for an extensive, multipart project. We believe this technology positively influenced the virtual team because the tool helped facilitate a process by which the team could thoroughly explore options and "hear" everyone's opinions before making their decision. The impact of the electronic meeting was felt throughout much of the semester.

Despite these benefits, there are clear limitations of electronic meeting systems that warrant consideration. First, electronic meeting systems are costly. It would not be feasible for students to personally fund an electronic meeting system; access to such systems or services would have to be purchased by the instructor's institution. A second limitation is that electronic meeting systems are more complex and thus not as easy for the average virtual team member to use. Not only must meeting members be trained on the technology, but these systems usually require a skilled technographer to operate the system. For our course, we acted as the technographers. If the instructor is unfamiliar with the technology, however, a technographer would have to be paid to facilitate the meeting. Related to all this, these systems typically require advanced preparation and setup — which greatly restricts when they can be used by virtual student teams. Finally, we have noted as we facilitated these meetings that some students and some teams appeared to appreciate the technology much less so than others — especially if a student had a difficult time convincing others of his/her favorite option. We know in some instances that teams decided to disregard the decisions reached using the GDSS/GSS and reverted to more traditional discussion and selection of topics.[4]

Summary

This section of the chapter focused on the benefits and limitations of technologies used by virtual teams in an educational setting. We first focused on synchronous and asynchronous tools for discussion, noting frequent use of tools such as listservs, discussion boards, and chat. Then, we addressed coordination/collaboration tools in groupware systems. Groups displayed substantial variation in the degree of use and value for these tools. The collaborative writing/reviewing features in word-processing tools were most valued by teams. This section of the chapter concludes by discussing the utility of electronic meeting systems for virtual teams.

Training

Having described the utility of various tools for virtual teams in an educational setting, we turn next to issues of training. Training related to proper technology use and collaboration skills is essential for students prior to participating in a virtual team (Brandon & Hollingshead, 1999; Macdonald, 2003). Educators should focus on how communication and collaboration technologies are used and how to otherwise function effectively in virtual teams. We address these issues next.

Technology Training

Throughout nearly a decade of instructing classes that incorporate virtual teams, we have found that students typically have only minimal experience with many of the group-based technologies. Although students have become more savvy users of e-mail and chat-based tools in the past few years, they are less familiar with collaboration tools such as the track-changes feature of word-processing programs. As a way of illustrating our training efforts, we describe three different ways in which we train students to help prepare them for their virtual team experience. Each of the levels differs in the intensity and detail of training for both the instructor and students, and could be adapted for a multitude of different situations.

Extensive Training

In our team-based communication course, we provide perhaps our most extensive training prior to the virtual team experience. For the past several years, we have held a technology-training week in this class at the beginning of each semester. This training is divided into two parts: general technology training and specific training for use of a GDSS. In the general training, we provide students with a detailed manual that addresses use of the various technologies described earlier in this chapter. Then, we meet with each section (approximately 24 students each) and provide them with laptop computers for a hands-on learning experience as we go through guidelines/tips about each of the relevant technologies. The wireless Internet laptops are ideal for training because we are able to conduct the training in the students' regular classroom and provide everyone with computer access—although similar goals could be accomplished in a computer lab even with students sharing terminals. We have found that students respond positively to having the laptops during the training. The ability to first demonstrate the technology on a public screen visible to the entire class and then have them experiment with the tool on their personal computers seems quite effective.

During the training, we briefly address topics such as using audio-conferencing, avoiding viruses in e-mail attachments (including where to download free virus protection software), and experimenting with Web-based groupware programs as described earlier. We more extensively demonstrate features of the courseware tool (e.g., chat and discussion board features specifically setup for each virtual team) and guide students through the process and subscribing to their team's listserv (which also has been setup in advance). We have found that taking time during the training to actually subscribe to the list helps to ensure students gain the benefits from this widely-utilized tool. Because these teams are producing written documents, we also spend time covering the various editing/tracking/saving features found in word processing systems such as Microsoft *Word*. Perhaps the most engaged response comes from students as we have demonstrated online collaboration tools such as *NetMeeting*. By exhibiting how the tool works during a demonstration between the instructor and a random student's computer, we are then able to invite others to engage in their own collaborative sessions during the training.

Finally, we teach students how to use a GDSS and then facilitate a team meeting using this tool. Our training centers on some reading about the tool, and then a hands-on practice session. For each student team, we walk through the purpose of the tool, how to use it for brainstorming, how to do voting, how to interpret results, and how to use that information to help reach effective decisions. Once the students become familiar with the tool, they complete a decision-making meeting. Each team decides on a topic for a multipart project they will complete over the next several weeks.

Moderate Training

A second type of training we conduct is geared for less intensive virtual teams. These groups spend a moderate amount of time in virtual teams completing a case study project (in the organizational communication course) and do not require as much training. Whenever this course is taught online (with physical meetings only for the training/orientation and exams), we still have a mandatory technology training session on the first day the course is taught. During the training, we focus on those technologies we expect teams to utilize for their project. Teams are instructed where to locate these technologies on the course Web site, how one makes posts/entries and responses, etc.

Two to three weeks after the initial meeting, we hold two follow-up training sessions. We first hold an online meeting to discuss the case studies. A key part of this meeting is spent going back over how to use the discussion board forums for this assignment. Second, we also conduct a week-long "practice case" for the entire class where they practice making initial and response posts to others. This task is ungraded, though it does count toward participation points for the course. Throughout this practice case we provide ongoing training by offering feedback on every student post. Students are informed what they are doing well and what should be improved.

Minimal Training

A final type of training, geared toward short-term virtual teams, we deem our minimalist approach. This approach is focused more on student self-learning than hands-on training by the instructor. Toward the end of the semester in our course on new communication technologies in the workplace, we invite student teams to experiment with some Web-based groupware tools that allow them to work virtually as they prepare a class training project. Although we spend about two weeks as part of the class talking about technologies that virtual teams use and have a couple readings on these topics, the specific training dedicated to the virtual teams is minimal. We assign each team a commercial web-based groupware tool (e.g., *SmartGroups*) and ask them to experiment with it to conduct team meetings and other group work. This training is also tied to an assignment students complete for a grade. Each team is obliged to use the groupware tool and to consider its benefits and limitations — drawing on course readings and lecture when possible. Students then report their experiences on a discussion board accessible to the entire class. This assignment helps students begin to develop strategies for evaluating the merits and limitations of different technologies available to virtual teams. When the technology is used in beneficial ways, the virtual team experience also helps the team to better prepare for their upcoming training assignment.

In summary, there are many different ways to train students about use of the technologies they will need for their virtual team experience. In some instances where the experience is intensive and involves use of multiple tools, extensive training is warranted. In other situations where the virtual team experience is more limited or the range of technologies to be used is restricted, more minimal training is required.

General Training Issues

Virtual teams not only need training about the technologies they can use, but also about how to communicate in general with other dispersed team members and how to create a functional virtual team. In fact, Timmerman and Scott's

(2004) work suggests that desirable team outcomes depend more on having certain communication competencies than on using certain communication technologies. We see this more general training taking three forms. First, there needs to be some general orienting to the team and the task. A great deal of the conventional wisdom about virtual teams in general suggests that it is ideal to have them meet team members in advance of working together. In all of our courses, we provide opportunities/time for students to get to meet one another and to know the names/faces of those members with whom they will be working virtually. Additionally, because tasks are often less clear for virtual teams, we make efforts to first explain them when we are physically together. From there, we also provide written information about the tasks and opportunities for ongoing conversation/clarification to help ensure the virtual team is clear about the assignment.

Second, there are a number of challenges that are amplified in the virtual team environment. Although these have been most discussed largely outside the classroom (see Connaughton & Daly, 2004; Kirkman, Rosen, Gibson, Tesluk, & McPherson, 2002), such challenges also apply to virtual teams in educational settings. Two key challenges that can be addressed via training include overcoming feelings of isolation/detachment and building trust. Because our virtual teams have not been completely virtual in most cases, we have not experienced these challenges to any real degree. However, in the online course where there is little (if any) non-mediated interaction, we have taken steps to train students in these areas. We begin by helping students recognize that they may experience a disconnect from others and an initial lack of trust—clarifying that such reactions are understandable. To remedy such concerns, we make it clear that social interaction is acceptable during online discussions and inform students that they will be working together for multiple projects. We also encourage teams to select a team name/identity and to initially work on low-risk activities to help build trust. The key idea we try to articulate throughout these procedures is that trust is essential for effective collaboration in virtual teams.

Finally, when teams are more dispersed across geographic regions, time zones, and different cultures, additional challenges needing more detailed training arise. For these more globally dispersed virtual classroom teams, additional training is perhaps most needed to address cultural differences. Virtual team members are most likely to blame members from other cultures for problems (Cramton, 2001). Jarvenpaa's (Jarvenpaa et al., 1998; Jarvenpaa & Leidner, 1999) work with global virtual student teams also indicates a number of challenges related to culture. Although we have not employed virtual teams with this degree of diversity, valuable efforts to do so must also include training to help members recognize cultural differences in ways that help them better work together. Teams must be trained about the unique practices and cultural norms of all members.

Instructor/Student Responsibilities in Training

Of course, effective training takes more than a simple understanding of its importance. Without the necessary skill and motivation from both instructors and students, any training can be problematic. For the trainer/instructor, our experience suggests several guidelines. First, one must simply make the time to do the training correctly. As noted above, the training can vary in its intensity —but even the least amount of training will require additional instructor effort that goes beyond typical responsibilities. Providing the necessary detail and facilitating hands-on training require advanced planning and practice. And, as technologies and our knowledge about what works evolves, such training must be regularly updated. Every semester we have tools to add or delete in our training and are regularly adjusting how we use virtual teams in the various classes. Ideally, instructors in classes related to teams, technology, and organizational communication should be able to learn and then help teach such skills to their students. However, when an instructor is not able to do this, it may be wise to bring in another trained instructor or outside expert who can help conduct the needed training.

Second, we are increasingly realizing that training need not be one or more isolated events completed prior to the virtual team's work together, but it should be ongoing. By monitoring logs of virtual team activities—which is much easier to do than tracking meetings of more traditional student teams—one can even make interventions designed to improve virtual team performance. As one example, data gathered from virtual teams in our new technologies course suggests that teams who began very early on clearly outperformed slower-starting teams (Scott & D'Urso, 2003). We have incorporated this finding into our initial training *and* monitor teams for slow starts so as to caution them during the project about the need to begin more quickly.

Third, we caution instructors that some of the efforts to train students about the technology and more general issues related to their virtual team can be met with ambivalence. Perhaps because some students do not see the value of working in virtual teams, they do not always see the need for training either. Inevitably, we have students who do not take the training as seriously as others or who assume they will figure this out as they go — all of which creates additional challenges for the trainer. Despite these concerns, we firmly believe that the training is an essential element in helping to achieve desirable virtual team outcomes.

Throughout the training process, students should play an active part. Accordingly, we offer three key guidelines highlighting the role of students. First, students who take the training seriously are most likely to retain desired information from these efforts. We encourage question-asking and hands-on experimentation during the training as a way to help get students involved. Second, the students can sometimes be the trainers as well. In some instances this happens during classroom training when a student has some specialized experience on virtual work teams or has used a certain technological feature in key ways that go beyond the instructor's knowledge (e.g., when a new version of *Word*'s track changes function arrived, we had a student who knew shortcuts that we had not yet discovered). More often, this training comes from one virtual team member who can train others on how to use certain technologies or communicate competently in the virtual team environment. These latter training opportunities arise during and between team meetings when instructors are not available. Thus, this sort of informal peer training represents a critical source of information for the virtual classroom team. Finally, students must continue the training/education that begins in the classroom. We believe our training provides them with resources and initial experience/knowledge. Over time, it will be up to the student to update his or her own skills. By making students aware of such possibilities and providing some initial training in this area, we help make future exploration more likely.

Summary

This section of the chapter has examined issues related to training virtual teams in education. Assuming that students have access to the technologies and basic computer skills, we first focused on three approaches to training. These forms of training vary in their intensity as well as the amount of preparation and delivery time required for each. Next, we discussed three types of more general training (team/task orientation, challenges such as isolation and mistrust, and concerns related to team dispersion) that likely have as much — if not more — to do with successful virtual teams than does technology use itself. Finally, several guidelines were suggested concerning the role of both instructors and students in the training process.

Future Trends: Virtual Team Technology and Training in Education

Scholars studying the social implications of new technologies know as well as anyone the challenges of making predictions about the future (see Norman, 1993). Such efforts are no less problematic when it comes to the use of virtual student teams. With this caveat, we identify some possible future trends/directions that are essential for moving work in this area forward.

First, the simultaneous rise of online courses and growing use of virtual teams in various organizational contexts strongly suggest that virtual student teams will become increasingly common and necessary in the future. Thus, we as educators must continue to provide opportunities to experience virtual teamwork (for its own sake and because of the potential for greater collaborative learning) in those classes where it is appropriate. Resources such as this text can serve as a useful guide to instructors attempting to integrate virtual teams into their courses.

Second, the range of technologies available to support virtual teams is also likely to grow, morph, and combine on a single device. Reviews of work on group technologies suggest this area is poised for growth (see Scott, 1999). Keeping up with such changes can be quite challenging, and providing experiences with certain tools (e.g., GDSS) can be especially expensive early in a tool's development. One solution is to focus on dimensions/attributes of technology (e.g., time, space, interactivity, content capacity, etc.), which then allows one to better understand seemingly new technologies that actually share familiar characteristics with existing media. Through focusing on key features of new technologies, both instructors and students will be better suited to evaluate and use tools developed in the future.

Third, this growth in technology and in virtual teams also demands greater attention to coordinated training efforts in the future. Working/learning this way remains unfamiliar to most people and guidance about how to collaborate virtually is essential. One way to address this issue is for educational institutions to begin training students not only in media literacy and communication competency, but in virtual literacy as well. Certification efforts for virtual workers and their managers can also be offered to interested students. The key is that more comprehensive efforts for training potential virtual team members are essential.

Finally, we caution that increased use of virtual student teams creates additional demands for quality evaluation of such teams. One concern about virtual work in almost any environment is adequately evaluating performance—and this is indeed a potential concern for instructors whose students' work is less visible (and for students who may fear instructors have fewer opportunities to observe their contributions). As one uses more and more virtual teams, one solution is to rely heavily on technological records (login information, number of posts, time spent on a course site, etc.). Increasingly this information is recorded and available to the instructor. Although this data provides some useful information for evaluation, it is obviously a very incomplete measure of project work. We suggest that instructors supplement that information with reading posts/comments for content, observing occasional face-to-face meetings of such groups, and asking for students to reflect on their virtual team experiences. We see nothing wrong with using the detailed information provided by the technologies that the teams use—assuming we let students know in advance that this sort of information will be a part of their evaluation. Yet, we must never rely solely on discussion logs or the number of posts made by students as a measure of involvement or participation (which we feel will be an increasing temptation as the technology advances and the number of virtual student teams grows). Instructors should balance the increased information available about virtual teams with more traditional methods of evaluation.

Conclusion

Scott (2003) sums up the importance of virtual teams and new communication technologies (NCTs) arguing that, "There is little doubt that the movement toward teams—in educational and organizational contexts especially—and the technologies to support them is more than a fad… [and] demands that students…. [have] a solid working knowledge of NCTs for groups and teams" (p. 145). Given the growing use of virtual teams, it is essential to examine their use in the education context. This chapter contributes to this objective through assessing the affordances of new technologies in virtual teams and examining the importance of training for these teams, as well as making some predictions about future trends in these areas. The virtual team can be an important experience for students as they prepare for work beyond the classroom — and by considering what technologies to provide and what level of training to offer, we can help make that experience all the more valuable.

Acknowledgment

The authors would like to acknowledge undergraduate research assistant Kanishka Ramyar for his efforts in preparing this chapter.

References

Aubert, B. A., & Kelsey, B. L. (2003). Further understanding of trust and performance in virtual teams. *Small Group Research, 34,* 575-619.

Bauer, J. F. (2002). Assessing student work from chatrooms and bulletin boards. *New Directions for Teaching and Learning, 91,* 31-36.

Benbasat, I., & Lim, L. H. (1993). The effects of group, task, context, and technology variables on the usefulness of group support systems: A meta-analysis of experimental studies. *Small Group Research, 24,* 430-462.

Brandon, D. P., & Hollingshead, A. P. (1999). Collaborative learning and computer-supported groups. *Communication Education, 48,* 109-126.

Brown, H. G., Poole, M. S., & Rodgers, T. L. (2004). Interpersonal traits, complementarity, and trust in virtual collaboration. *Journal of Management Information Systems, 20,* 115-143.

Chidambaram, L. (1996). Relational development in computer-supported groups. *MIS Quarterly, 20,* 143-163.

Connaughton, S. L., & Daly, J. A. (2004). Long distance leadership: Communicative strategies for leading virtual teams. In D. J. Pauleen (Ed.), *Virtual teams: Projects, protocols and processes* (pp. 116-144). Hershey, PA: Idea Group Publishing.

Coppola, N. W., Hiltz, S. R., & Rotter, N. G. (2004). Building trust in virtual teams. *IEEE Transactions on Professional Communication, 47,* 95-105.

Cramton, C. D. (2001). The mutual knowledge problem and its consequences for dispersed collaboration. *Organization Science, 12,* 346-371.

Ferris, S. P., & Minielli, M. C. (2004). Technology and virtual teams. In S. H. Godar & S. P. Ferris (Eds.), *Virtual and collaborative teams* (pp. 193-212). Hershey, PA: Idea Group Publshing.

Jarvenpaa, S. L., Knoll, K., & Leidner, D. E. (1998). Is anybody out there? Antecedents of trust in global virtual teams. *Journal of Management Information Systems, 14,* 29-64.

Jarvenpaa, S. L., & Leidner, D. E. (1999). Communication and trust in global virtual teams. *Organizational Science, 10,* 791-816.

Johnson, S. D., Suriya, C., Yoon, S. W., Berrett, J. V., & La Fleur, J. (2002). Team development and group processes of virtual learning teams. *Computers & Education, 39,* 379-393.

Joinson, C. (2002). Managing virtual teams. *HR Magazine*, 47, 69-73.

Kayworth, T. R., & Leidner, D. E. (2002). Leadership effectiveness in global virtual teams. *Journal of Management Information Systems, 18,* 7-40.

Kirkman, B. L., Rosen, B., Gibson, C. B., Tesluk, P. E., & McPherson, S. O. (2002). Five challenges to virtual team success: Lessons from Sabre, Inc. *Academy of Management Executive, 16,* 67-79.

Krebs, S., Hobman, E. V., & Bordia, P. (2003). Virtual teams and group member dissimilarity: Consequences for the development of trust. *Australian Journal of Psychology, 55,* 134-139.

LaFasto, F., & Larson, C. (2001). *When teams work best: 6,000 team members and leaders tell what it takes to succeed.* Thousand Oaks, CA: Sage.

Macdonald, J. (2003). Assessing online collaborative learning: Process and product. *Computers & Education, 40,* 377-391.

McLeod, P. L. (1992). An assessment of the experimental literature on electronic support of group work: Results of a meta-analysis. *Human-Computer Interaction, 7,* 257-280.

Norman, D. A. (1993). *Things that make us smart.* Reading, MA: Addison-Wesley.

Ocker, R. J., & Morand, D. (2002). Exploring the mediating effect of group development on satisfaction in virtual and mixed-mode environments. *E-Service Journal, 1,* 25-41.

Pauleen, D. J. (2004). *Virtual teams: Projects, protocols, and processes.* Hershey, PA: Idea Group Publishing.

Piccoli, G., & Ives, B. (2003). Trust and the unintended effects of behavioral control in virtual teams. *MIS Quarterly, 27,* 365-386.

Rains, S. A. (2005). Leveling the organizational playing field—virtually: A meta-analysis of experimental research assessing the impact of group support system use on member influence behaviors. *Communication Research, 32,* 193-234.

Robyler, M. D., & Wiencke, W. R. (2004). Exploring the interaction equation: Validating a rubric to assess and encourage interaction in distance courses. *Journal of Asynchronous Learning Networks, 8,* 25-37.

Scott, C. R. (1999). Communication technology and group communication. In L. R. Frey, D. Gouran, & M. S. Poole (Eds.), *The handbook of group communication theory and research* (pp. 432-472). Thousand Oaks, CA: Sage.

Scott, C. R. (2003). New communication technologies and teams. In R. Y. Hirokawa, R. S. Cathcart, L. A. Samovar, & L. D. Henman (Eds.), *Small group communication theory and practice: An anthology* (8th ed., pp. 134-147). Los Angeles, CA: Roxbury.

Scott, C. R., & D'Urso, S. C. (2003, November). Virtual teams, viable decisions? Message timing and thoroughness in online problem-solving groups. Paper presented to the annual convention of the *National Communication Association Convention,* Miami Beach, FL.

Timmerman, C. E., & Scott, C. R. (2004, May). Virtually working: Communicative and structural predictors of media use and key outcomes in virtual work teams. Paper presented at the *International Communication Association Convention,* New Orleans, LA.

Warkentin, M., & Beranek, P. M. (1999). Training to improve virtual team communication. *Information Systems Journal, 9,* 271-289.

Endnotes

1 Throughout the chapter we identify specific companies that offer communication tools for illustrative purposes. *Blackboard* and *WebCT*, for example, offer course management software that can be used to compliment and facilitate an academic course. These two companies are cited only as examples. We do not intend to advocate any particular company's product. There are other companies that make tools such as these that should be examined before making purchase or adoption decisions.

2 We make a concerted effort to expose students to those types of tools that they are likely to encounter during their professional careers. Indeed, there is a great deal of overlap in the tools used by our students and those used in contemporary organizations. E-mail, chat, discussion boards, file-sharing, and track-changes are all features that are used in our class as well as organizations. However, we do not have students use the exact same tools they might encounter in any specific corporation — this is not possible given the range of specific products/vendors and the customization of tools each employer might have. Our aim is to have them experience the types of tools typically used in contemporary organizations to provide the necessary foundation for their professional career.

3 We did provide extensive guidelines on ideal posting frequency and timing and used that for assessment of student participation. However, uneven participation still often resulted. For more discussion of rubrics used to assess interaction online, see Bauer (2002) and Robyler and Wiencke (2004).

4 In these instances, students seemed to be frustrated by not being able to communicate their ideas orally. The process of typing out their ideas seemed to distress a small number of students as they felt that they could not communicate as effectively. It is important to note that instances in which students reverted to traditional (oral) discussion were fairly rare.

About the Authors

Sharmila Pixy Ferris (PhD, Pennsylvania State University, 1995) is professor and graduate program director in the Department of Communication, William Paterson University, USA. Her research brings an interdisciplinary focus to the study of computer-mediated communication, where she studies gender, small groups, orality and literacy, and adoption patterns. She is co-editor of *Virtual and Collaborative Teams* (2004, Idea Group Publishing) and co-author of *Beyond Survival in the Academy* (2003, Hampton Press). She has published in a variety of paper and electronic journals including *Qualitative Research Reports, The New Jersey Journal of Communication, The Electronic Journal of Communication, Interpersonal Computing and Technology,* and *The Journal of Electronic Publishing*.

Susan H. Godar is associate professor and chairperson in the Department of Marketing and Management Sciences, Christos M. Cotsakos College of Business, William Paterson University, USA. Her research, primarily on virtual teams, business ethics, and marketing pedagogy, has appeared in such journals as *Journal of Business Ethics*, *Journal of International Management*, *Industrial Marketing Management*, and *Services Marketing Quarterly*. With Dr. Ferris, she has edited a book titled *Virtual and Collaborative Teams: Process Technologies, and Practice* (Idea Group Publishing, 2004). Dr. Godar served as a consultant to numerous companies and organizations in the aviation industry, and has been a member of the National Academy of Sciences' Transportation Research Board. Prior to joining academe, she marketed light airplanes and helicopters. She holds a BA in sociology from Creighton University, an MBA from the University of Iowa, and a PhD in international business from Temple University.

* * *

Lilianna Aniola-Jedrzejek, Senior Lecturer at the Poznan University of Technology (Poland), teaches English for specific purposes with the Department of Foreign Languages. She has a PhD in physics and became interested in online teaching/learning when she took a one-semester online course on designing Internet courses at Heriot-Watt University, Edinborough, Great Britain (1999). Since then she has coordinated three European Union projects within the Leonardo da Vinci program (one project currently underway), with the purpose of introducing instructional technology components to language learning. Since 2002, she has conducted, with Boehm, four online projects between students of the Poznan University of Technology and Saginaw Valley State University, Michigan (USA).

Rashmi H. Assudani will be joining the faculty at Williams College of Business, Xavier University, Cincinnati (USA) in Fall 2005. This chapter was written during her doctoral dissertation at the Faculty of Management, McGill University, Montreal, Canada. Her research interests lie in understanding the issues and challenges associated with the management of knowledge in organizations, especially across dispersed units. Her research has been published, and has been regularly awarded at leading academic and practitioner conferences.

Diane Boehm is director of instructional support programs at Saginaw Valley State University (USA), a regional state university in east-central Michigan. Her responsibilities include directing a university writing center in which approximately 25% of all sessions are conducted with nonnative speakers of English from other cultures. This experience, together with frequent travels to visit friends and universities in former Eastern European countries and Russia, led to the desire to open the world of other cultures to her students. Since 2002 she has conducted, with Aniola-Jedrzejek, four online projects between students of Saginaw Valley State University, Michigan (USA), and Poznan University of Technology, Poland.

Pieter du Toit is senior lecturer in the Department of Curriculum Studies at the University of Pretoria (South Africa). He specializes in teaching and learning in higher education, with a research focus on learning styles. He leads the Postgraduate Certificate in Higher Education (PGCHE) program and is involved in other postgraduate programs that focus on adult learning. He is a member of the Managing Committee of the Australian-based Association for Action Learning, Action Research and Process Management (ALARPM) and a registered HBDI-practitioner with the USA-based Ned Herrmann Group. He was awarded a postdoctoral grant from the University of Antwerp, Belgium.

Anne-Laure Fayard has a background in philosophy and earned a PhD in cognitive science from the Ecole des Hautes-Etudes en Sciences Sociales (Paris). Since 1999, she has been working as an assistant professor in technology management at INSEAD (France). Her research interests involve socio-technical practices, technology-mediated communication, distance collaboration, online communities, and space. She designed a distributed elective on Managing global teams and projects, where students — located on INSEAD's two campuses (Singapore and France) — work in virtual teams. Teaching this course has provided her with the opportunity to explore issues related to distance learning and collaboration in virtual teams.

Mark A. Fuller is an associate professor and chair of the Department of Information Systems at Washington State University (USA). His major research interests include virtual teamwork, technology mediated learning, and consumer trust in e-commerce. Dr. Fuller's past research has appeared in outlets such *as Information Systems Research*, *Group Decision and Negotiation*, *Decision Support Systems*, the *Journal of Information Systems Education*, the *Journal of Management Education*, and the *Journal of Management Information Systems*. He has been honored with a number of teaching awards, and has been very active in both MBA and Executive MBA programs during his career.

Terri L. Griffith (PhD, Carnegie-Mellon) is a professor of management in the Leavey School of Business, Santa Clara University (USA), and program director within the Center for Science, Technology, and Society. Her research interests include knowledge transfer in virtual work and "negotiated implementation". Her current field research includes a National Science Foundation sponsored project to study three of the Fortune 100. Her work is published in journals such as *Organization Science*, *Information Systems Research*, *MIS Quarterly*, and the *Academy of Management Review*. She coedited the book, *Research on Managing Groups and Teams: Technology* (2000, JAI Press). She is a senior editor for *Organization Science.*

Noriko Hara held a position as an NSF postdoctoral research fellow in the School of Information and Library Science, University of North Carolina at Chapel Hill, before joining the faculty of the School of Library and Information Science, Indiana University (USA) in 2002. She is currently an assistant professor of information science and also a fellow in the Rob Kling Center for Social Informatics. Her research focuses on topics within social informatics, more specifically on mobilization of resources. Her studies examined the roles of the Internet in mobilizing civil society movements, online learning, and communities of practice in a digital environment.

Kathryn Hashimoto has been a faculty member at the University of New Orleans (USA) for the past 10 years. Because she specializes in understanding people's behavior, her graduate degrees in psychology, management, and marketing aid her in teaching the service management and hospitality marketing courses. Dr. Hashimoto's career began in resort management where she worked in training and marketing management for ten years. The next 12 years found Dr. Hashimoto teaching marketing at business schools in various universities in New Jersey. Her major research interests are in cross-cultural communications/advertising, consumer behavior, and service management.

Andrea L.R. Lassiter is an assistant professor in the Industrial and Organizational Psychology Program at Minnesota State University, Mankato (USA). She earned her PhD in 2004 from George Mason University and was a consortium research fellow at the U.S. Army Research Institute for Behavioral and Social Sciences in Arlington, Virginia. Her current research interests are in the areas of team training, collaborative learning, and program assessment.

Andrea is an active member in the Society for Industrial and Organizational Psychology and an associate member of the Association of American Colleges and Universities.

Jean-marc Lehu is an associate professor in the Gestion Sorbonne Department at Paris 1 Panthéon Sorbonne University in Paris (France) where he teaches marketing. His research interests include brand management, marketing communications, and consumer behavior. He is also a marketing and communication consultant for French and multinational firms, and author of several books on marketing and brand strategy published at Editions d'Organisation, Paris.

Gregory B. Northcraft is the Harry J. Gray professor of executive leadership in the Department of Business Administration, and Institute of Labor and Industrial Relations, University of Illinois (USA). His major research interests include collaboration and diversity in teams, negotiation and conflict management, managerial decision making, and employee motivation and job design, particularly in high-technology manufacturing settings. Professor Northcraft has published widely in management research journals and has done consulting and management training for a variety of manufacturing and service-sector firms. He has been honored with a number of teaching awards, served as editor of the *Academy of Management Journal,* and currently is Senior Editor at *Organization Science*.

Patricia J. O'Connor is an associate professor of philosophy at Queens College, City University of New York (USA). She earned a PhD in philosophy from the University of Exeter, UK. After three years as associate provost at Queens, during which she worked with academic programs on outcomes assessment, she spent three years on loan to Brooklyn College, CUNY, leading academic assessment there. Her research interests include business ethics, the ethics of academic administration, and the scholarship of teaching.

Kara L. Orvis is a post doctoral consortium research fellow at the U.S. Army Research Institute in Arlington, Virginia (USA). Her main research interests have been in the realms of teams and leadership, concentrating on technology, training, and development. In addition to her postdoctoral work, Kara teaches for the George Mason University School of Management and works as an independent consultant, helping organizations overcome cultural barriers in international training. She has co-authored/authored more than 35 presentations and publications, two of which received awards in 2004. Recent publications include *Leadership in Virtual Teams*, *Communication Patterns During Synchronous Web-based Military Training in Problem Solving* and *Overcoming Barriers to Information Sharing in Virtual Teams.* Kara earned her PhD and MA in industrial/organizational psychology from George Mason University (2004 and 1999, respectively), and her BA from Ohio Wesleyan University (1997).

Stephen A. Rains (PhD, University of Texas at Austin, 2005) is an assistant professor in the Department of Communication, University of Arizona (USA). His research focuses on the uses and implications of new communication technologies and social influence. His work on computer-mediated teams has been published in *Communication Research*.

Craig R. Scott (PhD, Arizona State University, 1994) is an associate professor of communication studies at The University of Texas at Austin (USA). His research and teaching focus on the use of new communication technologies at work, issues of identity/identification (especially in dispersed organizations/teams), and communication among virtual workers. His research on virtual workers and teams using technology has been published in *IEEE Transactions on Professional Communication*, *Communication Quarterly*, *Communication Reports*, *Western Journal of Communication*, *Small Group Research*, and several edited handbooks. Scott is a member of the Association of Internet Researchers, Academy of Management, International Communication

Pnina Shachaf is an assistant professor at the School of Library and Information Science, Indiana University - Bloomington (USA). She earned her PhD from the School of Information and Library Studies at the University of North Carolina, Chapel Hill (2003). Her dissertation focused on "Global virtual teams: The effect of cultural diversity and information and communication technology on team effectiveness." Her research areas focus on the use of technology by distributed virtual teams in a multicultural environment.

Karen Rohrbauck Stout (PhD, University of Utah) is an assistant professor of communication at Western Washington University in Bellingham, WA (USA). Her research focuses on organizational and instructional communication, technology, and gender. Her pedagogical research has focused on how various teaching practices and tools (like technology and service-learning) improve student learning and communication in the classroom. Her organizational research has focused on how socialization practices can exclude and marginalize newcomers, as well as how gender and race are constructed in the workplace. She directs research and teaches courses in organizational communication, emerging communication technologies, instructional communication, and research methods.

Peter van Petegem is a senior professor in education at the University of Antwerp (Belgium). He specializes in teacher education and related areas, such as educational leadership, educational change, learning styles and alternative assessment. The research group EduBROn at the University of Antwerp operates under his leadership. As a scholar he authored, co-authored and edited numerous scientific publications on various topics. Nationally and internationally he acts as mentor to young scholars. Over the past few years he has taken leadership in several European and international research projects, and is currently taking part in African capacity building projects in Botswana, Zimbabwe and South Africa.

Robert Zheng, EdD, is an assistant professor of instructional and learning technology at Temple University, Pennsylvania (USA). He received his doctorate in curriculum and instruction from Baylor University (1998) with a concentration in educational technology. His research agenda include online learning and pedagogy, multimedia and cognition, and educational technology and assessment. He was the recipient and principal investigator of PT3 grant ($250,000) awarded by the U.S. Department of Education. His publications have appeared in refereed journals including *Educational Technology Research and Development*. He has presented extensively at national and international conferences.

Index

www.ingramcontent.com/pod-product-compliance
Lightning Source LLC
LaVergne TN
LVHW062117200926
848484LV00007B/1691
* 9 7 8 1 5 9 1 4 0 7 0 8 9 *